Captain James Cook: Claiming the Great South Land

Captain James Cook

Claiming the Great South Land

John Molony

Connor Court Publishing

Published in 2016 by Connor Court Publishing Pty Ltd

Connor Court Publishing Pty Ltd
PO Box 7257
Redland Bay QLD 4165
sales@connorcourt.com
www.connorcourt.com
Phone 0497-900-685

Printed in Australia

ISBN: 978-1-925501-28-5

Front cover design: Maria Giordano

Front cover painting: H.M. bark, Endeavour [picture] / Oswald Brett
Author: Brett, Oswald, 1921-
year: 1972
http://nla.gov.au/nla.obj-136015149

All maps in this volume have been set down by Nik Fominas, and are based on the wonderfully clear maps that appear at the National Library of Australia South Seas Voyaging Maps website: http://southseas.nla.gov.au/index_maps.html.

Contents

In grateful memory,
to
The Little Old Man of the Guugu Yimithirr people

Maps

Introduction

Some years ago it was not uncommon to meet people in Europe, and remarkably so in Italy, who, on ascertaining one's Australian nationality, often replied with 'Ah, Capitano Cook', or a similar acknowledgement of the famous captain. The response revealed that Cook was so closely identified with Australia that no more needed to be said. He was accepted as the discoverer of Australia. Cook was not that, however; he was much more.

His first voyage on the *Endeavour* (1768–1771) had two purposes. The principal, public one was to observe the Transit of Venus across the sun at Tahiti in 1769. That mission was almost a disguise for Cook's main objective, which the Admiralty, unavailing however, wished to keep secret. He was to sail south-west from Tahiti in high latitudes in search of the Great South Land. If he failed to find it, which proved to be the case, he was enjoined to proceed to New Zealand, the west coast of which Abel Tasman had touched in 1642, and chart its whole coast.

Once that was done, in the event successfully and thoroughly, he was free to decide on what passage he would take to return home. The obvious choices would involve either going back on his tracks to Cape Horn or sailing south of Van Diemen's Land to the Cape of Good Hope and thence to home.

Cook was not, however, given to opting for the obvious. First, he was conscious of the fact that the east coast of New Holland had not been charted, although its position was generally well established. The Dutch had charted the west coast of the Gulf of Carpentaria, but it was uncertain how far its east coast, as did the remainder of that coast below Carpentaria, stretched into the Pacific. There was also the important question as to whether there was a strait between the tip of its northern coast and New Guinea, which had not been satisfactorily answered.

Thus Cook knew that, were he to opt to return home by sailing further west until he reached the east coast of New Holland and then sailed north to chart it, he would achieve his two objectives. The map of New Holland would be a settled matter to a significant degree as would the existence or otherwise of Torres Strait.

Cook would have been gravely discomforted were there no strait because he was determined to get to Batavia as quickly as possible for repairs and to replenish supplies. Should there have been no strait, he would be forced to sail further north and pass along the north coast of New Guinea to reach his destined port, Batavia, where the needed repairs to the *Endeavour* could be undertaken in the well-equipped Dutch shipyards there. That done he could set sail for home by sailing to Cape Town and around the Cape of Good Hope. In the event he found the strait at Cape York, named it Endeavour's Strait and all was well — temporarily. So many of his crew died at, or in the aftermath, of the stay at Batavia that Cook was hard put to man his ship.

Although Cook had grave doubts about the existence of the Great South Land, as an obedient officer of the Admiralty he followed his instructions to the letter. The matter was of utmost importance, as proven by the determination of the Admiralty to find the fabled land. Belief in its existence stemmed back to antiquity and Ptolemy's maps, which joined Africa to Antarctica thus landlocking the Indian Ocean, seemed to confirm the matter. More recently belief was heightened by the realisation of the vastness of the Pacific, which could surely hide huge, as yet undiscovered, land masses in its immense embrace of a third of the world's surface.

Cook was in no position to deny the existence of the undiscovered treasure trove. All he could do was suggest that further voyages had to be made to find it. The mystery is that a huge land, Cook called it 'the largest island in the world', had already been discovered and named New Holland. But those earlier mariners, the Dutch and the Englishman, William Dampier, had pronounced it worthless, indeed repulsive in respect of its natural qualities and even more in people. It did not measure up in any sense to the expectations of finding vast deposits of silver and gold, endless veins of sparkling gems in a fertile land peopled by amiable inhabitants eager to share their wealth with the northerners. Thus it was logical to reject it as worthless and continue to search for the fabled paradise.

Cook dealt only in reality and he spelled it out. He wrote, 'In this extensive country it can never be doubted but what most sorts of grain, fruit, roots, etc. of every kind would flourish here once brought hither, planted and cultivated by the hand of industry, and here are provender for more cattle at all seasons of the year than ever (can) be brought into this country.' He did not speak of sheep. As a former farm boy, Cook had not come to know that handmaiden of early Australian development, the Merino.

Cook took possession of what was to become, despite all, the Great South

Land and given the name Australia. It was enriched further and greatly by the later addition of the immense western part of the continent. Australia possessed in abundance all the riches envisaged of it by the northerners, as well a stark but immeasurable beauty even in its deserts. Ironically the very spot on Possession Island in Torres Strait where Cook claimed the land later proved to have a gold mine beneath its surface.

What this Great South Land did not have was a meek and placid people anxious to allow the newcomer to exploit and ravage it. Although he was derided for doing so, Cook wrote with deep admiration and almost affection of the land's first inhabitants, the Aborigines, whose origins stretched back to the very beginnings of the human race. In their inviolable integrity as the custodians of the land, which they embraced as their country, to Cook they were among the happiest of people on the earth.

The narrative of Cook's voyage primarily depends on his own journal. A voyage of any kind, especially one at sea where landmarks are lacking, must rely on maps. In Cook's case there were no maps for an immense section of his long passage. He had to make them from Tahiti to Batavia, so that others could follow. We follow with them and, for every league of that passage, we know when and where we are by looking at the maps. Nik Fominas set them down here with patience and high skill, but we acknowledge and are indebted to the cartographers of the National Library of Australia whose wonderfully clear maps we cite as the basis for those in this book.

Although it rests with the author to take responsibility for the contents of this work, and in particular for its lapses, it does not belong to him. It belongs to the small team of the East Coast Project in the Emeritus Faculty of The Australian National University who worked alongside him with knowledge, forbearance, good grace and, above all, lasting friendship. There are no boundaries to my gratitude to them.

I thank Bob Dixon and Alexandra Aikhenvald, Loretta and Bob Sullivan, John MacDonald and Mayor Peter Scott, as well as all those who keep alive the memory of Cook and the *Endeavour* at Cooktown, Hope Vale and at James Cook University in Cairns.

Finally there are the descendants of those who met Cook in 1770 from whom I came to understand their precious heritage and especially the late Eric Deeral (1932–2012), his daughter Erica and Alberta Hornsby. Their words to me whispered with the Dreamtime of the centuries.

Portrait of Captain James Cook RN 1782, by John Webber (c 1752–1793), oil on canvas.

Source: Collection: National Portrait Gallery, Canberra. Purchased 2000 by the Commonwealth Government with the generous assistance of Robert Oatley AO and John Schaeffer AO.

Portrait of Sir Joseph Banks, 1970, by Joyce Aris, Sir Joshua Reynolds.

Source: Te Papa (1000-0000-59).

A view of Endeavour River, on the coast of New Holland, where the ship was laid on shore in order to repair the damage which she received on the rock, 1773, by William Byrne.

Source: nla.obj-135951500.

1

Captain and his Ship

At 11 am on Friday 27 May 1768, James Cook made a simple entry on the first page of his journal. He stated that he 'took charge of the Ship', renamed H.M. Bark *Endeavour*, which lay at Deptford Yard near Greenwich on the River Thames. The Royal Yard at Deptford had seen many famous commanders do as Cook had done, including Francis Drake and Walter Raleigh. Indisputably great as those others were, Cook was about to set out on a voyage because of which he would stand tall with them. The *Endeavour*, although in Cook's estimate she had been built to hold her own against any massive sea she might encounter, was ungainly in appearance, small and, in some waters, sluggish. Nevertheless, as a former collier plying the English coast, in her humble way she lived up to her new name and fully merited her master's confidence. Thus she contributed to the fulfilment of his destiny, as did those who sailed with him. James Cook was destined to become one of the great mariners of the ages.[1]

Named after his father, a Scottish farm worker, James was born on 3 November 1728 at Marton-in-Cleveland, Yorkshire. His mother Grace, née Pace, was of Yorkshire stock. The humble homes in which the family dwelt at Marton-in-Cleveland and, after 1753, at nearby Great Ayton, saw the death in infancy of four of James's seven siblings. Young James showed a thirst for learning, especially mathematics, at the little school in Great Ayton.

---

[1] J.C. Beaglehole (ed.), *The Journals of Captain James Cook on his Voyage of Discovery*, vol. 1, *The Voyage of the Endeavour 1768-1771* (1955, opposite p. 1). Cook used official naval time, known as 'ship time', which ran from noon to noon, for his journal entries, which I adopt also. Joseph Banks, Sydney Parkinson and other civilians who wrote journals on the voyage adopted the normal usage from midnight to midnight. If Cook, however, speaks of an event that took place after noon and before midnight on, say, his 1 September 1768 , it would be dated 31 August 1768 by civilians. This means that the part of the day shared by all in dating was from midnight to noon. I use Cook's date to avoid confusion, given that his journal is the main source for this account. For the same reason I do not give dates for the other journals. When citing Cook I use the name, date and page number as it appears in Beaglehole. For Banks, I use his name, volume and page number. Daniel Solander used tongue and pen sparsely, and declined to write a journal.

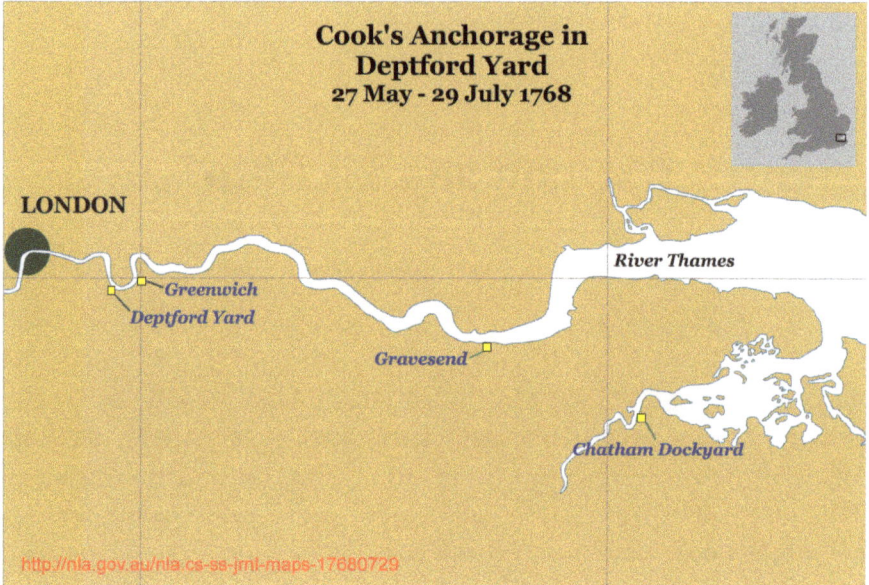

**Cook's Anchorage in
Deptford Yard
27 May - 29 July 1768**

LONDON

River Thames

Greenwich

Deptford Yard

Gravesend

Chatham Dockyard

http://nla.gov.au/nla.cs-ss-jrnl-maps-17680729

His days as a farm labourer ended when, aged 17, he took a position with a grocer in the fishing town of Staithes. There he came to the notice of a generous and warm-hearted Quaker, John Walker, who became a friend for life. Walker was one of two brothers who owned vessels that worked mainly in shipping coal from Newcastle to London, but also in taking cargo to ports in the Baltic and the North Sea. Aged 20, James put away his grocer's apron to stand before the mast at sea on a Walker brothers' vessel. On the frequent runs along the English coast and on longer trips in the Baltic, James learnt the rudiments of navigation as well as some advanced mathematics, which helped decisively to define his life.

Cook's career progressed rapidly and, in 1755, Walker offered him command of a vessel. His rejection was not merely verbal. On 17 June 1755, James Cook joined the Royal Navy with the full blessing of John Walker. The Seven Years' War between England and France did not begin until a year later, so it was not an onrush of patriotism that prompted his action. Any prospect of advancement to officer rank in the Royal Navy to a lowly born, 26-year-old member of the merchant navy whose main occupation had been toiling on a coal-laden cat in mainly coastal waters was, at best, dismal. Ambition, therefore, was not the driving force behind Cook's decision, either, nor was the paltry wage of £1 4s a month.

Cook was driven by the call of the oceans of the world. He wanted to know and conquer them and thereby widen knowledge of the lands that lay within them. His reward came almost instantly. Within a month of joining

HMS *Eagle* as an able seaman, Cook became its master's mate. This meant that he had to report to the master, the highest non-commissioned officer in charge of the navigation of the ship, on the vessel's condition, sails, masts and all else that made it seaworthy. Instead of coal, the *Eagle* carried 400 men and 58 guns, and she began to play a role in what increasingly became a real war in the English Channel. Fortunately for Cook, Hugh Palliser, only four years older than Cook, was appointed the *Eagle*'s commander. He quickly realised that in Cook he had a genuinely trustworthy seaman with whom he established bonds of a strength that were never broken.

By 1757, Cook had been promoted as master of a new vessel, HMS *Pembroke*, which carried 64 guns. The war soon shifted to Canada, where the British had decided to take the French possessions of Québec and Louisbourg at the head of the Gulf of St Lawrence. To that end they sent a large fleet, including the *Pembroke*, to Halifax, the British base in Nova Scotia. Louisbourg was taken on 26 July 1758. After the victory, Cook struck up a warm friendship with the Dutch-born engineer Samuel Holland, who was surveying parts of the east coast of North America for the British. From Holland, Cook rapidly learnt how to use a tripod and a plane table to take sights on the features of the land, and he used his newfound skill to chart Gaspé Bay in preparation for the attack on Québec. This became Cook's first published chart. His initial mastering of celestial navigation using a sextant was also learnt under the watchful eye of Holland at Halifax during the following severe winter. On 12 September 1759, Québec fell to the British so that North America would never be French and its new future was beginning to unfold. Cook was rewarded with £50 for 'making himself master of the pilotage of the River St Lawrence'. Back in London by December 1762, he received his back pay of £291 19s 3p and was highly praised at the Admiralty for the charts he prepared, with their draughts and observations of the St Lawrence as well as of some parts of the coasts of Nova Scotia and Newfoundland. Cook was now in a position to undertake another step of his own choice.

Elizabeth Batts, born in 1742, was the only child of a Quaker couple, Samuel and Mary Batts. Their respectable establishment, the Bell Alehouse, at Execution Dock in Wapping was run by Mary after Samuel died while Elizabeth was still an infant. The Quaker connection between John Walker and the Batts meant that Walker's seamen often stayed there between voyages; Elizabeth might well have come to the notice of Cook in her teens. As an elderly widow, Elizabeth Cook destroyed all the private correspondence of her husband and speculation as to whether the couple remained in contact during

Cook's four years in North America is idle. Elizabeth well knew that to be the wife of a seaman involved the acceptance of long absences. Nonetheless, two weeks after his arrival home Elizabeth, aged 21, married James, aged 34, at St Margaret's Church in Barking on 21 December 1762. By a happy sequence of official mishaps, they were able to spend their first three months together before Cook was off again to survey the islands of Newfoundland, St Pierre and Miquelon off the east coast of Canada. From their marriage until Cook's departure for the Pacific in 1768, three children — James, Nathaniel and Elizabeth — were born. The union between James and Elizabeth was to be one of partings and reunions, but nothing healed the sorrows of the absences.

Cook's time in Newfoundland was brief, and atrocious weather reduced to only a few months the period that he could devote to practicing his skills as a marine surveyor. Back again in London, he put his papers, charts and observations together to present to the Admiralty, bought a modest but pleasing terrace house at 88 Mile End Road and cherished proudly his newborn son James. This home became his heartland for the remainder of his life and that also of Elizabeth. Of their children, three died in infancy, James and Nathaniel died at sea as young members of the Royal Navy, while the youngest boy, Hugh, died in college as a student at Cambridge. One of James Cook's sisters, Margaret (1742–1804), married James Fleck of Redcar, Yorkshire in 1764. They had eight children whose descendants live on into the present although the surname, Cook, was lost after the deaths of the sons of James and Elizabeth, none of whom married. After 53 years of widowhood, during which she treasured the memory of James and mourned so many deaths, Elizabeth died in 1832.

From Mile End Road, Cook went to and fro to Newfoundland each summer, until his final visit in 1767. Cook rejoiced in the appointment of Palliser as Governor of Newfoundland in 1764, but he suffered a serious wound when a horn filled with powder blew up in his hand on that same visit. A skilful doctor on a nearby French vessel repaired the damage with considerable success but, at times, and in the John Webber portrait of him held by the National Portrait Gallery, Canberra, his right hand was gloved. In 1766 he was asked to observe an eclipse of the sun on the Burgeo Islands off the south coast of Newfoundland. His observations of the transit were intended to allow members of the Royal Society to calculate the distance in longitude between the islands and Oxford, which was an important step in the hitherto uncertain calculation of longitude. This purpose was in itself sufficient proof of Cook's outstanding mathematical and astronomical knowledge to recommend him highly to the Admiralty. Furthermore, to have come so noticeably to the attention of the Royal Society was also a vital step in Cook's own passage to fame.[2]

That Cook possessed all the qualities expected of an officer by the Royal Navy, except a suitable family background, was clear. He was intelligent, diligent and trustworthy and those who had worked under him respected his leadership. That he would be capable of guiding a ship safely in unknown waters on the other side of the world had yet to be proved, but that his navigational skills were of a high order was unquestionable. To send him back repeatedly to Newfoundland, as Cook expected would occur, was an option, but perhaps he could be better used elsewhere. There was, in fact, another option. Shortly before Cook returned from Newfoundland on his last voyage the Council of the Royal Society met to consider what action to take in respect of the forthcoming transit of Venus across the sun. It would take place on 3 June 1769 and, thereafter, not again until 1874. The council had only 18 months to decide on action and make the necessary preparations for recording the transit, and they were forthright in pointing out to the king that, given the French, Danes, Swedes and Spaniards were making their own preparations to ascertain the exact length of time Venus took to transit the sun, Britain would be dishonoured should she neglect to do so likewise.

The variation in time at which the transit occurred, measured from three distant locations, would be an essential element in the calculations and, if done properly, the results would permit scientists to calculate the distance from Venus to the sun, as well as the distance between the sun and the earth. Based on those calculations it would be possible eventually to calculate the distance on earth between, say, Greenwich near London and Rio de Janeiro in Brazil, provided the exact time at Greenwich was known. In effect the problem of longitude would be solved, once accurate clocks at a reasonable price became available to ships at sea, by calculating the distance in times. In that way a vessel would know precisely where it was at any given moment as well as how far it had travelled from one destination to another.

---

[2] I have drawn on many of the biographies of James Cook for his life up to 1767 as well as for those of his wife and family. Beaglehole's scholarly *Life of Captain James Cook* (1974) remains paramount among them. The best short summary is in the *Australian Dictionary of Biography* (Cook, James (1728-1779), *Australian Dictionary of Biography*, National Centre of Biography, The Australian National University, adb.anu.edu.au/biography/cook-james-1917/text2279, published first in hardcopy 1966, accessed online 19 February 2016). The entry is unsigned, which means that its author was one of the staff of the dictionary. For more recent and eminently readable accounts see Nicholas Thomas, *Cook; The Extraordinary Voyages of Captain James Cook* (2003); Richard Hough, *Captain James Cook* (1994) and Rob Mundle, *Cook* (2014).

The North Cape in Norway and Hudson Bay in Canada were chosen as suitable places in the Northern Hemisphere from which to view the transit, but it seemed imperative that an observation also be made in the Southern Hemisphere. Where better, it was thought, than in the Pacific? Nonetheless, two vital elements of the proposed expedition had to be addressed. An appropriate ship had to be chosen and work on fitting it out for the voyage needed to commence immediately. The other element proved to be troublesome. It was imperative to appoint a commander with the proper qualifications and no time should be lost in so doing. In Alexander Dalrymple, the council thought they had the right man. He was learned, active, experienced and determined. Indeed he might have been somewhat too determined. Above all he was a man with a fixed idea. To him, taking celestial observations mattered, but they were of secondary importance to achieving the great objective. Out there, somewhere in the Southern Hemisphere — he thought he knew where — Dalrymple believed that there was a Great South Land. It was there because it had to be there, otherwise the world would spin unbalanced in its orbit because the massive proportion of its earth was situated in the north. This manner of speculation seems to have paid little or no account to the extent of both those parts of Africa and the American continent lying below the Equator, as well as of the Antarctic itself.

Nonetheless the council was sure of their choice and let the Admiralty know that Dalrymple would command the expedition. The high officials in that august body would have none of this, however; the thought of having a civilian in command of a naval vessel was, to them, preposterous. To Dalrymple, the rejection of his role as sole commander was unacceptable; he would go only as sole commander. There were other captains available, in particular John Byron and Samuel Wallis, both of whom had recently been to the Pacific. In fact Wallis had returned at that very time with HMS *Dolphin* and he was able to pinpoint accurately the location of an eminently desirable place in the Pacific, Tahiti, from which observations could be made. In the event, the choice of a commander was quickly made and remarkably so because the chosen candidate was not even a commissioned officer. Cook was promoted to lieutenant and put in command of the vessel with responsibility for carrying out the orders given to him by the Admiralty. His pay was to be five shillings per day. Dalrymple became a forthright and unrelenting critic of all that followed.

No time was lost in acquiring a vessel, either. A ship of the Royal Navy was not regarded as desirable given that naval vessels were built to go to war at sea, while this was to be a voyage in a time of peace with strictly scientific and geographical objectives. The final choice proved that, although in the immediate sense unusual, it had been a wise decision in all respects. On 27 March 1768, after five other vessels had been rejected as unsuitable, the then-named *Earl of Pembroke* was bought by the Admiralty. She was a cat-built bark with a square stern and a wide bottom suitable for careening on beaches where the tide was favourable. She had been launched at Whitby less than four years previously, after which she served her time ploughing up and down the east coast delivering coal from Newcastle to London. She could transport 368 tons, which was deemed sufficient for the purpose of the intended voyage. Her owner, Thomas Milner, sold her to the Admiralty for £2,800 and an immediate decision was taken to change her name. To put her down on the naval list of vessels as *Endeavour* Bark was necessary given that an *Endeavour* Cutter was already on the list. The modifications and additions demanded by her purpose included fitting her out with a few guns so that, if necessity demanded, she could engage in some moderate action at sea. Modifications were also undertaken to provide some material comfort for the officers who had to be displaced from their accommodation in favour of the civilians who were to come aboard. This necessitated the building of a new deck and the spending of a lengthy and expensive period in dock during which all the refitting was done at the cost of £5,394 15s 4p. Cook had no role in the choice of the vessel, before whose mast he stood first on 27 May 1768, but both vessel and master sailed proudly together. She was the kind of ship in which he had grown to the sea on the English coast. He trusted her.[3]

The purpose of the voyage was clear. The transit of Venus in the following April was to be observed at Tahiti and, once that was done, Cook was to sail south to about 40° latitude and then west in search of the fabled Great South Land. If it was not discovered he was to proceed to New Zealand, which Abel Tasman had touched upon in 1642, and chart its coast. He was then to return home, but some degree of choice was left to him as to the optimum passage by which to do so.

To ready the ship for this lengthy voyage, two months passed lying at Deptford while 'fitting the ship (and) taking on board stores and provisions, etc'.[4] Having paused at Plymouth Sound on 26 August, he welcomed his

---

[3] Numerous publications deal with the *Endeavour*. I have principally relied on Ray Parkin's scholarly and painstaking work, *H.M. Bark Endeavour: Her Place in Australian History* (2006).

[4] Ray Parkin, *H.M. Bark Endeavour: Her Place in Australian History* (2006). In order to avoid the repeated use of [sic], I adopt contemporary spelling in instances when Cook's use differs. In this instance he has 'takeing' rather than 'taking'. When there is a conflict as to sense, the exact spelling of Cook and the other journal writers is preserved. I also use the lower case rather than the sporadic, at times inexplicable, use of capitals that occurs in the journals.

gentlemen passengers aboard in the persons of the land-holding gentleman, Joseph Banks, who was determined to test his mettle as a botanist in regions little or totally unknown to European science, and Doctor Daniel Carl Solander, former pupil of the great Carl Linnaeus and already possessed of far greater knowledge of botany than the younger Banks. After berthing the ship's company by assigning them their narrow sleeping quarters, Cook made them open their sea chests and all that he considered unnecessary for the voyage was cast overboard. All was ready, but Banks was quickly critical of the vessel, which he decided was better fitted for carrying stores on coastal voyages rather than sailing the high seas. Indeed her capacity to do so ought to have pleased him given the vast amount of gear he brought aboard. Banks spent the last night in London at the opera with his fiancée, Miss Harriet Blosset, who was 'quite gay', being unaware that it was to be their last meeting, for her at least, of a loving nature.[5] There is no record as to how Cook's wife, Elizabeth, felt about her parting with James. When Cook returned home in 1771 he was told that, a few weeks after his departure for the lands of the far south, another son was born and had died.

The number of persons aboard the vessel now amounted to an unexpected 95, as well as near '18 months provisions … carriage guns, 12 swivels with [a] good store of ammunition and stores of all kinds'. Two fictitious members were added to the crew who were each put down simply as a 'Widow's Man' with their pay and maintenance going humanely towards the pensions for the widows of deceased members of the Royal Navy. The combination of men and materials filled the *Endeavour* to its gunnels. About 16,000 kilograms of bread and 6,000 pieces of pork, together with biscuits and salted beef were the main provisions. There were also 3,500 kilograms of sauerkraut (spelt by Cook as 'Sour Krout') to combat scurvy, as well as 5,500 litres of beer, described as 'four tons of beer', and 7,300 litres of rum. Other requirements, such as sails and all manner of necessities to maintain the vessel, goods for trading, the workings for a carpenter's and blacksmith's shops, medical equipment and the scientific instruments involved in observing the transit of Venus at Tahiti, as well as those required by Banks for his botanical pursuits, had to be fitted in. One machine 'for sweetening foul water' was supplied because water stored in wooden casks tended to rapidly become undrinkable. This contraption consisted of a boiler heated by wood in which

---

[5]   For Banks, my principal source is Beaglehole's *Endeavour Journal of Joseph Banks 1768–1771* (1962). For his masterly work on Banks, Beaglehole used both the journal and extracts from the multitudinous papers on Banks in the Mitchell Library, Sydney, and other repositories in Australia and England. This excerpt is taken from vol. 1, fn. 1, p. 153.

the foul water or sea water was heated to boiling point and condensed into pipes from which it was bottled.[6]

Of necessity, vessels undertaking lengthy voyages in that period were floating zoos containing domesticated animals and birds. Thus three cats, 17 sheep, four pigs, Banks's two dogs (which slept in his cabin), and an unspecified number of poultry were aboard. A well-travelled goat, which had just arrived home after an around-the-world voyage with Wallis on the *Dolphin*, also took passage to ensure that the officers had fresh milk for their coffee. In effect, the *Endeavour* was fully laden, and certainly to excess in respect of the number of persons aboard her, so that to move with ease whether by day or night became difficult, if not hazardous, in heavy weather. On Friday 26 August 1768, Cook recorded with his customary detachment, 'At 2 pm got under sail and put to sea'. The first of his great voyages had begun with no fanfare or acclaim.[7]

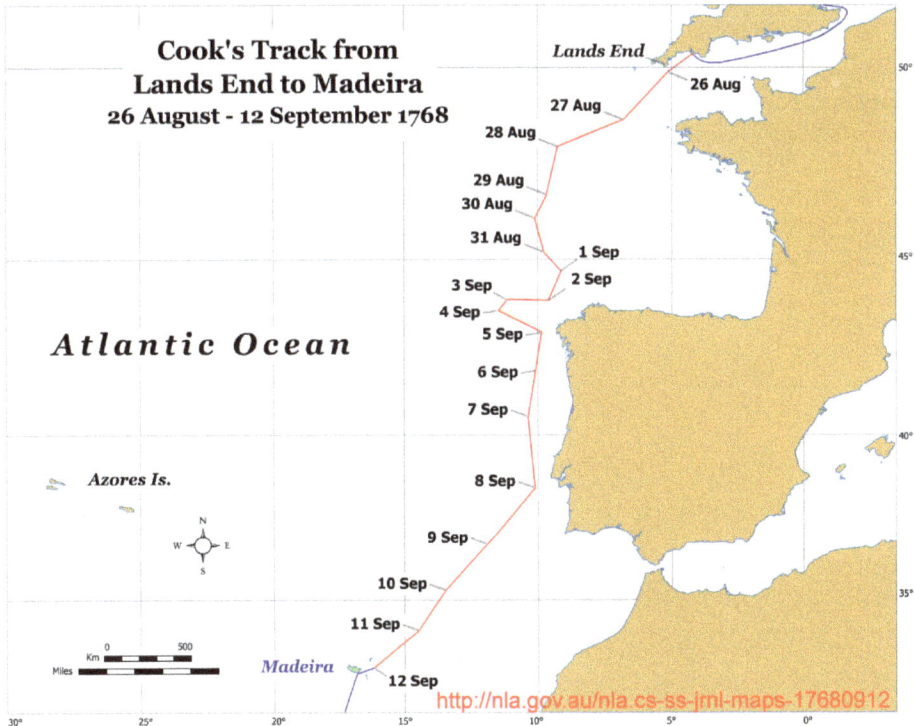

Cook's Track from Lands End to Madeira
26 August - 12 September 1768

Atlantic Ocean

Azores Is.

Madeira

http://nla.gov.au/nla.cs-ss-jrnl-maps-17680912

---

[6] For the reference to tons of beer, I used the 'Anonymous Journal' in *Cook*, p. 549. See also Alistair MacLean, *Captain Cook* (1972, p. 35) for a list of provisions taken on at Deptford and *Cook's Endeavour Journal; The Inside Story* (2008, pp. 32–33). For the water condenser, see Navy Board Warrant, 10 June 1768, in *Cook*, Appendix 5, p. 612, and Alan Villiers, *Captain Cook, The Seaman's Seaman: A Study of the Great Discoverer* (1967, p. 115).

[7] *Cook*, 26 August 1768, p. 4.

2

Madeira to the Cape

A week after departure, the first minor disaster occurred on 1 September 1768. Cook was not unduly distressed when a small skiff belonging to the boatswain was swept overboard. Presumably some of the poultry nested in the skiff and thereby 'between 3 and 4 dozen of our poultry' were drowned. To him this loss was the 'worst of all' that could have happened. Every egg they laid was a precious addition to the largely unchanging daily diet.[1]

The first anchorage was at Funchal, the capital city of Madeira, where the master's mate, Alexander Weir, was accidentally drowned having become entangled in an anchor rope. Cook recorded the event without comment but he immediately replaced him with John Thurman, who was 'impressed into His Majesty's service' from a nearby New York-based vessel, which possibly meant that he had been forcibly persuaded to change his 'service'. The Admiralty had ordered Cook to take on board as much of the local, and already famous wine, he could 'conveniently stow for the use of the ships company'. Cook duly purchased 13,800 litres costing £64 3p, but he also charged £40 5s to the Royal Society 'being for the purchase of wines and other necessaries for the use of Mr Green and myself'. Charles Green was 33 years of age and had been appointed as an assistant at the Royal Observatory in Greenwich in 1761. He was so highly regarded that the Royal Society did not hesitate to secure his service as the principal observer of the transit of Venus. Generous in all manner of things, perhaps too much so in respect of drink, he quickly became invaluable to Cook and especially in fixing positions at sea, to which end he tried, with varying success, to teach the basic elements of a scientific and mathematical nature to some of the crew.[2]

---

[1] *Cook*, 26 August, 1 September, pp. 4, 5.

[2] *Cook*, 14, 16 September 1768, p. 7; *Banks*, vol. 1, p. 168. The two accounts are in *Cook* to the Royal Society, Madeira, 17 September 1768, p. 480. For Green, see Beaglehole in *Cook*, pp. cxxxiii–iv.

Banks went ashore with a party to visit a winery where he saw and described the primitive manner of making the wine for which servants pressed down on the grapes with their feet and elbows, thus squeezing out the juice. Banks promptly decided that this was very probably the way Noah had made it after the flood. The group also visited a Franciscan friary where the 'good fathers' showed them refined hospitality, proving that 'they were not bigots to their religion'. He was especially impressed by the friary's clean and well-ordered infirmary containing one bed only in each of the small 'wards', which had floors lined with white Dutch tiles. The friars had eaten but promised to roast a turkey for dinner the next day, despite it being a Friday and, therefore, a day on which they were obliged not to eat meat. At the convent of Saint Clare the nuns showered them with questions to the extent that 'there was not a fraction of a second in which their tongues did not go at an uncommonly nimble rate'. Despite these occurrences Banks formed decided views of the local people who seemed to be 'as idle, or rather uninformed a set as I ever saw'. On the other hand, he was vastly impressed by the fertility of the island and deplored the neglect of the Portuguese, whom he judged to be even less prompt than the Spanish in the development of the lands that they claimed to possess.[3]

Fresh beef and a live bullock weighing 600 pounds were brought aboard and the bullock was immediately dispatched and consumed. An able seaman and a marine had already been given 12 lashes respectively because they refused to consume their allowance of 'fresh beef'. While Cook could do little to prevent an accidental death, as in the case of the unfortunate Weir, he could, and did, do a great deal to ensure the health of all those under his command. He did so not merely by injunction but by his own behaviour in that he regularly set an example in consuming whatever was put before him, excepting bananas, which he refused to eat although they were plentiful on Madeira. In all else he insisted that his officers follow his example at the table, which left the lesser crewmen no option but to do likewise. Hence the sentence to floggings, mild as they were in the eyes of the old tars who had been accustomed to witness and perhaps endure far worse atrocities. Cook even procured a vast quantity of onions of several varieties and had them dealt out to the whole ship's company in lots weighing 13.5 kilograms each because he thought that they would serve a useful purpose in helping to prevent scurvy. Whether they were expected to eat them raw is not stated.[4]

---

[3]   *Banks*, vol. 1, pp. 161, 164, 165.

[4]   *Cook*, 19, 27 September 1786, pp. 8, 10.

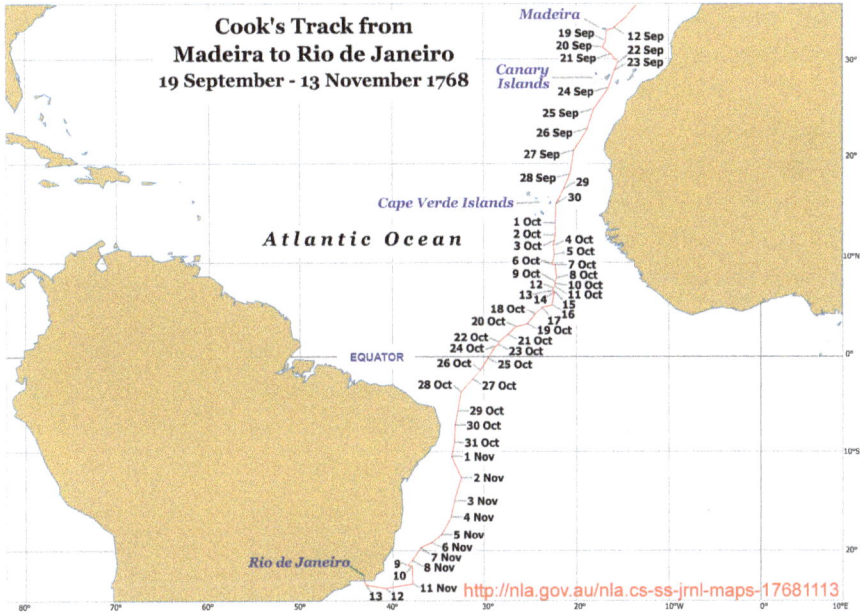

Cook's Track from Madeira to Rio de Janeiro 19 September – 13 November 1768

http://nla.gov.au/nla.cs-ss-jrnl-maps-17681113

The *Endeavour* left Madeira on 19 September and they sighted the 'pike' or 'peak' of Tenerife as they passed on 23 September. The day-to-day routine of the seemingly endless business of manning the ship fell naturally into place. The crew undertook a variety of tasks that gave order to their days such that no periods of idleness, with the possible consequence of unrest, were permitted among them. In recompense they were rewarded with a ration of wine because, by 27 September, the beer had been reduced to two small barrels that Cook deemed to be of such fine quality he saved them for a later occasion. On their way towards the Equator, a young shark was caught and stewed for dinner. Banks and Solander judged it to 'have very good meat', but some seaman rejected it 'probably from some prejudice founded on the species sometimes feeding on human flesh'. No flogging is recorded in consequence of this behaviour, indicating that Cook respected the feeling of his crew in that matter.[5] On 26 October the *Endeavour* passed the Line (Equator) when:

> the Ceremony … practised by all Nations was not omitted; everyone that could not prove on a Sea Chart that he had before crossed the Line, was either to pay a bottle of Rum or be ducked in the sea (and) this ceremony was performed on about 20 or 30 to the no small diversion of the rest.

All living things, including the cats and dogs, were included in the ducking.

---

[5]   *Cook*, 27 September 1768, p. 10; *Banks*, vol. 1, p. 168.

Banks, who had brought brandy aboard for his own use, paid in that spirit for himself, two dogs and his servants. In the various journal accounts of this 'Ancient Custom of the Sea', there is some confusion as to the nature of the fine with one account by the newly appointed master's mate, Francis Wilkinson, asserting that the price exacted was '4 days allowance of wine'. The amount of alcohol generally consumed prompted the author Alistair MacLean to remark with some justice that 'one marvels that the *Endeavour* got as far as the Isle of Wight, far less round the world'. Given that the captain was numbered among the novices who had never crossed the Line, one assumes that Cook paid with his ration of rum. It seems that the money accruing from this ceremony was kept by the master's mate, who used it to buy wine at the next available port for the consumption of the 'ancient' seamen, presumably meaning those who had been to the far south previously.[6]

By early November, the *Endeavour* had reached into the western Atlantic and Cook was aware that he was approaching the coast of Brazil. He expressed his determination to pause at Rio de Janeiro to restock and augment his provisions and he 'doubted not that we should be well received'. By noon on 13 November he was in the harbour. Contrary to his high expectations, the Portuguese Viceroy of Brazil, Dom Antônio Rolim de Moura, opposed a landing by anyone except Cook. It rapidly became evident that de Moura and his subordinates were unwilling to accept Cook's commission and doubted that his true purpose was to observe the transit at Tahiti, of which they knew nothing. In all likelihood they concluded that his ship resembled a pirate vessel rather than one of the British Navy. The latter conclusion was at least understandable, given the humble appearance of the *Endeavour*, and Cook did nothing to dispel the causes of suspicion. Lieutenant John Gore recorded in his journal that the Portuguese authorities were unable to accept Banks and Solander as mere 'naturalists', given their obvious learning and that the *Endeavour* was 'a trading spy'. Among the local seaman it was said, with justification, 'That ship don't look like an English man of war nor have her officers the same dress'. Perhaps in order to live up to the expectations of the Portuguese authorities, whose behaviour increasingly outraged Cook, he took pains to record in detail the harbour and its entrance, all its fortifications and similar matters that could prove useful in the event of a future conflict. To that specific end, also, no less than 45 detailed charts were drawn up of Rio de Janeiro and its surroundings, including the harbour

---

[6] *Cook*, 26 October 1768, p. 16; Beaglehole in *Cook*, fn. 2, p. 16; Alistair MacLean, *Captain Cook* (1972, p. 39); and, *Banks*, vol. 1, pp. 168, 176–77 and fn. 1, p. 177.

itself. Ever careful as to accuracy in maritime matters, Cook remarked that, although the bay at Rio de Janiero was called a river (as its name indicated), such use was improper because it was 'nothing more than a deep inlet of the sea, into which no considerable fresh water empties itself'. In all other respects he carefully refrained from expressing any negative judgements about the Portuguese control and management of Brazil.[7]

In the event, an uneasy three weeks passed during which, after protracted and testy negotiations conducted through tedious and lengthy written communications that remained remarkably courteous on both sides, provisions were procured including fresh beef, vegetables and fruit, some poultry and 1,900 litres of rum. Banks was outraged at the whole sorry affair but he managed, with Solander and Parkinson, to steal time ashore to botanise almost daily. He described the Portuguese authorities as 'illiterate impolite gentry', although he found the civilians he met quite otherwise. He recorded that the 'township of Rio' was said to have 37,000 white inhabitants and 629,000 'negroes' making up 666,000, and that it had 'long been infamous for the unchastity of its women', which assertion, perhaps with regret, he had to accept as true 'as I had not even the least opportunity to go among them'. His generalisation regarding the Portuguese was remarkable only in that it remained a mere assertion. They were 'the laziest as well as the most ignorant race in the whole world'. The *Endeavour* sailed out of the harbour on 7 December 1768 after a further tragedy took place when Peter Flower, who Cook described as 'a good hardy seaman and has sailed with me above five years', fell overboard and perished. He was immediately replaced with a Portuguese seaman whose prompt acceptance of a new role was not explained.[8]

---

7   *Cook*, 13 November–7 December 1768, pp. 22-34; *Banks*, vol. 1, pp. 183, 193. For the charts of Rio de Janeiro and its surroundings see Andrew David, Rüdiger Joppien & Bernard Smith (eds), *The Charts and Coastal Views of Captain Cook's Voyages*, vol. 1, *The Voyage of the Endeavour, 1768-1771* (1988, pp. 16-45).

8   Cook's correspondence with the viceroy is at pp. 481-97; for the reference to Flower, see p. 28; *Banks*, vol. 1, pp. 198-99, 205.

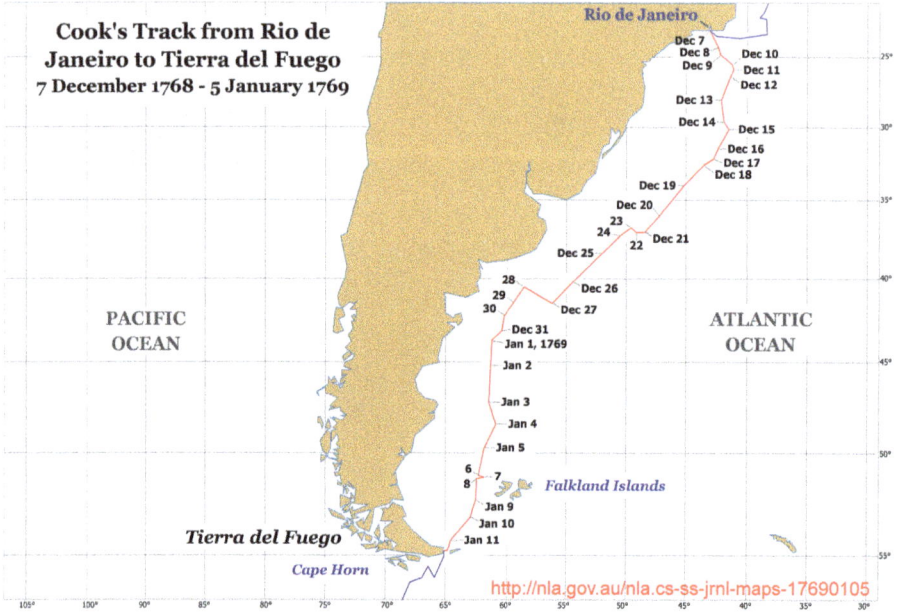

Cook's Track from Rio de
Janeiro to Tierra del Fuego
7 December 1768 - 5 January 1769

Rio de Janeiro

Dec 7
Dec 8   Dec 10
Dec 9   Dec 11
        Dec 12
Dec 13
Dec 14 Dec 15
        Dec 16
        Dec 17
        Dec 18
Dec 19
Dec 20
  23
24   Dec 21
  22
Dec 25
28   Dec 26
29
30   Dec 27
Dec 31
Jan 1, 1769
Jan 2
Jan 3
Jan 4
Jan 5
6   7
8   Falkland Islands
Jan 9
Jan 10
Jan 11

PACIFIC
OCEAN

ATLANTIC
OCEAN

Tierra del Fuego

Cape Horn

http://nla.gov.au/nla.cs-ss-jrnl-maps-17690105

Sailing further south with the temperature dropping, although it was high summer, they saw numerous sharks, whales, porpoises, seals, penguins, shoals of red crawfish and sea lions, which created much general interest among those who had never sailed so far south before. On Christmas Day, Cook, always careful to retain full use of his senses, admitted that 'the People were none of the Soberest'. Banks was more forthright in asserting that 'all good Christians, that is to say all hands, got abominably drunk', so drunk that he thanked God that the wind was mild otherwise 'the Lord knows what would have become of us'. By 6 January 1769 the cold had become intense and Cook issued 'Magellan Jackets' and heavy trousers to all hands except the officers, who apparently fended for themselves. Banks donned a waistcoat and 'thick trousers', which possibly put him in a better frame of mind because he now admitted cheerfully that the *Endeavour* rode the seas with comfort when subjected to gale force winds. With botanising in mind, he had hoped to visit the Falkland Islands but Cook, to the discomfort of his esteemed passenger, showed no inclination to make port again.[9]

Cook decided to sail against the mighty gales rounding Cape Horn rather than pass through the narrow Straits of Magellan, which that valiant explorer had named more modestly as the Straits of All Saints in 1520. The straits

---

[9]   *Cook*, 26 December 1768, pp. 36-37; *Banks*, vol. 1, p. 213. For the charts of Tierra del Fuego, Strait Le Maire, the Bay of Good Success and Cape Horn see Andrew David, Rüdiger Joppien & Bernard Smith (eds), *The Charts and Coastal Views of Captain Cook's Voyages*, vol. 1, *The Voyage of the Endeavour, 1768–1771* (1988, pp. 48-70).

had, thereafter, been used as a gateway from the Atlantic into the Pacific, but they were bordered by channels and mountains which affected the passage of vessels through the straits and sudden, but violent, gusts ravaged their waters. It was still unclear during Cook's voyage whether the land below the straits formed part of the continent or it stood as a separate landmass.

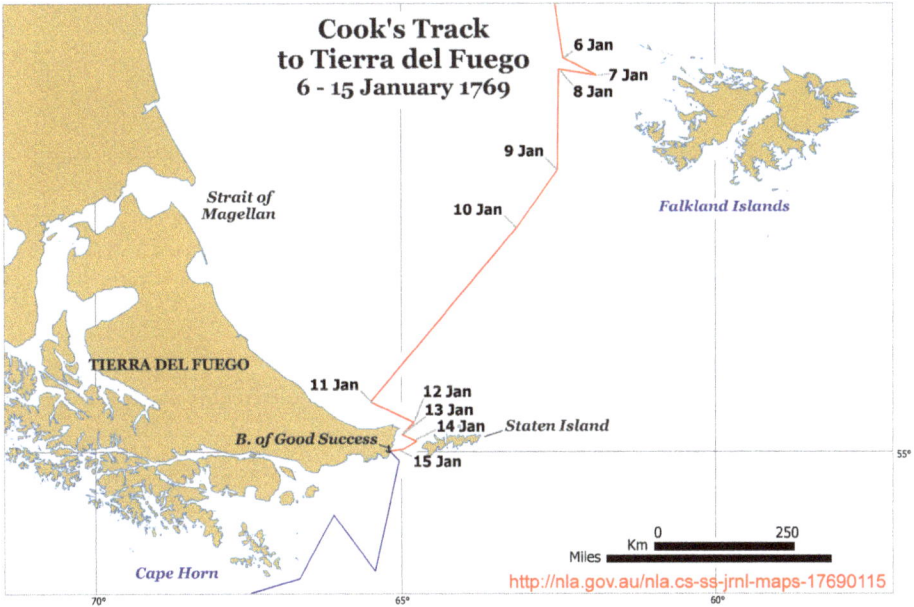

Cook's Track to Tierra del Fuego 6 - 15 January 1769

In search of the fabled Great South Land with its promise of gold, silver, spices and other sought after riches, Willem Schouten and Jacob Le Maire had formed the Australian Company at Hoorn in Holland. In that way they wanted to circumvent the monopoly held by their government in the name of the Dutch East India Company on the use of the Straits of Magellan. They thought it possible that there was a more southern strait by which they could enter the Pacific. Passing by the Magellan Straits with two ships, one of which, the *Hoorn*, was lost in a fire, they named Staten Land and entered the passage called by them the Strait of Le Maire. By 29 January 1616, they sighted the extremity of the southern land and Schouten had his own reward by naming it Cape Hoorn in honour of his birthplace and his lost ship.[10]

Many mariners who passed through the Strait of Le Maire later judged the Straits of Magellan to be a more favourable and safer passage. But Cook had often been in wild and menacing seas. Not for nothing had he grown to manhood on coal-laden vessels plying the perilous coast of England from

---

[10]   J.C. Beaglehole, *The Exploration of the Pacific* (1966, pp. 127-30).

the Humber to the Thames, and he had also mastered the North Sea and ocean stretches in North America. Thus he stuck to the sea route and they were off Tierra Del Fuego by 11 January 1769. The weather was vile with gales, squalls, rain and hail but, by the late afternoon, they were passing Capo San Diego in the Strait of Le Maire. Because Cook knew that they were 'so near to the extremity of South America' in Tierra del Fuego, he determined to calculate the longitude of the place which he decided was 66° west of Greenwich while the latitude was 54° 39' south. His quadrant was out of order and Green had to calculate the distance of the sun and moon, which, under the extreme conditions, must have been difficult and resulted in slight errors. The true position is 65° 8' west and 54° 40' south.[11]

On 12 January 1769 they passed the Three Brothers (Tres Hermanos) and he later remembered them and gave their name to three large hills south of Port Macquarie on the coast of New South Wales. Coming closer to the land they saw a few 'Natives' and Banks and Solander, anxious to go 'botanising', landed with a few others on 15 January. In a deserted hut they came across scraps of European broad cloth, collected about a 100 plants, shot several birds, and returned greatly pleased with their discoveries.[12]

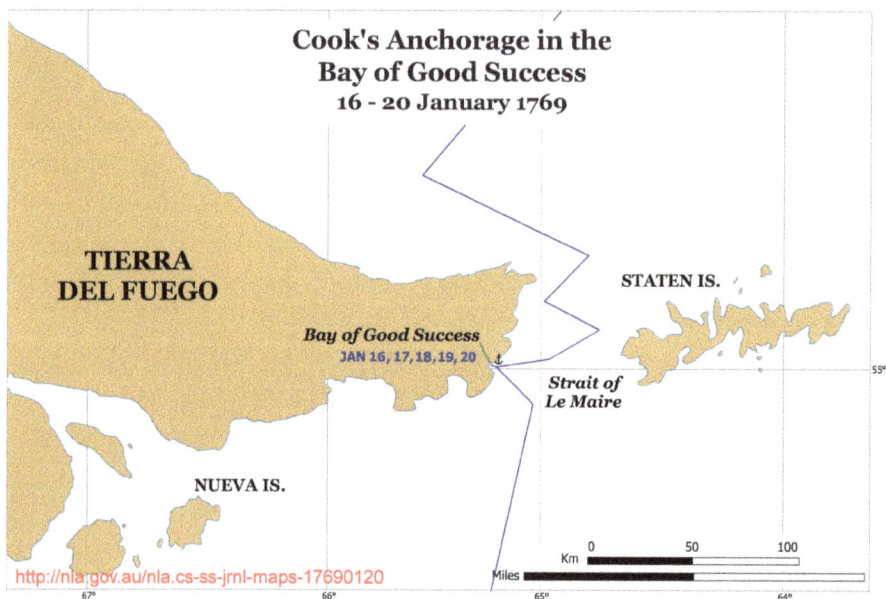

Cook's Anchorage in the Bay of Good Success
16 - 20 January 1769

TIERRA DEL FUEGO

STATEN IS.

Bay of Good Success
JAN 16, 17, 18, 19, 20

Strait of Le Maire

NUEVA IS.

http://nla.gov.au/nla.cs-ss-jrnl-maps-17690120

---

[11] *Cook*, 11, 14 January 1769, pp. 40–41, 43; *Banks*, vol. 1, pp. 207, 209, 212, 213, 214.
[12] *Cook*, 12, 24 January 1769, pp. 42, 50.

By 17 January the *Endeavour* had anchored in the Bay of Good Success, where Cook was determined to get wood and water, and he took his instruments ashore to survey the bay. Wood was always needed to keep a main fire going and to operate the primitive, but effective, distillery, while the barrels carried aboard had to be replenished regularly with fresh water. Cook also wanted to meet the local people and he soon encountered about 40 of them. The total population was only between 50 and 60 and they had no obvious form of government or even chieftain to protect and guide them. They had no fear of their visitors and three later came on board without hesitation. Dressed only in llama or seal skins and almost naked, their bodies were painted with red and black streaks. To Cook, their living in primitive conditions in huts open to the prevailing extreme elements invoked his sympathy, which he expressed by remarking that they were 'perhaps as miserable a set of people as this day are upon Earth'. They were disinclined to drink or eat the liquor or food offered to them but they were much attracted to the cheap but colourful, especially red, beads. Banks said that he visited their 'village' where he saw no sign of their having any boats. He recorded them as living in huts with no furniture, and without vessels for cooking or eating and surviving on little else than shellfish. Undaunted, he spent a day in the nearby high country pursuing plants. Cook, having little knowledge of botany and its intricacies, was inclined to take a less enthusiastic view of such proceedings.

Nevertheless Cook had mellowed and invariably made every effort to assist Banks in his quest, but he declined to accompany the party of 12, which was forced to spend the night in the mountains in the midst of a blizzard. Banks returned with the grim tidings that his two 'Black servants', alleged to have been rendered senseless and paralytic by liquor, had perished from the cold in the snow during the night. He suffered the loss of his male greyhound, which also perished in the snow and was found lying by the corpses. Nonetheless he had 'the satisfaction ... to make a valuable collection of alpine and other plants hitherto unknown in natural history'. While the others fell exhausted into their hammocks, Banks, with his customary unrequited zeal, hauled the seine immediately for further sea specimens. He was unsuccessful.[13]

On setting sail again, the *Endeavour* ploughed through thick fog and strong westerlies which blew her from off the land. By 25 January 1769, Cook and

---

[13] *Cook*, 16, 17 January 1769, pp. 40–41, 44–45; *Banks*, vol. 1, pp. 217–22. See also a reference to Molyneux's journal in *Cook*, p. 46, fn. 3.

Green calculated that they were in the vicinity of Cape Horn 'lying 55° 59' latitude and 68° 13' longitude'. They were, in fact, only a minute out in latitude and less than a degree in longitude and the cape was rounded with difficulty, but safely. Cook was almost nonchalant in his attitude to having conquered the cape without mishap and he deemed it to have been no great feat. Notwithstanding, he stood ready to declare all previous charts as 'imperfect' and 'incorrect' when compared to those done by himself and Green. A week later the winds forced Cook to sail 960 kilometres west from the cape and as far south as the latitude of 60° 10'. He must have been unaware that in 1721 Jacob Roggeveen had sailed through the Strait of Le Maire in search of the great continent and had gone south beyond 60° of latitude. Cook, however, and with justice, was quietly proud that his own latitude was 'the fartherest south' he had ever been. No bonds to man or land could tie down the driving force of Cook, whose spirit belonged to the sea and his ambition spurred him on to sail forth on the vast oceans of the world. They became his true home and one among them, the Pacific, was both his lodestar and his destiny. It had its own right to be foremost because the surface of the Pacific covered one third of the earth and was larger than all the land combined.[14]

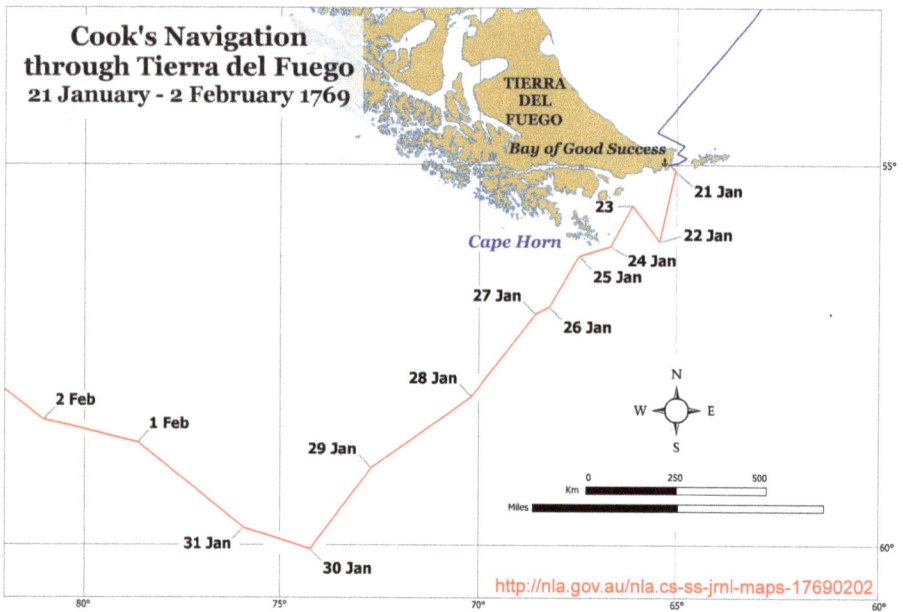

Cook's Navigation through Tierra del Fuego
21 January - 2 February 1769

TIERRA DEL FUEGO

Bay of Good Success

21 Jan
22 Jan
23
24 Jan
25 Jan
Cape Horn
27 Jan
26 Jan
28 Jan
2 Feb
1 Feb
29 Jan
31 Jan
30 Jan

N
W — E
S

0   250   500
Km
Miles

http://nla.gov.au/nla.cs-ss-jrnl-maps-17690202

---

[14]   *Cook*, 25, 26, 31 January, pp. 48–53, 55; *Banks*, vol. 1, p. 215; J.C. Beaglehole, *The Exploration of the Pacific* (1966, pp. 180–81) for Roggeveen.

After the passage through the South Atlantic and the rounding of Cape Horn, no doubt was left in anyone's mind as to whether the *Endeavour* had measured up to the wildest of seas, gales and storms. She might not have carried her excessive burden of fittings, stores and men with grace, but she did so with dogged persistence and an element of dignity.

By late March, Cook was well to the north-west of Cape Horn and thus far out into the Pacific. All the wine had been drunk and 'grog' (presumably rum), took its place. Although Banks disputed the widely held theory that the land masses of the northern world had to be counterbalanced by a large southern continent, he became nonetheless anxious by 24 March 1769 that the line they had sailed from Cape Horn had not thrown up the continent. Cook had his own estimate of the matter. Despite the alleged evidence by 'one of the people' that land was nearby in the form of what could have been a log in the sea, the ever sceptical captain remarked, 'I did not think myself at liberty to spend time in searching for what I was not sure to find'. A more serious matter diverted attention on the next day when a young marine, William Greenslade, either fell, or more probably jumped, overboard. This deplorable event deeply troubled Cook who felt that Greenslade had been persecuted by his 12 fellow marines because of a minor theft, if indeed it was a theft at all, of a seal skin. The deed had gravely embarrassed the other marines who, fearful lest their reputation was tarnished, pursued him relentlessly with insults. Banks dwelt at considerable length on the event, which outraged him because William was 'a very young man scarce 21 years of age, remarkably quiet and industrious' who was driven 'almost mad' by his fellows who represented his trifling behaviour in 'the blackest colours ... [as] an inexcusable crime'. Throughout the whole voyage thereafter, the marines as a group rarely warranted any mention by Cook and Banks in their journals.[15]

---

[15] *Cook*, 24, 26 March 1769, pp. 66, 67. For the grog see *Cook*, 25 March 1769, fn. 1, p. 67; *Banks*, vol. 1, pp. 239–43.

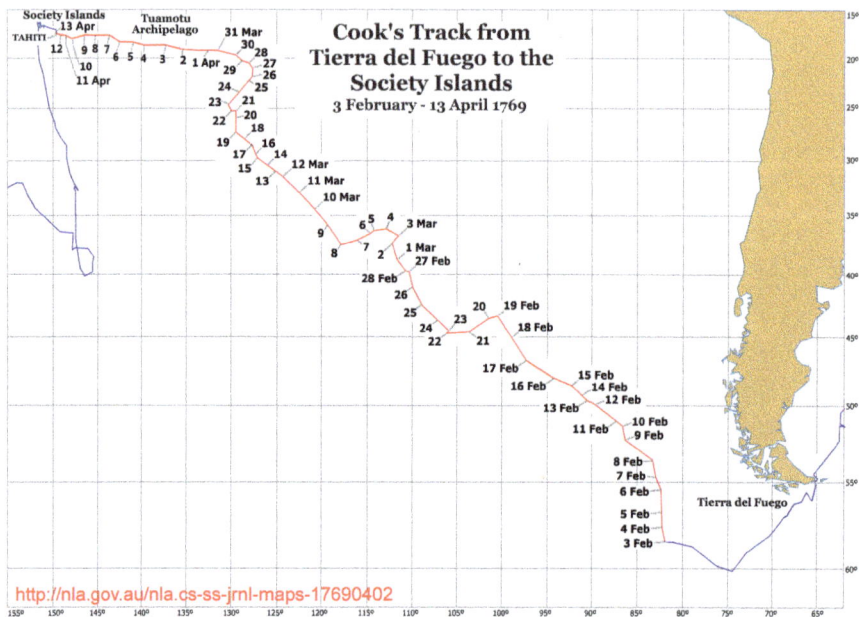

Cook's Track from
Tierra del Fuego to the
Society Islands
3 February - 13 April 1769

3

Garden of Eden

Cook's lack of enthusiasm in respect of a dubious continent was rewarded in early April when the *Endeavour*'s charts made it plain that they were approaching their chosen destination from which to observe the transit and no land mass of any description had been sighted in that long voyage. On 4 April 1769 they sighted Vahitahi, the easternmost island of the Tuamotu Archipelago. Cook was well aware that the *Dolphin* under Captain Samuel Wallis, who was also sent to find the Great South Land, had come among these regions and, on 19 June 1767, Wallis had named King George the Third Island, which was in fact Tahiti or, as it is named on many early charts, Otaheite. There, after some initial hostilities, generally good relations had been established with the inhabitants. Wallis remained a month during which he had charted Tahiti and gave an accurate estimation of its longitude, which, knowing its latitude, made possible Cook's direct voyage there. On his departure, Wallis took ample provisions aboard that he obtained by bartering or by exchanging gifts, through which exchange the islanders had become better acquainted with Europeans. In fact, some of Cook's crew had sailed with Wallis, among them being Cook's second officer, John Gore, and three others, which meant that first-hand knowledge of the island and its inhabitants was available.

Between the period of Wallis's and Cook's visits, Louis Antoine de Bougainville had passed through the Straits of Magellan in January 1768. In April he landed at Tahiti where he was so taken with its beauty that he named it Nouvelle Cythère after one of the main Greek islands. Indeed Bougainville thought he was 'transported into the Garden of Eden' where he and his men were treated with great kindness, despite the islanders' daily habit of pilfering from the French. Unnamed murderers among Bougainville's crew had killed several islanders, despite which, tears were shed at his departure after a stay of a little over a week. Cook was also conscious that as early as 1606 Pedro Fernandes de Quiros had probably reached these same parts and, on 24 March, he was already remarking that 'I thought myself not far from those islands discovered by Quiros in 1606'.[1]

About 24 inhabitants on Vahitahi were observed, 'stark naked of a brown copper colour', but they were armed with long clubs and behaved as if they would oppose a landing, which Cook decided he would not make. For several days many islands were passed and more islanders were seen, but no landings were made, which pleased Banks who had no wish to land among strangers. To him it was far better to arrive at King George the Third Island among people 'who already know our strength and if they do not love at least fear us', and he even hoped to 'persuade one of them to come with us as interpreter'. That latter remark is perplexing, given that he had no idea whether anyone at Tahiti spoke English or whether the language spoken there would be used elsewhere. On 13 April 1769 Cook anchored in Matavai Bay on King George the Third Island. He had arrived at his destination, Tahiti, in good time and thus had ample time to prepare for the transit. He showed no exhilaration in attaining his objective, however, and prosaically marked the conclusion of this first part of the voyage by deciding that, for the duration of his stay at Tahiti, it would be appropriate to switch to civil time in reckoning his days in his journal.[2]

Cook did, however, take great comfort and some justifiable pride in the fact that not one case of scurvy had occurred so far on a voyage of eight months length, which he put down principally to the daily diet of sauerkraut and malt. He had inveigled his initially reluctant men into consuming the sauerkraut with such alacrity that he was forced to ration it. On 17 April he regretted the death from an epileptic fit of Banks's landscapist, Alexander Buchan, 'a Gentleman well skilled in his profession and one that will be greatly missed'. Understandably Banks, surely excessively delighted as he came before 'the truest picture of an arcadia of which we were going to be kings', also lamented the 'irretrievable loss of an ingenious and good young man', which would thereby shatter 'his airy dreams of entertaining his friends in England with the scenes I am to see here'. His eulogy spent itself bewailing that 'had providence spared him a month longer what an advantage it would have been to my undertaking, but I must submit'.[3]

---

[1] *Cook*, 4 April 1769, pp. 69-70. For Wallis and Bougainville see *An Historical Account of the Circumnavigation of the Globe: And of the Progress of the Discovery in the Pacific Ocean, From the Voyage of Magellan to the Death of Cook*, Oliver & Boyd (1836, pp. 186-87).

[2] *Banks*, vol. 1, pp. 244, 247-48, 252, 256–58; *Cook*, 13 April 1769, pp. 73, 74, 81.

[3] *Cook*, 14-17 April 1769, pp. 77-81; *Banks*, vol. 1, pp. 257–58. For the charts and illustrations done during, or about, the period at Tahiti see Andrew David, Rüdiger Joppien & Bernard Smith (eds), *The Charts and Coastal Views of Captain Cook's Voyages*, vol. 1, *The Voyage of the Endeavour, 1768-1771* (1988, pp. 74-125).

Given his upbringing, Banks was disposed to accept that society had its ranks and that his own family stood on a high level. Whether as large landowners, or as members of parliament and the Royal Society, they were well known and respected in the right places. Joseph, born on 13 February 1743, was subjected, fruitlessly, at Harrow and Eton to vast measures of Latin and Greek. He opted for botany, which he pursued untaught and continued his studies in it at Oxford, but came down without a degree and henceforth devoted his mental energies to natural science. Having inherited his father's wealth at the age of 21, he used £10,000 of it to finance his voyage with Cook. Some of his friends thought his proposed venture south with Cook preposterous and advised him instead to take the Grand Tour of Europe. He replied, 'Every blockhead does that; my Grand Tour shall be one round the whole globe'.[4]

Although the 'Hints' given to Cook before his departure by James Douglas, 14th Earl of Morton and President of the Royal Society, in which Banks and Solander held membership, were unofficial, they nonetheless came from the head of the body responsible in the first instance for the voyage of the *Endeavour*. In any event, Morton's 'Hints' prompted Cook to set down a short list of rules for the behaviour of his men while at Tahiti. The principal one was 'To endeavour by every fair means to cultivate a friendship with the Natives and to treat them with all imaginable humanity'. With very few exceptions this rule was maintained, some might argue that it was excessively so in respect of the friendships that were rapidly established between the sexes. Cook refrained from overt criticism of the prevailing sexual mores, including those of Banks, while Sydney Parkinson, the draftsman and illustrator employed by Banks, was almost prudishly censorious at the fact that most of the crew quickly established relationships with women.

Nonetheless, Cook was not able to refrain from remarking on the widespread habit among the islanders of stealing 'everything that came within their reach'. Indeed, the only act of extreme violence committed on Tahiti was the fatal shooting of an islander who had manhandled a sentry and made off with his musket. The marines who happened to be on the spot were commanded by a mere boy, though a midshipman, who ordered the shooting in a fit of juvenile impetuosity. The affair ended rapidly with good relations restored because the islander chiefs agreed that a serious form of retaliation was demanded by such an act of thievery. On a less serious

---

[4]   For *Banks*, see vol. 1, pp. 1–54. For the remark on the Grand Tour, see Patrick O'Brian, *Joseph Banks: A Life* (1997, p. 23).

note the ship's butcher, Henry Jeffs, was flogged after threatening to cut the throat of a woman who refused to give him a stone hatchet in exchange for a nail. Cook explained at length the reason for the punishment but, as soon as it commenced, the islander burst into tears while the woman in question, named Tamide, 'was in the greatest agonies and interceded for him'. Cook refused to cede to her entreaties.[5]

Cook revealed a less stern element of his nature in an episode with an imposing woman whom the Dolphins (Cook's name for those on the *Endeavour* who had been at Tahiti with Wallis) had come to know as the Queen. Queen Obariea came aboard the *Endeavour* where Cook gave her a present in the form of a child's doll and pretended that it was a representation of his wife. Delighted with such a precious memento, she pinned the doll to her breast and took Cook ashore where, pointing out the doll and explaining its importance, she led him around among the crowd that had gathered. Having acted the tease, Cook observed with intense interest some of the traditional practises of the islanders in respect of the dead, although he found difficulty in deciding other than that they made an offering for them. From this he deduced that 'it should seem that these people not only believe in a Supreme being, but in a future state also'. He concluded somewhat laconically that 'the Mysteries of most Religions are very dark and not easily understood even by those who profess them'. Nonetheless, Cook saw to the celebration of divine worship on three Sundays during the three months stay at Tahiti in response to the recommendation of Morton and the injunction of the Admiralty to do so, although he refrained from taking a role in any ceremony himself. There is no record in the journals of a ceremony on any Sunday at sea, or of a funeral at sea, at which a ceremony was conducted by the captain. Both Cook and Banks, however, were moved by the many local people present on this Sunday, 14 May 1769, who behaved with 'great decency' and who furthermore bade those outside the tent in which the service was held to remain silent throughout. Afterwards the people neither asked nor wished for an explanation of the ceremony. This led Banks to conclude that there was no evidence of religion 'among these people, maybe they are entirely without it', which was manifestly false if Cook is to be believed. The other event celebrated, although some days late, was the king's birthday. Attempts to teach the pronunciation of George proved ineffective but Tupia, who later left Tahiti aboard the *Endeavour*, nonetheless showed his enthusiasm for the absent monarch by becoming 'most enormously

---

[5]   *Cook*, 13, 15 April, pp. 75, 78-80; see Molyneux's journal in *Cook*, 29 April 1769, p. 554; see also Sydney Parkinson, *Journal of a Voyage to South Seas* (1773).

drunk'.[6]

Before his departure from home, the Royal Society had paid Cook a gratuity of 100 guineas to act with Green and others as an observer of the transit of Venus and he went to great pains to ensure that a strongly built fortress sufficiently large as to be able to 'accommodate about 45 men' was erected from which to observe same. He did so with the help of the islanders, despite the fact that they were not permitted to visit it upon completion. The structure was named Fort Venus and it contained, as well as the equipment for the transit, a forge, ovens and 'pens for our sheep'. Perhaps disappointed with the eventual results, Cook passed over almost casually the proceedings involved in undertaking the transit itself. He sent out two parties tasked with making an observation from nearby islands while, together with Solander and Green, he did so himself from the main base. The whole point of the exercise, being undertaken simultaneously by teams of international scientists at various places on earth, was to calculate if possible the exact length of time it took Venus to pass over the sun. The day, Saturday, 3 June 1769, was 'hotter than it had ever been before', rising at noon to 119°F which was due clearly to the fact that 'the thermometer [was] in the sun'. However, the heavens were cloudless and the sky 'perfectly clear', which implies that there was no natural impediment to success. Nevertheless Cook reported that the results in the time of transit taken as Venus passed over the sun differed from one another 'much more than could be expected'. Cook was clearly displeased and partially ascribed the differentials to 'an atmosphere or dusky shade round the body of the planet', although it is surely possible that the extreme heat might have affected the instruments and even the sun and the planet were perhaps partly obscured by heatwaves. He made no further reference to the matter in his journal at that time. Banks merely reported that the sun rose 'as clear and bright as we could wish him'. After shopping for provisions he was delighted to be able to entertain 'three handsome girls' in his tent but was quick to express 'his great satisfaction', when informed that the observation had been attended with 'much success'.[7]

---

[6]   *Cook*, 14, 15, 21 April; 14 May 1769, pp. 77, 79–80, 84, 93; *Banks*, vol. 1, p. 277; on 21 May Queen Obariea and many others were present and all 'behaved very decently', *Banks*, vol. 1, p. 279; for the birthday see *Banks*, vol. 1, p. 286.

[7]   *Cook*, 1–3 June 1769, pp. 81–4, 97–98, *Banks*, vol. 1, 'the day being perfectly clear with not so much as a cloud intervening', pp. 285–86; Sydney Parkinson, *Journal of a Voyage to South Seas*, (1773, p. 38.)

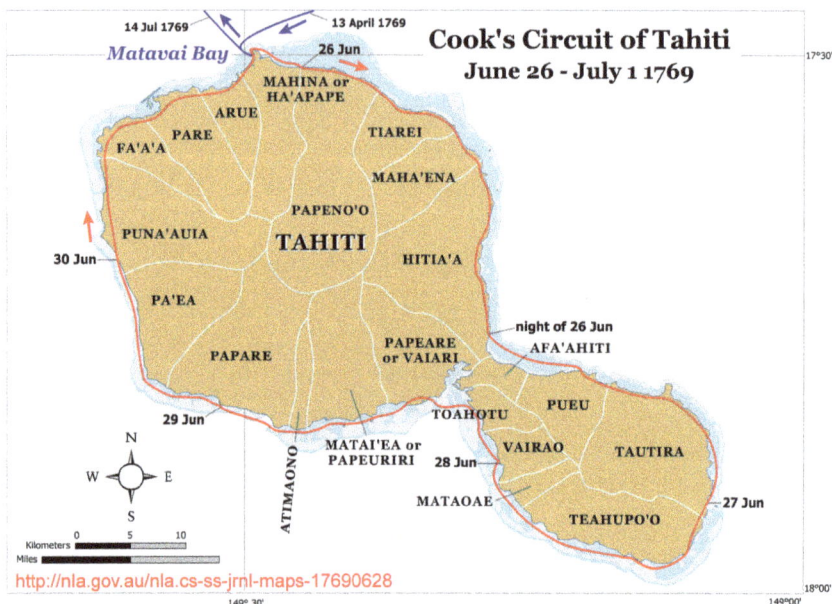

Cook's Circuit of Tahiti
June 26 - July 1 1769

An unusual length of time passed in preparation for leaving Tahiti, which was punctuated by the eating of a dog cooked to perfection by Tupia in an underground oven. It proved to be a 'most excellent dish', while Cook and others who ate it decided that they 'never ate sweeter meat (and) resolved for the future not to despise dog's flesh'. Banks ascribed its sweetness to the fact that, unlike European dogs, 'these scarce in their lives touch animal food'. Parkinson, however, found the odour of the flesh objectionable and asserted that very few of the crew partook of the meal. Parkinson also said that there was not the same reluctance to eat rats, once fried, and that the islanders ate mainly breadfruit and bananas, while flesh of any kind was rarely taken and even fish eaten sparingly, which, because no salt was available, they dipped in sea water to strengthen its taste.[8]

Another event moved Cook and Banks to conclude that there was evidence of the visit of a Spanish ship to Tahiti in January 1768. Banks encountered islanders who had an iron tool that he claimed had not been carried to Tahiti on either the *Dolphin* or the *Endeavour*. The explanation by the islanders was that a Spanish ship had called there, and remained for eight days anchored nearby, although the place in question did not seem to be a suitable harbour. The Spaniards came ashore, erected tents and, departing to the west, took with them a young man who was a chieftain's younger brother

8   *Cook*, 20 June 1769, pp. 102–03; *Banks*, vol. 1, pp. 292-93; Sydney Parkinson, *Journal of a Voyage to South Seas*, (1773, pp. 45-60).

whom they promised to bring back when they returned in nine months. They also said that the Spaniards had a woman aboard with them. In fact, Bougainville's expedition had a woman aboard who had managed to conceal her sex until they arrived at Tahiti, where the islanders immediately perceived the deception. Banks questioned the locals thoroughly as to whether they were in fact Spaniards they had seen, which they proved by picking out the Spanish flag and insisting repeatedly that it was the one flown by the visitors. This was followed up by a visit to the place where the visitors had camped and where they met the local chieftain, Orétté, whose brother had been carried away. There were holes at the place where the tents were erected and Banks said that they showed him one corner in 'which they set up a cross I had made for them and said Turu turu which in their language means the knees', seeming to indicate that the Spaniards prayed before it. Banks fossicked about and found 'a small piece of potshard or tile', which he took as proof that the islanders had not deceived him. Cook has a more modest variation of this account, but agreed with it in essence. He even went further and said that among the islanders they saw iron tools as well as jackets, shirts and other garments 'usually worn by Spanish seamen, [which] proves beyond doubt that they must have been ships of that nation and come from some port on the coast of South America'. When he reached Batavia, Cook was told that Bougainville and his two ships were at Tahiti two years before and that the young man taken aboard was waiting at Mauritius for a French vessel to return him to his home. Bougainville, however, later stated firmly that he had never flown a Spanish flag so that, to some extent, the episode remained a mystery given the tendency of the Spanish to secrecy as to where they voyaged in the Pacific. Moreover the flags of Spain and France in that period are so different that it is difficult to reconcile the accounts, given the normally acute degree of observation among the islanders.[9]

The thought of an imminent departure proved to be a sufficient incentive for two young marines, Clement Webb and Samuel Gibson, to abscond into the nearby mountains with young ladies to whom they had formed strong attachments. Banks asserted that one of them 'is already married and become an inhabitant of Otahitte [Tahiti]'. The by now regular practise of impounding islander possessions, such as canoes, in return for stolen items was well established with varying and less positive results over the three months of the sojourn at Tahiti. This episode warranted a more serious step so that royalty in the persons of Queen Obariea and her husband the

---

[9]   *Cook*, 6, 11, 20, 26 June 1769, pp. 98–99, 100, 102–03, 105–06, 139; *Banks*, vol. 1, 286-87, 294-95.

king, from whom she was separated in bed and board, together with several chieftains, were detained on the understanding that they would be released immediately upon the return of the wayward youngsters. This transaction took longer than Cook would have liked and caused temporary animosities on both sides. Doubtless with their ardours cooled, the young suitors were brought to heel and Cook was not disposed to punish them excessively beyond a short confinement and two dozen lashes each.[10]

On 13 July 1769 the *Endeavour* sailed from Tahiti and Cook's responsibility to both the Royal Society and the Admiralty had been fulfilled. He had observed the transit of Venus, but to what good end he remained uncertain. Although several islanders 'were daily offering to go away with us', Cook agreed to take Tupia who, on the eve of their departure had come aboard together with his servant, Tiata, a young boy. Thereby Banks had his early wish fulfilled of obtaining the services of an interpreter, indeed of much more than a mere interpreter. He promptly offered to be responsible financially for Tupia, thinking that he would profit later in England much more than his neighbours who, allegedly, kept lions and tigers for their amusement and to show them off to their friends. Tupia's ability to learn English was clearly remarkable and he had been constantly in attendance to the needs of the visitors from the beginning of their stay. Cook said that he was 'a Chief and a Priest ... a very intelligent person', aged about 45, whose knowledge of the area, its geography and its peoples, their religion, laws and customs was greater than anyone else Cook had met. Furthermore Cook clearly hoped that Tupia would assist him in the search for the Great South Land. Banks was well aware that Tupia undertook to go with them only after a period of indecision during which he struggled to master his emotions. Eventually he 'stood firm at last in his resolution of accompanying us' but he 'parted with a few heartfelt tears'. Parkinson described the emotions of the departure well: 'On our leaving the shore, the people in the canoes set up their woeful cry, Awai, Awai; and the young women wept very much. Some of the canoes came up to the side of the ship, while she was under sail, and brought us many cocoas.'[11]

Before leaving Tahiti, Cook and Banks both wrote summaries of the land, of its people and their customs. Their accounts contain clear evidence of collaboration, which is not surprising. Cook was strictly enjoined by the Admiralty to write a daily journal and to fill in the log, which combined tasks

---

[10] *Cook* 10, 11 July 1769, pp. 114–16; *Banks*, vol. 1, pp. 310–12; *Cook*, 13 July 1769, p. 117.
[11] *Cook*, 13 July 1769, p. 117; *Banks*, vol. 1, pp. 313–14, Sydney Parkinson, *Journal of a Voyage to South Seas*, (1773, p. 95).

added a further and weighty burden to all the other duties his role as captain of the vessel entailed. He knew he would have an official readership, which demanded high standards. Banks was answerable only to himself, which gave him greater freedom of expression. It is remarkable that, apart from a fleeting classical reference by Banks, there is little difference in the use of the language between the two journals. That they would discuss their entries in the main cabin after the chores of the day were done and thus overlap and draw from each other was both natural and almost inevitable. This explains why a particular example of sexual relations between 'more than half of the better sort of inhabitants of the Island' was described in much the same words. It was the practise of 'enjoying free liberty in love without a possibility of being troubled or disturbed by its consequences' because 'those who are so unfortunate as to be thus begot are smothered at the moment of their birth'. Both were told of its prevalence repeatedly and noted almost with horror that its practitioners took pride in it. Both condemned it in the same words, although Cook omitted to refer to the intervention of the devil. He, however, agreed with Banks who wrote that it was 'founded upon a custom so devilish, inhuman, and contrary to the first principles of human nature' that they expected that the account they gave of widespread infanticide would be believed only with difficulty and reluctance. Whatever reaction to the above account may have been evidenced among the men of foresight in the Admiralty, it is certain that Cook's summary of the future prospects of Tahiti would have given them little if any joy. He summed up his judgement with 'notwithstanding nature has been so very bountiful to it yet it does not produce any one thing of intrinsic value or that can be converted into an article of trade, so that the value of the discovery consists wholly in the refreshments it will always afford to shipping'. It could well have been the case that the old tars among his readers might have pondered more happily on the varied nature of the 'refreshments' on offer at Tahiti besides pigs and yams.[12]

The remainder of the time spent in the islands from 14 July until 15 August passed without drama although Banks was less taken with the inhabitants of the other four islands where they landed out of the 16 they had seen besides Tahiti. He said of the inhabitants of the latter that they were 'a people so free from deceit that I trusted myself among them almost as freely as I could do in my own country.' Cook was happy to state that while in the Society Islands they had used up very few of their provisions having been 'plentifully supplied with Hog, Fowls, Plantains and Yams'. Given his added role as purser,

---

[12]   *Cook*, July 1769, pp. 127-28, 136; *Banks*, vol. 1, pp. 351-52.

Cook had been granted £120 to victual the *Endeavour* before sailing and was also authorised to 'be at liberty to draw upon the Society for any sum not exceeding £120' whilst on the voyage. Pigs seem to have been available in good measure at Tahiti and throughout the Society Islands and, although they were small as compared to the European pig, their flesh was agreeable. Otherwise and apart from fish, the Pacific was almost a meatless world, which proved to be a trial for Europeans who ventured there. Cook tried to obtain food at the lowest possible cost, especially by barter with nails, indeed with any iron object or tool of even minimal value. Thus little drain was made on his accounts. The fact that he would attempt to profit by virtue of his role casts no reflection on him. Unlike Banks, especially, Cook's only income lay in the exercise of his profession. Furthermore, as captain, his primary responsibility was the welfare of his crew. Long leagues at sea lay before them and fresh food, especially meat, was precious. In any event he seemed well satisfied with the outcome of his stay in the islands and, on 17 July, he permitted himself to record an event with a degree of uncustomary levity. At a harbour called Owharre on the island of Huahine, Tupia made an offering intended for 'the God of this people'. They responded with a pig and coconuts as an offering 'for our God'. Cook remarked 'thus they have certainly drawn us into committing sacrilege for the Hog hath already received sentence of death and is to be dissected tomorrow'.[13]

Tupia's knowledge of a large segment of the neighbouring Pacific bordered on the prodigious, much of it drawn from what his father had taught him. Unsurprisingly he knew nothing of a 'Continent or large track of land' in those parts so that, by 15 August, Cook 'now fully resolved to stand directly to the Southward in search of the Continent' was determined to set out on his main task of discovering the Great South Land long dreamt of by many northern Europeans and firmly believed in by many accepted authorities, including the foremost proponent of same, Alexander Dalrymple. Although Cook's private attitude to the existence of the continent bordered on incredulity, as a loyal servant of the Admiralty, which had ordered him to search for it, he had no hesitation in doing so even though he seemed to have considered it a mere vanity. In any case his time among the Society Islands, which he named in honour of the Royal Society and of which he had taken possession on 21 July 'in the name of His British Majesty', had come to a close. He was ordered to take possession when he came across new islands that had not hitherto been claimed by Europeans and then to

---

13 Royal Society Council meeting, 19 May 1768, in *Cook*, vol. 1, p. 513; *Cook*, 9, 17 July, pp. 150, 151; Andrew David et al. in *The Charts* have seven sketches of views of Huahine, pp. 136-39, 140.

do so only under the specific circumstances laid down by the Admiralty. Had he so acted when taking possession of the Society Islands he made no attempt to explain the manner in which he went about the act or ceremony and more importantly whether he had discussed the matter with the local chieftains. It is not inconceivable that the orders of the Admiralty in this matter were issued on the understanding that common sense would prevail. After all it would be in most cases likely that any meaningful negotiations between people possessing no common language would prove unprofitable. Why then engage in them, especially if the outcome was to be the same regardless of any protest on the part of the inhabitants in question?[14]

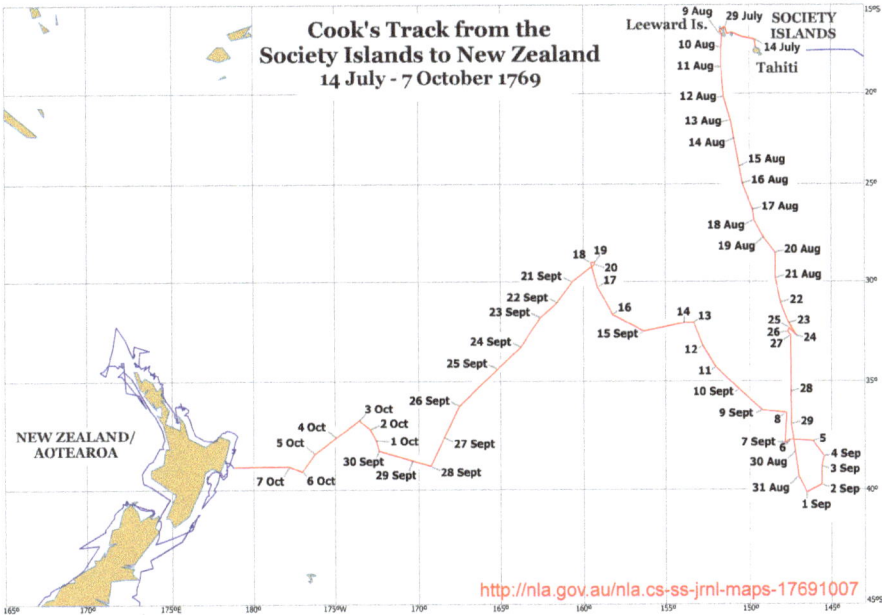

Cook's Track from the Society Islands to New Zealand 14 July - 7 October 1769

NEW ZEALAND/ AOTEAROA

http://nla.gov.au/nla.cs-ss-jrnl-maps-17691007

Before his departure from home, a set of so-called 'Instructions' were given to Cook, which help in understanding and appreciating his behaviour in respect of relations with the islanders as well as his taking possession of the Society Islands, New Zealand and the east coast of New Holland. The first set of instructions, dated 30 July 1786, was marked 'Secret', meaning that they were directed to him alone, but presumably he was free to discuss them with his officers at his own discretion. Given by the commissioners acting on behalf of the 'Lord High Admiral of Great Britain', they deal directly with the voyage as far as Tahiti. He was, however, instructed 'to endeavour by all means proper to cultivate a friendship with the Natives', as well as giving presents to them, exchanging provisions and 'Showing them every

---

14   *Banks*, vol. 1, pp. 333-34; *Cook*, 21 July 1769, p. 144; 9 August 1769, pp. 150-51.

kind of Civility and regard'.[15] It is reasonably clear that Cook's disposition as a human being was inclined to civility and the cultivation of friendship as well as the avoidance of bloodshed, while prudence indicated that the establishment of good relations was a prerequisite to the absolute necessity of obtaining the provisions demanded by a long journey at sea. The death of the islander at Tahiti in the incident involving the theft of a firearm was neither undertaken at Cook's command nor with his approval.

The additional instruction of the same date, also marked 'Secret', was opened by Cook after observing the transit of Venus. It addressed the matter of the discovery of the Great South Land. Using elevated terminology, the commissioners assert that 'there is reason to imagine that a continent or land of great extent may be found to the Southward of the tract lately made by Captain Wallis … or of the tract of any former navigators in pursuits of the like kind', which probably referred to Quiros. Were it, therefore, possible to transfer from the imagined to the real such would 'redound greatly to the honour of this nation as a maritime power, as well as to the dignity of the Crown of Great Britain and may tend greatly to the advancement of the trade and navigation thereof'. To further this end Cook was ordered to sail south to 40° latitude. If unsuccessful he was to proceed further west and south to the latitude of 35° and thence to New Zealand, 'the land discovered by Tasman'. In the event that he did discover the continent, he was to examine it carefully, chart its coasts, bays and harbours and, were he to find 'any mines, minerals or valuable stones', he was to bring home specimens of them. Finally he was to 'observe the Genius, Temper, Disposition and Number of the Natives' and cultivate a friendship and alliance with them, which would presumably be brought at least partially to fruition by 'making them presents of such trifles as they may value'. That done, and with their consent, he was to 'take possession of convenient situations in the name of the King of Great Britain; or, if you find the Country uninhabited take possession for His Majesty by setting up proper marks and inscriptions, as first discoverers and possessors'. Should he fail to fall upon the continent, he was to explore as much of the coast of New Zealand as possible. The commissioners revealed their own humanity by insisting that all this be done 'as the condition of the Bark, the health of her crew, and the state of your provisions will admit of'. The ultimate caveat was that nothing he did was to divert him from his principal objective which was 'the discovery of the Continent so often mentioned'. He was then to return home either around

---

[15]   See Beaglehole in *Cook*, pp. cclxxix–cclxxxiv.

the Cape of Good Hope or Cape Horn, dependent on his judgement of 'the most eligible way'.[16]

Despite the secrecy surrounding the import of Cook's voyage, knowledge circulating of it in London came into the hands of the press, possibly via Dalrymple, who certainly knew of it. The *London Gazetter* of 18 August 1786 informed the public that:

> The gentlemen, who are to sail in a few day's for George's Land, the new discovered island in the Pacific Ocean, with an intention to observe the Transit of Venus, are likewise, we are credibly informed, to attempt some new discoveries in that vast unknown tract above the latitude of 40° degrees.

No mention was made in the instructions or in the press of visiting or charting the east coast of New Holland, the existence of which in some form was already accepted as running north to south between New Guinea and Van Diemen's Land, although to what degree it extended in an eastern longitude had yet to be established.[17]

On 10 August 1868 James Douglas, 14th Earl of Morton and President of the Royal Society, the body financially responsible for much of the costs involved in the voyage, wrote a series of 'Hints' addressed to Cook, Banks, Solander 'and the other Gentlemen who go upon the Expedition'. Clearly the society had no desire to enter into the responsibility of the Admiralty to control the *Endeavour* and its crew, but Cook was a servant of the society insofar as he accepted payment to carry out its wishes in regard to the transit of Venus. Morton began by stating that they needed 'to exercize the utmost patience and forbearance with respect to the natives of the several Lands where the Ship may touch'. He added words of such high import, indeed of humanity and nobility, that some of them deserve to be set down in full:

> To have it still in view that shedding the blood of those people is a crime of the highest nature.
>
> They are the natural, and in the strictest sense of the word, the legal possessors of the several Regions they inhabit.
>
> No European Nation has a right to occupy any part of their country, or settle among them without their voluntary consent.
>
> Conquest over such people can give no just title, because they never could be Aggressors.

---

16   Beaglehole in *Cook*, pp. cclxxix–cclxxxiv.
17   Beaglehole in *Cook*, p. cxxxvii.

They may naturally and justly attempt to repel intruders, whom they may apprehend are come to disturb them in their quiet possession of their country, whether that apprehension be well or ill founded.

Therefore should they in a hostile manner oppose a landing, and kill some men in the attempt, even this would hardly justify firing among them, 'till every other gentle method had been tried.[18]

In some measure Morton was heard and acted upon.

Cook sailed south for about 2,400 kilometres through raging seas, gales of the Roaring Forties, and an increasingly dipping thermometer. Reaching the latitude of 40° south without any success in his quest for the continent, he decided enough was enough. The seven weeks of an uneventful voyage from Tahiti was broken only by the death of John Reardon, the boatswain's mate who was rendered 'speechless and past recovery' after consuming a quantity of rum given to him 'out of sheer good nature by the Boatswain'. It is just to remark that the six deaths on the *Endeavour* since departure were not due to neglect or a lack of provisions. Banks spent some time making an inventory of the provisions he still had available aboard in late September. It appears that he and his party had a private stock of sheep, an English boar and sow with a litter, a few surviving 'South Seas hogs' and North American apples from which pies were made. Among the provisions available to officers and crew were salted beef and pork which were 'still excellent' as were the flour, oatmeal, peas, soup and 'sourcrout' while wheat was boiled for breakfast on some week days but the bread, being riddled with vermin, was increasingly unacceptable. Banks still had some beer and porter on tap but the wine was not up to his expectations. The ship's cook suffered no complaint despite his limitations. Before departure Cook had remonstrated with the Admiralty when they provided him with a one-legged cook. Cook concluded that he would not stand up to the voyage. Someone in authority must have had his own sense of wry humour when the replacement proved to be one- armed.[19]

Home was constantly on the minds of even the old hands aboard and, on the first anniversary of their leaving England, a modest feast was had in Banks's cabin. A piece of Cheshire cheese, reserved for this occasion, was consumed and 'a cask of porter tapped which proved excellently good', so good in fact that 'we lived like Englishmen and drank the health of our friends in England'. On another occasion, Parkinson recorded that a birthday

---

[18]   *Cook*, pp. 514-19.
[19]   *Cook*, 28 August 1769, pp. 159–60. For the provisions, see *Banks*, vol. 1, pp. 393–94.

was celebrated by roasting a leg of mutton served with French beans for dinner and thus the fare of 'Old England afforded us a grateful feast'.[20]

On 6 October 1769 land was sighted from the masthead by a boy, Nicholas Young. Cook rewarded the lad and named the nearby promontory Young Nick's Head. Cook and Banks had both read Dalrymple's *An Account of the Discoveries Made in The South Pacifick Ocean, Previous to 1764*, which was published in London in 1767. The book contained in part Tasman's account of his contact with New Zealand. The result was that Banks stated firmly that 'all hands seem to agree that this is the Continent we are in search of' and Master's Mate Richard Pickersgill even contributed a chart to affirm the agreement, which he entitled 'A Chart of part of the So Continent'. Banks was gracious enough to grant that there was no evidence that Cook had arrived at the same conclusion as 'all hands' had done, and who remained convinced, at least temporarily, that they had come across the continent. That they had reached New Zealand was obvious to Cook from studying Tasman's charts and he was pleased to come upon it with such ease.[21]

---

[20]   *Banks*, vol. 1, p. 388.

[21]   *Cook*, 15, 28 August 1769, pp. 155-57, 159-60; 7 October 1769, p. 167; *Banks*, vol. 1, pp. 397, 399. See also Alexander Dalrymple, *An Account of the Discoveries Made in The South Pacifick Ocean, Previous to 1764* (1767); Sydney Parkinson, *Journal of a Voyage to South Seas* (1773, p. 119). For Pickersgill, see Beaglehole in *Cook*, fn. 5, p. 262.

Cook's Track around New Zealand
8 October 1769 - 31 March 1770

29 Nov - 5 Dec
Bay of Islands

15-28 Nov

5 Dec 1769 - 10 Jan 1770
Bay of Islands to
Woody Head

5-14 Nov
Mercury Bay
30 Oct - 4 Nov

Woody Head

Tolaga Bay 20-29 Oct

11-14 Jan
Woody Head to
Queen Charlot Sound

Poverty Bay 8 Oct

Hawken Bay

31 Mar 1770

15 Jan - 6 Feb

18 Mar - 26 Mar
Abut Head to
Low Neck Bay

*Queen Charlot
Sound*
C. Foulwind

C. Palliser

7-14 Feb
Queen Charlot Sound
to Banks Peninsula

TASMAN SEA

Abut Head

Banks Peninsula

Cascade Point

Milford Sound

Cape Saunders
Cape Providence

NEW ZEALAND

Stewart Is.

15 Feb - 17 Mar
Banks Peninsula to Abut Head

155°   160°   165°   170°   175°E   180°   175°W

35°

40°

45°

50°

4

Meeting the Maori

In 1642, Abel Tasman, with two ships, the *Heemskerk* and the *Zeehan*, was sent by the Dutch East India Company from Batavia in search of the Great South Land. On 24 November they encountered land. It was the south-western part of a new land that he named Van Diemen's Land after the Dutch Governor at Batavia. Sailing further south, Tasman passed along the southern coast and then anchored on the eastern coast for two days in an unsuccessful search for water. Tasman was determined, however, to claim the land for the company and, by extension, for the Dutch, to which end 'we carried with us a pole with the Company's mark carved into it, and a Prince-flag to be set up there, that those who shall come after us may become aware that we have been here, and have taken possession of the said land as our lawful property'. Not finding it safe to land he ordered the carpenter, a strong swimmer, to set out for the shore with the pole and the flag to 'plant said pole with the flag at top into the earth', which ceremony was keenly watched by Tasman and his officers. Having seen no Aborigines but only the smoke from their fires, he set out again on 4 December with the coast tending towards the north-west and the wind strongly blowing against him from that quarter. There was no reason for Tasman to continue charting the east coast of New Holland to his north because it had already been accepted that it was not the fabled continent, or at the very least no one had claimed that it was. He sailed east with the prevailing winds and thus remained unaware of Bass Strait. He hoped to reach Fiji and the Solomons in searching further for the continent.[1]

On 13 December 1642, Tasman came to 'a large land, uplifted high'. It was New Zealand, a name given to it later in unknown circumstances — possibly because it sat well with that of nearby New Holland. Tasman named it Staats Landt and said that 'This land seems to be a very fine country and we trust that this is the mainland coast of the unknown South Land', while also remarking that it had 'very fine timber'. That he did not pursue the matter

---

[1] See J.E. Heeres (ed.), *Abel Janzoor Tasman's Journal* (2006, pp. 13, 15, 16).

further by sailing south to resolve the question of how far it extended in that direction is puzzling. While he was ready to obey his instructions to behave in a humane manner with the natives of wherever he landed, his spirits were dampened when seven of his crew, crossing a bay in a small boat, were set upon by a larger number of Maori. Four of the crew then perished when they were intercepted as they rowed between Tasman's two vessels. Clearly the Maori regarded the Dutch as a threat to their land as well as to their lives. Tasman, having no understanding of the motives of the Maori, named the place Murderers' Bay and concluded that he was permanently unwelcome. He never set foot on New Zealand as, indeed, he had not at Van Diemen's Land and he was unable to refresh his provisions and water in either place. Tasman had made no discovery of the continent that he had been sent to locate and his later reception at Batavia was distinctly cool.[2]

Although it is unlikely that the Maori on the east coast had ever received or driven away alien invaders in the past, Cook's own reception in 1769 was ferocious and the reason for such must lie in their perceived need to repel all potential invaders, regardless of their origins. In the past on the eastern coast there were other Maori groups, and encounters between them had long proved to bring fatal results on both sides. On this occasion the bloodshed began on the very first day. Wood and fresh water were needed after the long run from the Society Islands and additional food supplies were always very welcome. Cook and others made an attempt to land and establish friendly contact with the Maori, which resulted on that and the following day in the death and wounding by shooting of at least nine, possibly more, Maori. Cook rapidly decided to leave this place which he named Poverty Bay 'because it afforded us no one thing we wanted'. In fact no supplies were forthcoming and friendly contact proved impossible despite the efforts of Tupia to initiate them. About 500 years had passed since the departure of the Maori from their homelands in eastern Polynesia. Yet Tupia 'found that the language of the people was so like his own that he could tolerably well understand them and they him'. Cook was delighted with this outcome, but his conscience was troubled. The slaughter of the Maori in the first days of contact prompted him to write 'most humane men who have not experienced things of this nature will censure my conduct ... nor do I myself think the reason I had ... will at all justify me'. He explained that he would never have landed had he imagined his doing so would have provoked such a hideous outcome but 'I was not to stand still and suffer either myself or those that were with me

---

[2] Alexander Dalrymple, *An Account of the Discoveries Made in The South Pacifick Ocean, Previous to 1764* (1767, pp. 63-63). He says that only three of the Dutch seaman were killed.

to be knocked on the head'. For his part, Banks said 'thus ended the most disagreeable day my life has yet seen. Black be the mark for it and heaven send that such may never return to embitter future reflection.'[3]

Cook turned south from Poverty Bay and came to a cape on the southern end of an inlet that he named Hawke's Bay after the First Lord of the Admiralty. The first boat to come out to them sold Cook some 'stinking fish', probably dried, which he bartered for in the hope of encouraging trade. Then 'a large armed boat' approached the *Endeavour*. Other boats followed and Tupia's 'little boy' being in the water was seized and was about to be carried ashore. The vessel was fired on by a four pounder and, in the confusion, the boy managed to escape overboard and was rescued unharmed. Two or three Maori lay dead on the stricken vessel and Cook named the place Cape Kidnappers.[4] On the next day he decided to turn north at a place he named Cape Turnagain, which Cook thought would be a more profitable venture. This decision pleased Banks given that his botanising might yield better results with the likelihood of warmer weather there. The land looked like 'our high Downs in England' and was well inhabited with several villages dotted about. Things turned out for the better when five Maori came aboard, including two who seemed to be chiefs. The encounter extended overnight and was warm and friendly. The next encounter gave Tupia an opportunity to explain to two elderly chiefs 'the reasons for our coming here and that we should neither hurt nor molest them if they did but behave in the same peaceful manner to us'. Cook was able to water there and barter for their cloth with that from the Society Islands and England. The Maori much preferred the former.[5]

Celery grew in abundance and it was one item of food that delighted Cook. He had it boiled with 'Portable soup and oatmeal every morning for the people's breakfast ... because I look upon it to be very wholesome and a great antiscorbutic'. There were further pleasant encounters with the inhabitants at Tolaga Bay, although only fish and a few sweet potatoes were traded for cloth, beads and nails. No animals were sighted except for dogs and rats. It was later established that the dogs, brought originally from the home islands, were domesticated and were bred to be eaten. Parkinson observed, 'The country ... is agreeable beyond description and, with proper cultivation, might be rendered a kind of second Paradise'. One aspect of the promising paradise that did not escape the notice of Banks was the

---

[3]   *Cook*, 9, 10, 11 October, pp. 168-73; *Banks*, vol. 1, pp. 401, 403-14.

[4]   *Cook*, 15 October 1789, pp. 177-78.

[5]   *Cook*, 15–22 October, pp. 177-83; Beaglehole in *Cook*, p. 179, fn. 4.

behaviour of the women who were 'as great coquettes as any Europeans could be and the young ones as skittish as unbroken fillies' although Parkinson insisted that the women were not free with their 'favours'. Banks, however, turned to a more serious observation in remarking on 'a piece of cleanliness in these people I cannot omit as I believe it is almost unexampled among Indians'. He had observed that the houses, or a small 'knot' of them, had 'a necessary house where everyone repairs and consequently the neighbourhood is kept clean'.[6]

Perhaps Tupia's explanation for their presence had not been passed on to the neighbouring northern villages because Cook had to use muskets and the 'great gun', several times in the following days to drive off apparently hostile vessels. If naming Poverty Bay was in recognition of reality, the next English descriptive name he used was less respectful. After being fired on, the Maori escaped to the shore with great haste; Cook named the site of this encounter Runaway Bay. One death occurred when Lieutenant John Gore shot a man who stole a piece of cloth, which act earned Cook's disapproval, judging the punishment as 'a little too severe for the crime'. A little boy, Hore Ta-Te-Taniwha, came aboard the *Endeavour* and, as an old man, recounted his experience. He said, 'There was one supreme man in that ship. We knew that he was the lord of the whole by his perfectly gentlemanly and noble demeanour. He seldom spoke … He was a very good man, he came to us — the children — and patted our cheeks, and gently touched our heads.' Cook gave the child a nail, which he treasured for years, but Cook's most precious gift to the elders, as well as the example of his personal dignity and kindness, was seed potatoes, which rapidly flourished. One simple difference between the behaviour of the races was immediately noticed by the Maori who spoke of the whites as 'goblins' because they rowed backwards, but were able to see forward while they, using paddles, faced forward.[7]

On 15 November 1769, Cook came to a river that he found 'very convenient for wooding and watering' as well as abounding in oysters. He named it Oyster River and called the bay Mercury Bay 'on account of the observation made there' of the transit of Mercury. Before leaving he cut into a tree the name of his ship, the date and other details and 'after displaying the English colours I took formal possession of the place in the name of His Majesty'. He made no mention of any attempt at acquiring the consent of the Maori chieftains to his act of taking possession, even though it was clearly possible to do so given Tupia's ability to converse so readily

---

6   *Cook*, 28, 29 October 1769, pp. 185-87; *Banks*, vol. 1, pp. 417, 418; Parkinson, p. 134.

7   *Cook*, 28, 31 October; 4, 9 November, pp. 185, 187, 188, 193, 196; John White, *The Ancient History of the Maori: His Mythology and Traditions*, vol. 5 (1888, pp. 121-25).

with them. A few days later, when people travelling on three large canoes came aboard 'upon the very first invitation', he put it down to the fact that they had heard of 'the manner we had treated the natives'; it is evident that in many instances civil negotiations with the Maori were possible. In late November, trading in fish was still being undertaken, but Banks, using language more suitable to the parlour than exploration, expressed his alarm that the Maori were 'most abominably saucy continually threatening us'. Matters turned for the worse when, on 30 November, an instance occurred in which negotiations of any nature became impossible and the visitors were in grave danger. Cook and some of his party were confronted on land by up to 300 Maori, although those aboard the *Endeavour* with a clear view of the low hills behind the beach reported later that up to 600 men were involved. Initially the Maori seemed to pose no danger 'but in this we were very soon undeceived'. The war dance was engaged in and hostilities began with a considerable use of small arms. Lieutenant Zachary Hicks, aboard the ship, was able to turn it broadside quickly and had several four-pound shots fired from the *Endeavour* resulting in the wounding of several of the men on the beach but no deaths. All conflict ceased, but from then on Cook became acutely aware that some of his crew were also not above uncivilised behaviour. He was determined to stamp it out, especially when it seemed likely to be received with disfavour by the Maori. He gave a dozen lashes each to three seamen who left their companions and dug up sweet potatoes in a Maori garden and he punished Matthew Cox with half a dozen lashes for an unnamed indiscretion, but of similar import.[8]

North Cape, which Cook judged to be 'the northern extremity of this country', was rounded on 19 December and the less eventful voyage south began. When he reached the southernmost part of the north island, instead of continuing south Cook sailed into what was presently revealed as a strait separating the two large land masses of New Zealand. There he entered a magnificent harbour and he was able to anchor on a perfect beach. It was imperative that he do so because the *Endeavour* seriously demanded to be careened — in effect a thorough cleansing of the hull — and any necessary repairs effected, for which an appropriate partial beaching and use of the tides were necessary. The work took several days during which Cook was fully occupied in examining the area. On such occasions, 'Tupia always accompanies us in every excursion we make and proves of infinite service'. From a large hill Cook was able to conclude that there was a strait

---

8   *Cook*, 15, 30 November 1769, pp. 201-04, 214-16; *Banks*, vol. 1, 439-41.

running from east to west and he 'resolved after putting to sea to search this passage with the ship'. Before his departure Cook, however, through Tupia, explained to an old man and several others that he proposed to set up a mark which would make it plain to anyone who chanced upon this place from abroad that he had been there before them. To this 'they not only gave their free consent to set it up, but promised never to pull it down'. After putting up the post and hoisting the Union Jack, Cook duly dignified this remarkable bay by naming it Queen Charlotte Sound and 'took formal possession of it and the adjacent lands in the name and for the use of his Majesty'. The company then drank a bottle of wine to Her Majesty's health and gave the empty bottle to the old man, who was highly pleased with the gift. It is uncertain whether Cook explained what this further ceremony implied beyond the mere raising of a post to signify their presence on the coast. Unquestionably the elder remained ignorant of the fact that the land he and his people had lived on for 500 years was now claimed as a possession of an alien and far distant people. Cook was then farewelled by another old man, of whom Tupia asked whether other ships like the *Endeavour* had ever called there. He replied that none had done so but that his ancestors had told him that two vessels, much larger than their own vessels, had come from a place called Olhemaroa. Oremaroa is marked north-east of Tahiti on one of the maps that Tupia drew for Cook. Banks recorded that the old man said that the vessels were totally destroyed 'by the inhabitants and all the people belonging to them killed'. Tupia arrived at the conclusion that this narrative formed part of a very old tradition among the Maori.[9]

By this time, early February 1770, supplies of beef, pork, flour and peas were running short. All hands were eating fish caught on lines or in a net, except when they were able to procure dried fish from the Maori, which added to the much greater number they caught themselves. Banks was able later to write that 'every mess on the ship that had prudence enough salted as much fish as lasted them many weeks after they went to sea'.[10] They passed through Cook's Strait, which had been named in honour of the captain, possibly by Banks, although he does not acknowledge doing so and Cook makes no mention of the matter. They rounded the southernmost point of the north island on 8 February and Cook named it Cape Palliser after 'my worthy friend' who had been his captain on the *Eagle* in 1755 and helped him to take his first steps in navigation and the lore of the sea. Some of Cook's

---

[9] *Cook*, 19–31 December 1769, pp. 224-43.
[10] *Banks*, vol. 2, 1 March 1770, p. 6. Clearly Banks wrote up his account of their time in New Zealand well after the salted fish had been consumed.

officers concluded that the north island was not in fact an island based on a supposition that the land between Cape Turnagain and Cape Palliser might extend to the south-east. Cook entertained 'no such supposition' and he decided to sail north-east along the lower part of south island to prove his point. When they were boarded by a group of Maori who asked for nails, Cook concluded that they knew strangers with appropriate gifts had come among them having received word from Cape Kidnappers and they also knew that iron was a valuable asset. Cook called his officers together and asked them whether they were satisfied 'that this land was an island', with which they agreed. With this it was finally established that New Zealand was not one land mass. On 11 February he turned south and, three days later, the southern island was clearly visible. They encountered four double canoes with 57 men aboard who began throwing stones; they would not come closer despite Tupia's attempts to entice them to do so. This led Cook to suppose, with good reason, that the people of the southern island had no contact with the northerners and did not know of the presence in their seas of the *Endeavour*.[11]

Keeping well clear of the coast and sighting occasional whales, they passed Cape Saunders on 4 March and, seeing no land to the south, Cook was hoping that they had reached the southern point of the island, thus proving that it was not joined to the mythical southern continent. This displeased Banks who, together with other believers, stuck to the conviction and thus still believed in the existence of a southern continent. They were delighted when, towards evening when the thick mists had cleared, 'we Continents had the pleasure to see more land to the southward'. On the next day Banks reported that even the unbelievers 'are inclined to think that continental measures will at last prevail', but shortly afterwards he was forced to admit that the land they had seen beforehand was 'nothing but clouds'. Finally he conceded defeat by writing that the belief in 'our aerial fabric called continent' was totally demolished. There is no evidence that Cook felt triumphant but he saw no benefit in searching further for a continent he had been ordered, once discovered, to possess for his king and especially when his supplies were beginning to run down rapidly. At noon on 10 February they passed the southernmost point of land which Cook afterwards named South Cape.[12]

Sailing north on the east coast of the southern island a short time later

---

[11] Cook, 5, 7, 8, 9, 11, 14, 15 February 1770, pp. 245, 247–53; for Hugh Palliser see Richard Hough, *Captain James Cook* (1994, p. 12).

[12] *Banks*, vol. 1, 5, 6, 8, 10 March 1770, pp. 471-42; *Cook*, 5, 10 March 1770, pp. 259-60, 262; *Cook*, 14, 23 March, pp. 264-66, 269-70; *Banks*, vol. 2, p. 4.

they sighted a possible harbour and appropriately named it Doubtful Sound. Despite urgent entreaties, and much to Banks's chagrin, Cook refused to enter the sound, and Banks ever afterwards harboured his resentment at the loss of further botanising. Cook, whose first duty was to his ship and its people, was sure that once inside the sound they would depend on a favourable easterly wind to sail out again. He concluded that this might detain them even for a protracted period, given that they already knew such a wind only blew very irregularly. They continued northward neither landing, nor encountering Maori, and the land was not 'distinguished by anything remarkable' except for the chain of mountains that Cook decided ran the length of the island. He graciously admitted that being out to sea in foggy weather and not having landed he could only see the mountain summits. Soon afterwards he landed again in Queen Charlotte Sound because water and wood were both needed. Five days later such tasks were completed and, having fished successfully, they were ready to depart New Zealand. They had circumnavigated the whole country, which Cook had charted so clearly and accurately that later navigators both used and praised his skills. Among them was the French naval officer, Julien Crozet, who had taken part in an expedition that charted part of the coast of New Zealand at the same time of Cook's voyage there. Crozet wrote that he 'found it of exactitude and of a thoroughness of detail which astonished me beyond all powers of expression, and I doubt much whether the charts of our own French coasts are laid down with greater precision'.[13]

Cook summarised his impressions of New Zealand in a lengthy but undated entry. Having spelt out Tasman's unhappy encounter with the Maori he said that 'This country, which before now was thought to be part of the imaginary southern continent' was in fact two islands and thus he dismissed the matter almost peremptorily. He was bold enough to assert that 'few parts of the world are better determined than these islands', which he generously put down to the observation of Charles Green, without referring to his own almost impeccable charting. He thought with everyone on board that all sorts of European produce would flourish in its soil and that were 'this country settled by an industrious people they would very shortly be supplied not only with the necessaries but with many of the luxuries of life'. In particular he thought highly of the fish, of lobsters — which were the

---

[13]   *Cook*, n.d., pp. 274-75, 286, 288-91. For Crozet see Beaglehole in *Cook*, f.n. 4, p. 274; David, Andrew, Rüdiger Joppien & Bernard Smith (eds), *The Charts and Coastal Views of Captain Cook's Voyages*, vol. 1, *The Voyage of the Endeavour, 1768-1771* (1988) has numerous charts of New Zealand, pp. 159-258.

best his crew had ever eaten — and of oysters as well as ducks. Timber was there in abundance, although it was not suitable for masts. Good relations could be established with the people and a settlement set down, provided kind and gentle ways were used with them. He admitted that they seemed to be 'very much divided into parties which make war with one another', but that 'all their actions and behaviour towards us tended to prove that they are a brave, open warlike people and void of treachery'. He also praised highly their boatbuilding skills and techniques and described the largest vessel he saw as being over 20 metres long and specifically built for war. Compared to the *Endeavour*, built in one of England's finest shipyards and 32 metres in length, the Maori vessel stood up well. He was not impressed by their dancing, during which 'they appear like madmen, jumping and stamping with their feet, making strange contortions with every part of the body and a hideous noise at the same time'. Although he concluded that, in respect of religion, they 'they trouble themselves very little about it', he conceded that they believed in a supreme being, together with lesser gods, and that they probably worshipped and prayed to their god, although he had never witnessed their doing so. Their notions and customs, including the creation of the world and of the human race, were the same as those he had observed in the South Sea Islands and their language proved conclusively that they all descended from people of one origin, to which Banks attested, having acquired some proficiency in the language spoken at both places. Although Cook claimed that he wrote his account of New Zealand together with his attitude to the further investigation of the existence or otherwise of the Great South Land 'Before I quit this land altogether', it is more likely that he wrote it either as he sailed to New Holland or at Batavia.[14]

Banks, who wrote his final account of New Zealand on the night before their final departure, was particularly taken with the modesty of the women, the physical strength of the people, the absence of disease among them and their high degree of intelligence, which was especially evident in their shipbuilding given that, in their isolation, they had not been able to draw on the experience of other peoples. He was more generous than Cook in that the songs sung in the *haka* pleased him as did the 'strength, firmness and agility of their motions'. While deploring the fact that the men made themselves 'most enormously ugly' by tattooing their faces, Banks acknowledged that generally it was impossible not to admire 'the immense elegance and justness of the figures' portrayed in the tattoos. Also they were

---

[14] Cook, n.d., pp. 273-78, 281, 283, 285-86. It is clear that both Cook and Banks used Dalrymple's, *An Account of the Discoveries Made in The South Pacifick Ocean, Previous to 1764* (1767).

'never as fat as the lazy inhabitants of the South Sea Isles'. The women had 'a peculiar softness of voice' and were 'more lively, airy and laughter loving than the men' and decently covered themselves by their dresses. Banks firmly stated that the 'disposition of both sexes seems mild, gentle and very affectionate to each other, but implacable towards their enemies'. Neither sex was addicted to stealing and 'tillage, weaving and the rest of the arts of peace', were undertaken more in the north island than in the south. He said that he had seen no other 'quadrupeds' native to New Zealand and that he had never seen a rat there, which confirmed its rarity. He saw no fruit except some insipid berries. Finally, he agreed with Cook in his judgement of their religion.[15]

In the first days of contact with the Maori, Banks and Tupia became aware of the possibility that cannibalism was practised when three young men, taken aboard and given food, had asked whether it was human flesh, not having ever encountered any animal as large as the sheep they had seen aboard. Banks and Tupia were appalled and initially were unwilling to even entertain the concept that the Maori ate the bodies of their fallen enemies. That they did so with relish and on both the north and south islands became increasingly clear and Banks finally accepted it to be true when an elderly chieftain made it plain that such was the case. At Queen Charlotte Sound they saw bodily evidence of the practise, which prompted Cook to name the place where this occurred as Cannibal Bay. Tupia was appalled at the revelation that his fellow people, as he acknowledged them to be, practised cannibalism. He endeavoured with all his strength to make them understand that they must desist from such behaviour, but he did so fruitlessly and aroused ire rather than acceptance among the Maori. The reaction of the crew of the *Endeavour* was 'better conceived than described' when this 'horror' was explained to them while poor Tupia, half ashamed, could only continue to lament its truth. At Tahiti, and throughout the islands, pigs were available in abundance to be eaten as meat. As Cook discovered, the Tahitian pigs could not survive at sea, so it is probable that, if the first Maori had sailed from their home islands with pigs, they had died on the voyage with perhaps only a remnant surviving to die out later. This left them with only one source of animal meat, apart from birds and a rare turtle, namely the native dog, which was even rarer and became extinct, as did the rats, with the later coming of a white population. To the Maori, cannibalism directed at their enemies had no basis in so-called ritualistic practises.[16]

---

[15] *Banks*, vol. 2, pp. 1, 4, 9, 11, 12.
[16] *Banks*, vol. 1, pp. 443, 455.

The evidence of seemingly semi-constant violence between Maori groups moved Banks to remark that they lived in a 'state of war', which in many places had 'taught them not only to live together in towns, but to fortify those towns'. To this end they surrounded them with a 'broad ditch and a palisade' and chose naturally defensive situations on an island, a peninsula or a steep cliff. These precautions were not taken about Hawke's Bay where they lived 'in a state of profound peace', which Banks put down to the fact that they were ruled by a strong chieftain or king whose authority generally descended by birth. On 24 January 1770 Banks wrote of seeing an object that drew his attention, but he made no comment on it. It was 'a kind of wooden Cross ornamented with feathers exactly in the form of a Crucifix cross ... we were told that it was a monument for a dead man'. Were it the case that a form of Christian influence had been brought to bear on the Maori, it could not have happened in their home islands because they had left them before the coming of Europeans.[17]

Cook was convinced that, if there was such a thing as a Great South Land, it had to be in a high latitude and he proceeded to weigh up the matter at some length. On the one hand, was it not the case that the continent had been proven not to exist in northern latitudes given the numerous voyages already made there? Thus he thought that it would have to be in a higher latitude than the southernmost portion of New Zealand and, as such, it would be in such a viciously cold climate it would be rendered of no value to the empire-making and mercantile interests of the day. He argued that the only unknown area vast enough to contain the northern section of the continent lay between longitude 110° and longitude 145° on about 40° of east latitude. This section of the Pacific was charted on his voyage from Cape Horn to Tahiti and thence south-west to New Zealand. Of this he stated firmly, 'But what foundation we have for such a supposition, none that I know of but this that it must be here or nowhere'. Despite his certainty on the matter, he used the accounts of other mariners, especially Quiros and Roggeveen, to sustain his argument. Of Quiros he remarked that his ultimate purpose was to find the famed continent that Dalrymple had claimed he saw evidence of in the form of clouds south of latitude 25° or 26° and longitude 130° and 140°. Quiros did not even turn south to examine the alleged evidence, which was thoroughly spurious in Cook's judgement, and who believed Quiros was unlikely to have taken any notice of it, given no one 'seems to have had discoveries more at heart than he

---

17   *Banks*, vol. 2, pp. 11, 13, 16, 30–32, 35–37; vol. 1, 445, 458.

had'. Despite a scepticism that was based on evidence and common sense, Cook proposed that a further voyage should be undertaken to clear up the matter and he strongly suggested that Tupia should be on board, thus giving 'a prodigious advantage over every ship' that might embark with a similar purpose. Cook was determined to command the Pacific. He could only do so with the support of the Admiralty in which case it was advisable to not rule out a further voyage in search of the continent, even though he knew that its existence was at the best highly unlikely.[18]

The captain, having fulfilled his orders, was free to stay as long in these seas as the safety of the ship and acquisition of provisions would admit. Cook decided, however, that the time had come to 'quit this country altogether', to which end he called his officers together, including Banks and Solander and probably Parkinson. The purpose of the meeting was to decide on the route to home, even though it is reasonable to suppose that Cook had already made up his mind on the matter. The basic question was what route would be the most suitable to the condition of the *Endeavour* and the availability of supplies. Surprisingly, Banks stated that they had six months of the latter provided they used them at two-thirds of the normal allowance each day. This surely implies that they must had some remaining livestock on board, including pigs, sheep and poultry, but there is no evidence that wine, for the crew at least, had survived the months in New Zealand. In his journal, Cook explained that his preference was to return by Cape Horn because that would help to settle the question of a southern continent provided they sailed in high latitudes. That would, however, put the ship at risk by taking a lengthy voyage across the southern Pacific at 40° or higher latitude in the 'very depth of winter', when it would expect to be exposed to gales and perhaps violent seas. Thus, he decided — with his officers' agreement — that, given the condition of the ship 'in all respects' and principally its sails and rigging, which had suffered much deterioration in the journey around New Zealand, to choose an alternative route to Cape Horn. The same argument worked against a direct return by the Cape of Good Hope for the opposite reason, that the supplies were sufficient to sail to the East Indies, preferably to Batavia. Why, then, waste them on a potentially dangerous voyage south of Van Diemen's Land and thence to Good Hope and home, which would provide no new discoveries? Parkinson put a less cheerful gloss on this matter asserting that 'we were in want of many kinds of provisions, particularly sugar, salt, oil, tea, and tobacco: our spirits also very low: and, as

---

[18]   *Cook*, pp. 288-91.

to bread, we had not had any for upwards of six months'. It would seem that he had the cheerful expectation of making up such deficiencies elsewhere by coming across, entirely by chance, 'a convenient refreshing place'.[19]

In any event, all agreed to a return by sailing directly to the coast of New Holland and then north along its coast to its extremity and 'if this should be found impractical' by not coming upon Torres Strait, they might at least fall in with the lands or islands discovered by Quiros in 1606, go north around the coast of New Guinea and thence to Batavia. The record of this decision is a clear answer to the vexed question of whether Cook and Banks took material from the other's account as, in this instance, their two journals overlay considerably in their account of Cook's meeting with the officers. Banks was able to relax at night once he had, with Solander, tabulated the results of their day's botanising. Cook enjoyed no such respite and, in instances when he was unable to write up his journal, perhaps having been forced to postpone the task for days if not weeks, that he would make use of the account made by Banks is unsurprising. If anything it clearly proves the trust that had been established between the men.

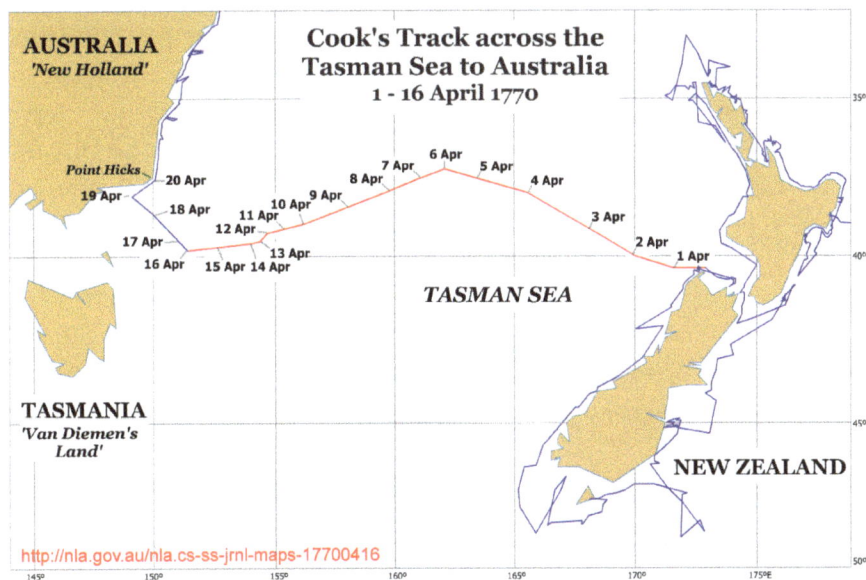

Cook's Track across the Tasman Sea to Australia 1 - 16 April 1770

http://nla.gov.au/nla.cs-ss-jrnl-maps-17700416

19 *Cook*, 31 March 1770, p. 272-73; *Banks*, March 1770, p. 38; Parkinson, Sydney, *Journal of a Voyage to South Seas* (1773, p. 167).

Cook did not come to his task of charting an unknown coast unaware of its ramifications. A vast coast lay before him and, with its charting, a chapter in the history of navigation would close by the addition of the last continent to its measure. The Admiralty left the acquisition of charts and printed sources to the commanders of their vessels when going to sea and Cook had gathered his to the extent that their availability and his own economic resources would permit. On 30 July 1768, however, the Lords of the Admiralty sent him copies of Doctor David McBride's *Experimental Essays on the Scurvy and Other Subjects* (1763) as well as his 'pamphlet' *An Historical Account of the New Method of Treating Scurvy at Sea* (1767) together with instructions on how to use malt to prevent scurvy. That the use of malt, highly recommended by McBride, was adopted with a considerable measure of success as an antiscorbutic by Cook is on record, although he was not entirely convinced that it could cure the ailment once it took hold.[20]

Despite any misgivings Cook might have had about the worn-out state of much of his vessel's rigging, as well as the running down of some of his provisions, he could set out with confidence on the final leg to home. The health of his crew was first rate, their confidence in his ability to lead them home was unfailing, and the *Endeavour* had given further proof of its capacity to master the seas with safety. All that remained was a coastline to be charted and a strait to be secured. He felt no unease as to the larger matter of the existence of a Great South Land, which so preoccupied his masters in the Royal Society and the Admiralty. It wasn't where they had expected that it would be, but he hoped to have one last throw of the dice at finding it on a later voyage. Little did he know then that he would not have long to ponder the question. Sail west he would, and chart a coast and, thereby, if he was ever going to find a great continent in the southern seas, he was about to encounter it. This continent was not one of frail and whimsical dreams. It lay there before him and in it a true Dreaming lived on.

---

[20] See Lords to Cook, 30 July 1768, *Cook*, pp. cclxxix–cclxxxi; Cook to Stephens, 12 July 1771 with enclosure from Perry, p. 631; Cook to Pringle, n.d. (early 1776), pp. 390-91, in *Historical Records of New South Wales: Cook 1762-1780*, vol. 1, pt 1 (1893).

5

Botany Bay

Although it had been decided at Cook's meeting with his officers to sight New Holland as near as possible to Tasman's point of departure from that coast, the wind and the sea had their role to play in the outcome. Cold weather was replaced by the kind of humidity that is experienced generally only in the tropics, while gentle breezes gave way to strong gales and heavy squalls. In fact, on 17 April, a strong gale blew up that continued into the night, ceasing for a period but, by 6 am on the next day, there were further 'heavy squalls'. A great sea finally settled down, although the Tasman had marked its reputation as an uneasy voyage in either direction. Makeshift repairs were engaged in daily and the judgement that had been made previously regarding the state of the sails was confirmed when a topsail, worn 'to rags', was used to repair the two topgallant sails both of which were in such a condition that using new canvas on them would have been a waste. In point of fact there was neither new canvas nor twine available so that, for the remainder of the voyage through to Batavia, ingenuity and the use of cast-off materials became the norm.[1]

---

[1]   *Cook*, 17, 18 April 1770, pp. 297-98.

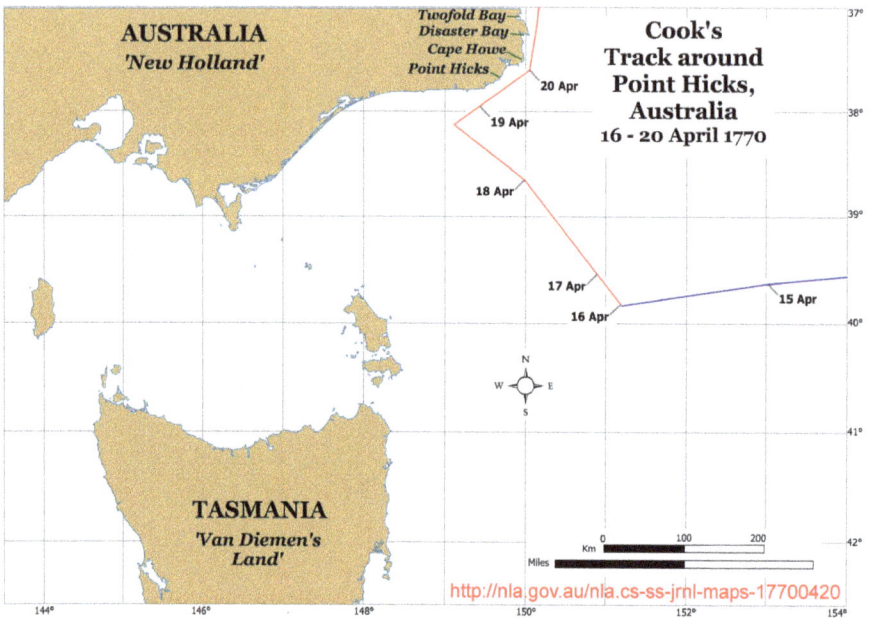

AUSTRALIA
'New Holland'

Twofold Bay
Disaster Bay
Cape Howe
Point Hicks

Cook's
Track around
Point Hicks,
Australia
16 - 20 April 1770

20 Apr

19 Apr

18 Apr

17 Apr

15 Apr

16 Apr

TASMANIA
'Van Diemen's
Land'

http://nla.gov.au/nla.cs-ss-jrnl-maps-17700420

By Wednesday 18 April, Cook, taking the sighting of a Port Egmont hen on the previous evening as 'a certain sign of the nearness of land', was sure that they were east of and close to Van Diemen's Land, but about 250 kilometres north of Tasman's departure point. Clearly he knew that they were about to come upon New Holland which duly happened at 6 am on the following day when Lieutenant Hicks sighted it. With an instinctive knowledge of the sea and its ways bought by long experience, Cook pondered as to whether Van Diemen's Land and the coast he was looking at were 'one land or not'. He doubted that it was so because of 'the soon falling of the sea once the wind abated'. In 1797 Cook's doubt was answered when George Bass went into the strait that now bears his name and Van Diemen's Land was thereby accepted as an island.[2]

There had been widespread rejoicing at sighting New Zealand, which Banks described, saying that he was by good fortune on deck at the time and was well entertained when 'the cry [land] circulated and up came all hands'. The boy who first sighted New Zealand, Nicholas Young, was rewarded with a gallon of rum as Cook had promised well beforehand. No such festivities took place at the sighting of New Holland. Although he named the nearest land Point Hicks 'as the first who discovered this land', no reward was given. The reason was simple; nothing but the expected had occurred

---

2   *Cook*, 18, 19 April 1770, pp. 298-99.

and thus the sighting did not need rewarding. In a letter of 13 September 1771 from Cook at his London home to John Walker, under whose care and protection he had served in his youth, Cook admitted that on leaving New Zealand he had 'steered for New Holland all the east part of which remained undiscovered' and his intent was to 'fall in with the southern part called Van Diemen's Land', but 'the wind forced me to the northward of it'. In effect he made it plain that he regarded Van Diemen's Land as part of New Holland irrespective of whether it was separated by a strait. Furthermore, he fully accepted that the Dutch had already charted the west coast of the Gulf of Carpentaria, as well as the continuation of the north coast to its western extremity, down the west coast and finally at least a long section of the south coast with the addition of the southern third of Van Diemen's Land. This rightly prompted Cook to remark that only the east coast remained 'undiscovered' and 'if New Holland can be called an island it is by far the greatest in the known world'. Cook was neither given to idle boasting nor fabricating a falsehood. He acknowledged that all that remained for him to do, and it was a larger task than even he could imagine, was to chart the east coast of New Holland. Its discovery was already an established fact. It has to be born in mind that the verb 'to discover' was also used at the time to mean the occasion of seeing land the existence and location of which was already well known. As they approached the English coast on the return of the *Endeavour* to home Banks wrote, 'this morning the land was discovered by Young Nick who first saw New Zealand: it proved to be the Lizard'.[3]

At sea, land is first sighted as a small cloud or faint smudge on the horizon. As a vessel comes closer to the shore a wondrous image gradually emerges. The land takes shape as if it were born from the sea, which it was in the beginning. Around the Mediterranean, the principal objective of the early map makers was to establish where vessels could make land safely, which was called a porta (door in Latin). Often the surface used on which to illustrate the position of a safe harbour was a dried sheep skin thus its name, portolano, being a combination of porta and lana or wool. Improvements in measuring instruments led to the increasing accuracy of maps and charts and, thus, by Cook's time, such records could be compiled with some degree of precision. Cook's task was to set down the contours of the land that would gradually reveal themselves day by day.

Banks was initially less interested in New Holland than he was in three

---

3   *Banks*, vol. 1, p. 399; *Cook*, 19 April 1770, p. 298-99; Cook to Walker, in *Cook*, p. 508. See the use of 'discover' by Parkinson in *Cook*, fn. 1, p. 324; *Banks*, vol. 2, p. 275.

water spouts that appeared between the ship and the land and he wrote at length about them. On 30 December 1771, however, he wrote a short account of the voyage to his friend the Count de Lauraguais and reported that, on 19 April 1770, 'we fell in with the coast of new Holland in Latitude 38 S. a coast which had never before been investigated by any navigator'. Thus the claim for investigation of the coast is asserted, rather than its discovery.[4] Cook dismissed the spouts in a sentence and commented on the land itself, which had a 'very agreeable and promising aspect' and his first description of the east coast was indeed promising. It was 'of a moderate height diversified with hills, ridges, plains and valleys with some few small lawns, but for the most part the whole was covered with wood'. He also started to name distinctive features of the land, being confident that no one had done so before him so that Cape Howe was followed by Mount Dromedary because of its shape. They passed a bay that Cook judged to be 'the only likely anchoring place I have yet seen upon the coast'. With his customary caution he did not enter it because he was uncertain as to whether it was sufficiently sheltered from the sea winds and was content to name it on his chart in honour of Captain Nathaniel Bateman under whom he had served as master.[5]

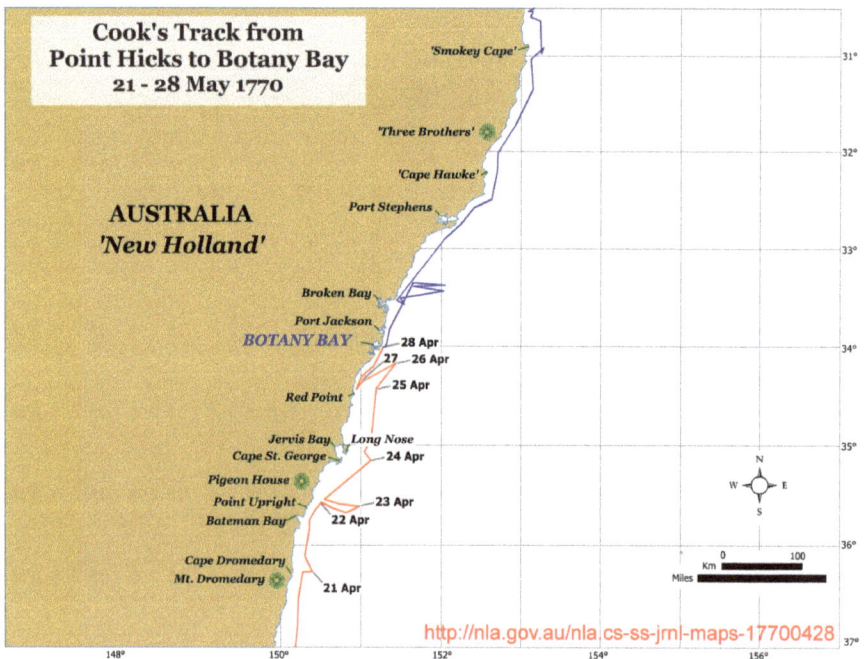

Cook's Track from Point Hicks to Botany Bay 21 - 28 May 1770

http://nla.gov.au/nla.cs-ss-jrnl-maps-17700428

4   *Banks*, vol. 2, pp. 49, 326.
5   *Cook*, 20, 21, April 1770, pp. 299–301.

Being already certain that the land was inhabited because of the several fires they had noticed, no surprise was expressed when the first sighting of the local inhabitants was made just north of Bateman's Bay, at Kioloa, adjacent to present day Bawley Point, on 22 April. They were close enough to the shore at 5 pm to see a small group on the beach. To Cook they 'appeared to be of a very dark or black colour but whether this was the real colour of their skins or clothes they might have on I know not'. According to Banks, the people seen through 'our glasses', appeared to be 'enormously black' although he admitted that 'the prejudices we had built on Dampier's account influenced us [so] that we fancied we could see their colour though we could scarce distinguish whether or not they were men'. This remark indicates that some preparation had been made for the encounter by reading William Dampier's accounts of his encounters with Aboriginal people on the coast of Western Australia nearly a century earlier, *A New Voyage Around the World* and *Voyage to New Holland*, in both of which the Aborigines were grossly depicted. Dampier's manuscript of the first volume, held in the British Library, shows him to have been more reserved in his judgment prior to publication:

> They are people of good stature but very thin and lean I judge for want of food. They are black yet I believe their hair would be long if it was combed out but for want of combs it is matted up like a Negros's hair. They have all that I saw two fore teeth of their upper jaw wanting both men women and children.

In his *Voyage to New Holland*, Dampier was less restrained stating that all the Aborigines he encountered 'have the most unpleasant looks and the worst features of any people that I ever saw'. His main concern seems to have been the abundance of flies, which he decided caused the Aborigines to close their eyes so repeatedly that their sight was impaired.[6]

Banks also said that he was unimpressed 'in favour of our future friends' because they did not 'clear the ground for cultivation' with 'large fires', as had been observed in the Pacific Islands and in New Zealand. By so doing he opted to ignore the 'few small lawns' noticed by Cook, who perhaps

---

6 *Cook*, 22 April 1770, p. 301; *Banks*, vol. 2, p. 50. I am indebted to Professor Robert Reece for the material drawn from the Dampier manuscript in the British Library (BL Sloan MS 3236 [ff. 233] [Title on binding] Dampier's Adventures in Darien Etc. [Written at beginning of ms] The Adventures of William Dampier with others who Left Capn. Sherpe in the South Seas and travelled back over Land through the Country of Darien. [Begins in 17 April 1681 — embarking from island of Plata for St Maria River — and ends in 1690 with return to England] ff. 220-223). Dampier was on the west coast near King Sound for five weeks from 4 January to 12 February 1688. See also William Dampier, *A New Voyage Round the World* (1697) and *Voyage to New Holland* (1699).

had concluded that burning off was not regarded by the Aborigines as a useful proceeding on the sandy soils of the coast line and especially in late autumn when little after-growth could be expected. Parkinson rightly wondered whether the fires they often saw were a kind of signal of the passing of the *Endeavour* because they were 'lit up one after another'. He further concluded that the five men seen through his glasses at Kioloa were 'quite naked'. He thought, furthermore, that, given no canoes were sighted, he incorrectly concluded that given in any case there appeared to be little chance of catching fish in the area, it was probable that the people of the area lived upon the direct produce of the earth. Banks gratefully remarked on one aspect of New Holland, noticed by all hands and still preserved in large measure, when he declared that the 'air in this Southern hemisphere was much clearer than in our northern ... some days at least it has appeared remarkably so'. Near to the coast at Kioloa there was a small island named on Cook's chart Brush Island. Given its proximity Cook had hoped to shelter the *Endeavour* between it and the beach on which he proposed to make his first landing at New Holland. The destiny of Kioloa remained unfulfilled. Cook wrote, 'we had a large hollow sea from the South East rolling in upon the land which beat everywhere very high upon the shore'. A landing was too hazardous for the prudent captain.[7]

On 24 April Cook named 'Cape St George ... having discovered it on that Saint's day' and on the next morning large fires were noticed, which prompted Banks to suppose 'that the gentlemen ashore had a plentiful breakfast to prepare'. His cheerfulness was short-lived, however, and he went on to describe a land which 'appeared in some places bare'. Waxing eloquent, and mindful perhaps of the lush meadows of home, he wrote ominously of a land often dried to its skeleton by drought. To him 'it resembled in my imagination the back of a lean cow, covered in general with long hair, but nevertheless where her scraggy hip bones have stuck out farther than they ought, accidental rubs and knocks have entirely bared them of their share of covering'. In any event, the first sighting of the inhabitants of New Holland and of the land itself by the men of the *Endeavour* was a blend of hope and uncertainty.[8]

More Aborigines were seen in the afternoon of 28 April at a place that Beaglehole considered to be just north of Bulli, north of Wollongong, New

7   *Banks*, vol. 2, p. 50; *Cook*, 22 April 1770, pp. 301-02; Sydney Parkinson, *Journal of a Voyage to South Seas* (1773, p. 178).
8   *Cook*, 24 April 1770, p. 302; *Banks*, vol. 2, p. 51.

South Wales. Four men were carrying a small boat that Cook and the others imagined was to be used to bring them to the *Endeavour*. However Banks remarked that, despite the hope that a meeting would occur, it was clear that it had to be ashore rather than on or near the *Endeavour*. Accordingly Cook, Banks and Solander set out in the yawl with four seamen manning the oars. As they approached the shore Banks said that the small party of Aborigines, whom he called Indians, 'sat on the rocks expecting us but when we came within about a quarter of a mile they ran away hastily into the country'. The word 'natives' rather than Aborigines, which was seldom used at the time, was frequently adopted by the journal writers aboard the *Endeavour*, although Banks sometimes called them Indians, which was a term often used when describing new peoples. Christopher Columbus, who sailed west to discover a shorter route to the Spice Islands than around the Cape of Good Hope, mistakenly thought that he had come upon India in 1492 rather than San Salvador, Cuba, Haiti and the Dominican Republic. He named the inhabitants Indios (Indians) and the word and the habit of using it took hold. It was not used as a mark of disrespect.[9]

On this event Cook wrote that a landing proved impossible 'by reason of the great surf which beat everywhere upon the shore', while the few people that they saw 'appeared to us exceedingly black' and 'took to the woods'. They left behind their three or four canoes which were 'not much unlike the small ones used in New Zealand'. Nakedness seems to have become a preoccupation among the Englishmen, and Parkinson, who was not with the party that had attempted to land, reported that the men 'were naked, and of a very dark colour' and that 'Our people also discovered several canoes drawn up on the beach, and a kind of house or wig-wam adjacent'. At this stage almost a month had passed since leaving New Zealand during which it had not proved possible to make a landing. This meant that finding a source of fresh water was becoming imperative.[10]

There is archaeological evidence that the Aborigines were living around Botany Bay some 5,000 years ago. There were three subgroups in the area with their own languages. The Kameygal lived on the northern part of the bay, the Gweagal were settled on the south and the Bidigal lived between the Cooks River and the Georges River. Although he very probably encountered each group, Cook had no way of knowing that there were any differences between these people and assuredly not that their languages differed. From

---

[9]   *Cook*, 28 April 1770, p. 304.
[10]   *Cook*, 28 April 1770, p. 304; Sydney Parkinson, *Journal of a Voyage to South Seas* (1773, p. 178).

the journals it is evident that the reaction of all the Aborigines at Botany Bay to the presence of the *Endeavour* and its crew was uniform, but open to differing interpretations.

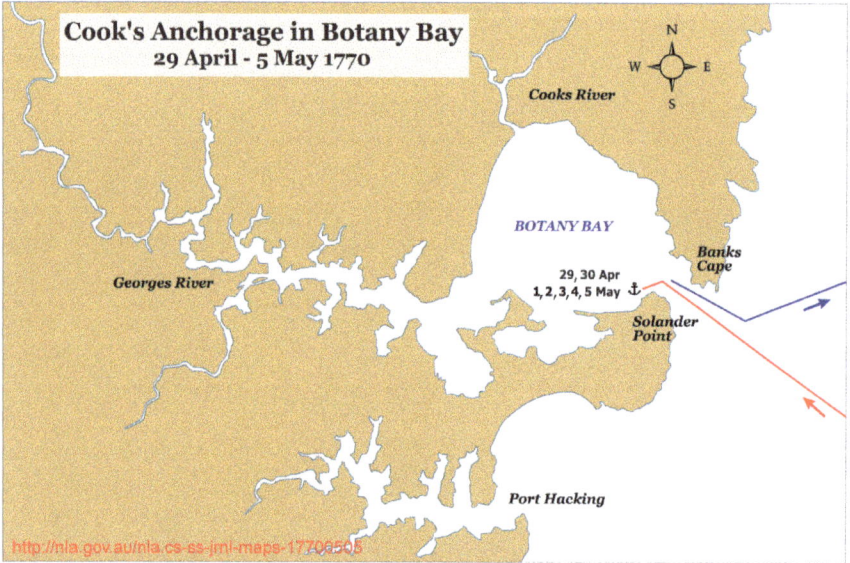

The *Endeavour* was moored in Botany Bay from 29 April to 6 May 1770. Many landings were made, but all hands remained aboard overnight rather than camping ashore. Over this period the relations between Cook and his men with the Aborigines, as well as of the reaction of the Aborigines to them, are detailed in the journals of Cook, Banks, Parkinson and Midshipman James Matra. The journals of the master, Robert Molyneux, and surgeon, William Monkhouse, do not have entries for that part of the voyage encompassing the east coast of New Holland, while those few written by others are scarcely worthy of notice consisting as they do of the same spare text and thereby adding little if indeed anything to that contained in the major journals.

It is clear that Cook and others on the *Endeavour* expected that they would be able to make verbal contact with the people of New Holland. This was not an unfounded expectation given that it had happened at New Zealand, where Tupia had been able to converse easily with the Maori, and there was some hope that the same would apply in this instance. This was possibly based on the reasoning that the Maori, who had undertaken a lengthy journey to reach New Zealand, could have visited the much closer east coast of New Holland, at least briefly. There is no evidence to support such a supposition and, in the case of Cook's early encounters with the Indigenous people of New Holland, the expectation of communication through the spoken language proved to be ill-founded.

On Sunday 29 April 1770 Cook wrote, 'At daylight in the morning we discovered a Bay'. He decided to enter it because 'it was tolerably well sheltered from all winds', which gave him an assurance that a passage out could be satisfactorily achieved later on. They anchored on the south shore near present day Kurnell, and Cook, Banks, Solander and Tupia approached the shore by boat. Near a few huts on the shore there were men, women and children, but 'they all made off except two Men who seemed resolved to oppose our landing'. Cook came in closer and Tupia attempted to speak to them 'but this was to little purpose for neither us nor Tupia could understand one word they said'. Some nails, beads and other trinkets were thrown to the men on the shore, which appeared to please them to the degree that Cook thought they wished him to land. He was mistaken because the men 'again came to oppose us'. Cook fired a shot between them upon which they retired to where their 'darts' lay and one threw a stone at them so Cook fired again. This time 'some of the shot struck the man' who, given the light shot Cook used, ignored any injury he suffered and took up a shield to defend himself. Cook decided to land and turned to young Isaac Smith, a cousin of Cook's wife, Elizabeth, to whom tradition has it that he said, 'Isaac, you shall land first'. Cook followed with Banks, Solander and Tupia, two 'darts' were thrown at them, another shot was fired and the Aborigines 'took off' but not in haste. Cook wanted to follow them, but Banks warned him to be cautious lest the darts be poisoned. The captain went further, nonetheless, and came across a few small huts made of bark. In one there were 'four or five small children' with whom he left some beads and other objects. There were many 'darts' (spears), Banks estimated 40 to 50, about the huts. The landing party took them as they departed for the *Endeavour*. Banks also twice described a wooden weapon 'made something like a short scymeter' which was clearly a boomerang. Before departure, Cook took the opportunity to examine three canoes on the beach that were made of bark tied together at each end and kept open with sticks. He pronounced them as 'the worst I think I ever saw'.[11]

A party organised by Cook to go ashore next morning found a source of fresh water sufficient for the ship's needs. The presents that had been left with the children lay there still and Cook thought that 'probably the natives were afraid to take them away'. After breakfast he took the pinnace to 'sound

---

[11]   *Cook*, 29 April 1770, pp. 304-05; *Banks*, vol. 2, pp. 53-55.

and explore' the bay and observed that several people 'fled at my approach'. He landed at a place where a meal had been in the course of preparation over small fires upon which fresh mussels were still being broiled. Nearby lay 'vast heaps of the largest oyster shells I ever saw'. This was the first recorded sighting of a midden.[12]

Banks' account of the same events was more elaborate. He says that while the *Endeavour* was entering the bay the land 'appeared cliffy and barren without wood'. About 10 people were seen who left their fire and retired to 'a little eminence' from which they could observe the ship and, presumably, carefully watch proceedings. Soon after, two canoes arrived with two men in each who hauled their boats ashore and went to join the others on the hill. One man, however, hid among rocks near the beach and remained there during the period that the men of the *Endeavour* were in the vicinity. Cook and his party landed while their boat went further along the shore with some 'Indians' following at a distance. On its return the officer aboard told Banks that in a small cove the men came close to the shore and 'invited our people to land by many signs and words'. They were all armed so that no landing was made. Banks then records his version of Cook's description of these episodes and agrees that the two men were belligerent in their opposition to a landing, although he makes no mention of Cook firing on them.[13]

By noon they were back aboard the *Endeavour* for 'dinner' and passed under the south head where four men were fishing, each in his own small canoe. Although the ship passed close by, they took no notice of it. This prompted Banks to speculate that they 'neither saw nor heard her go past them', given the sound of the surf and their attention to their task, which seems highly unlikely. The ship then came abreast of a small 'village' of '6 or 8 houses'. An elderly woman emerged from the bush with three youngsters carrying sticks, which were intended for a fire that was promptly lit to cook a meal. Three younger children came out of a house and the fishermen arrived with their catch so that preparation for the meal went on apace. Banks noticed that all this took place without any attention being paid to the looming presence of the *Endeavour*, while also observing the nakedness of the diners ashore, including the woman who 'did not copy our mother Eve even in a fig leaf'.[14]

Parkinson's narrative of these events was probably not written in the

---

12   *Banks*, vol. 2, p. 52; *Cook*, 30 April 1770, p. 306.
13   *Banks*, vol. 2, p. 53.
14   *Banks*, vol. 2, pp. 53–54.

immediate aftermath, but at a much later date when the use of the name Botany Bay had become customary. In fact Cook's journal for 29 April has a log entry stating that 'The great quantity of these sort of fish found in this place occasioned my giving it the name Sting ray's harbour'. Allegedly on the same day (although by his time reckoning it was 28 April) Parkinson wrote, 'From the number of curious plants we met on shore, we called the bay Botany Bay'. A week later, on 6 May, Cook wrote, 'The great quantity of New Plants etc Mr Banks and Dr Solander collected in this place occasioned my giving it the name Botany Bay'.[15] The new name gradually became acceptable and it was eventually adopted spasmodically by the journal writers aboard the *Endeavour*, except for James Matra.

Parkinson begins his account with 'We got into a fine bay, and some of our people went on shore on one side of it, where we saw some houses'. When they came near the shore, two armed and plainly hostile men made towards them threatening and 'often crying to us, Warra warra wai'. Making peaceful signs and offering trinkets to them availed nothing, but 'they kept aloof, and dared us to come on shore'. Firing a gun loaded with small shot failed to frighten the men, one of whom went to a house and emerged with a shield and a sword. Advancing 'boldly' they picked up stones and threw them at the shore party who then landed to receive two 'lances' one of which fell between Parkinson's feet. His own words best describe the remainder of the encounter:

> Our people fired again, and wounded one of them; at which they took the alarm and were very frantic and furious, shouting for assistance, calling Hala, hala, mae; that is, (as we afterwards learned,) Come hither; while their wives and children set up a most horrid howl. We endeavoured to pacify them, but to no purpose, for they seemed implacable, and, at length, ran howling away, leaving their wives and children, who hid themselves in one of the huts behind a piece of bark.

How Parkinson was able to give the meaning of the expression as 'Come hither' is inexplicable unless the later frequency of its use rendered the meaning plain.[16]

On the chest of one of the Aboriginal men sketched by Parkinson there is painted, in Matra's words, 'the rude figure of a man' but sufficiently clearly depicted as to permit some examination. In itself the figure is remarkable in that in no other instance is an image of a human figure depicted on any

---

[15] *Cook*, fn. 4, p. 310; Sydney Parkinson, *Journal of a Voyage to South Seas* (1773, p. 181); *Cook*, 6 April 1770, p. 310.

[16] Sydney Parkinson, *Journal of a Voyage to South Seas* (1773, p. 179).

part of an Aboriginal person. What is more remarkable is that the figure bears an undeniable resemblance to that of a crucified man, even though the cross itself is lacking. Be that the case, it might mean that the Aborigines of the Botany Bay area had in a previous contact seen a depiction of a crucified human being. If so the question then arises as to whether the figure appeared to have been of such importance to their visitors that it was deemed necessary to represent it again as a signal to Cook and his men that their kind had been encountered in the past. If there is any irony to be perceived in this matter, it surely lies in the fact that the near future would unfold into a grievous present for the Aborigines in which they would undergo their own passion.

Parkinson remarks more fully on some aspects of the Aborigines' comportment. He relates the trip to the north side of the bay 'where we had seen a number of people, as we came in, round a fire, some of whom were painted white, having a streak round their thighs, two below their knees, one like a sash over their shoulders, which ran diagonally downwards, and another across their foreheads'. Furthermore, 'Both men and women were quite naked, very lean and raw-boned; their complexion was dark, their hair black and frizzled, their heads unadorned, and the beards of the men bushy'. He describes their canoes much as Cook did, but added that each man used two small paddles and that some of their weapons 'had a kind of chisel fixed at their ends, but of what substance they were formed we could not learn'.[17]

The rest of Parkinson's journal entry for 28 April takes him through to the departure of the *Endeavour* from Botany Bay on 6 May and does not add to the first impressions except for the following which helps to fill out other accounts:

> The natives often reconnoitred us, but we could not prevail on them to come near to us or to be social; for, as soon as we advanced, they fled as nimbly as deer, excepting at one time, when they seemed determined to face us: then they came armed with spears, having their breasts painted white; but as soon as they saw our boat go off from the ship, they retreated. Constrained by hunger, they often came into the bay to fish; but they kept in the shallows, and as near as possible to the shore.[18]

On 30 April, Cook recorded in his journal that the 'wooders and waterers' — those responsible for cutting grass and for storing water in casks — came

---

[17] Sydney Parkinson, *Journal of a Voyage to South Seas* (1773, p. 179).
[18] Sydney Parkinson, *Journal of a Voyage to South Seas* (1773, p. 181).

aboard for dinner and 10 or more men appeared to rescue their canoes, but they did not touch the casks that had been left ashore. In the afternoon, 16, perhaps 18, armed men 'came boldly up to within 100 yards of our people at the watering place and there made a stand'. Although he was not present at this episode, it could well have been possible for him to observe it given the *Endeavour* was close inshore. Hicks was in charge of the shore party and he 'did all in his power to entice them to him by offering presents etc but it was to no purpose, all they seemed to want was for us to be gone. After staying a short time they went away.' Cook describes the weapons as 'darts' and 'wooden swords'. The darts, or spears, had four pointed prongs made of fish bones, which convinced him that they were used for fishing rather than 'as an offensive weapon'. It would also seem that some kind of test had been made on the 'darts' collected from the huts because the conclusion had been reached that they were not 'poisoned as we first thought'. Cook later more correctly identified the 'wooden swords' as throwing sticks. He also remarked that they had a defensive weapon, a shield, but that at Botany Bay it was seen once only.[19]

Again Banks has a lengthy and informative entry. After dinner, a party returned to the 'village' expecting that, from experience, no notice would be taken of them. On the contrary they met resistance. Two men appeared armed with spears and throwing sticks, which Banks identified as such. They shook their spears and 'called to us very loud in a harsh sounding language' that neither he nor Tupia understood. Meanwhile they made menacing gestures with their 'lances' in their resolution to prevent a landing 'to the utmost tho they were but two and we 30 or 40 at the least'. This episode lasted about a quarter of an hour 'they waving us to be begone' despite the fact that 'we [were] again signing that we wanted water and that we meant them no harm'. The men 'remained resolute' so a musket shot was fired over their heads, but to no effect. Small shot was then fired at the elder of the two, which he minded 'very little', although it struck him on the leg. He ran to his house, about 100 metres distant, returned with a shield and threw another lance, as did the younger man, which fell among the now landed party but did no harm. Two more shots were fired at them, the elder threw a final spear and they both ran away. In one 'house' they found children hidden behind a piece of bark and a shield. They did not disturb them but left them 'presents' and felt it 'no improper measure' to take 40 or 50 'lances'. Banks makes the point that, based on their hair, the people he invariably named

---

19   *Cook*, 30 April 1770, pp. 306, 396 for the throwing sticks.

Indians were not Negroes.[20]

In the afternoon of 1 May, 10 armed men were observed again visiting the watering place, so Cook went ashore and followed them for a distance 'alone and unarmed' indicating his confidence that he would remain unharmed. His courageous act was to no avail because 'they would not stop until they got farther off than I choose to trust myself'. That night Forby Sutherland, a seaman who had been stricken for some time with consumption, 'departed this life' and was buried in the morning near the watering place on the south shore of the bay, which was named after him while the headland itself was named Point Solander. The opposite point of entry into the bay was named after Banks. After the burial, but still before noon, Cook went with 'a party' to visit some huts where people had been seen each day and several useful objects, such as cloth, looking glasses, combs, needles and nails were left there. Penetrating into the 'country' they found it 'diversified with woods, lawns and marshes'. There was very little undergrowth beneath the trees, which were well spaced, and the soil was a 'light white sand' in which 'good grass' sprang up. The party concluded that the country, excepting the marshes, could be cultivated without the necessity of cutting down a single tree. Tracks were seen of what was probably a kangaroo and a dingo, but no sightings were made. Several trees cut down by the Aborigines, as well as others from which the bark had been cut by the same blunt instrument, attracted attention as did the gum of the eucalyptus, which was unnamed but seen clearly as the 'largest tree in the woods'.[21]

Dinner, clearly the main meal of the day, was perforce taken late at some time after three o'clock, after which Cook and others returned to the watering place and 17 or 18 men came into sight. Hicks recorded that two of the men 'advanced and talked much in an unknown tongue. I believe the purport was either commanding us to go away or daring to single combat.' They were the same group that had been encountered that morning by John Gore and a shipmate, but they did not come closer than 20 metres and stopped whenever Gore turned to face them. Although armed, they made no attack, but they threw three darts at Monkhouse and, soon afterwards, at another group from the *Endeavour* who pretended to beat a retreat from them. Solander, Tupia and Cook hastily made after the men but failed, by

[20] *Banks*, vol. 2, pp. 54-55.
[21] *Cook*, 1 May, pp. 306–08 and fn. 1, p. 308. Cook makes it plain that he had been reading Tasman by referring to gum and gum-lac. The latter word was used erroneously by Tasman in reference to the gum of the eucalyptus tree — our gum tree (p. 308). No reference is made to any use the Aborigines may have made of the gum.

words or actions, to prevail upon them to come close. Later again, Gore, now in a boat, saw more men further up the bay 'who by signs invited him ashore which he prudently declined'.[22]

More people were seen, but they retreated immediately they were aware of the presence of the men from the *Endeavour*. Cook remained determined to 'form some connections with the natives' so, taking the pinnace, he came upon 10 or 12 of them, each fishing in his own canoe, but they retreated into shallow water when he came near and fled in their canoes when he landed. In the late afternoon, smoke and canoes were seen, but the people fled as the crew approached. Six canoes and six small fires, still burning near the shore with mussels roasting on them and oysters lying about, led to the conclusion that six men, each with his own canoe, had disembarked to prepare a meal. Cook wrote, 'we tasted of their cheer and left them in return strings of beads, etc'. Cook again remarked on the condition of the soil which was 'much' richer than the sandy soil already encountered. Indeed it was 'a deep black soil which was capable of producing any kind of grain' while at that time, besides timber, it presented 'as fine a meadow as was ever seen'. He was, however, sufficiently cautious to remark that all the soil was not so attractive and that a few places were very rocky which would make it 'very proper for building'.[23]

In the evening, no people were seen at the watering place, but about 20 of them, out in their canoes and fishing, came close to the *Endeavour*. On the next morning Cook sent out 'some parties into the Country' in a final attempt to establish some kind of relationship with the Aborigines. A midshipman who strayed a long way from the main party came upon 'a very old man and woman and two small Children' who were close to the shore where several others were in their canoes taking up shellfish. The midshipman was afraid lest he be discovered to be alone, but he gave a bird, 'some Parrots' says Banks, that he had shot to the elderly people. They would not touch the offering, according to Banks, 'withdrawing themselves from his hand when he offered them in token of either extreme fear or disgust' and remained silent. The midshipman said that they seemed to be 'much frightened' and that they were 'quite naked even the woman had nothing to cover her nudity'. Monkhouse, with one companion, met six men who

---

22   *Cook*, 2 May 1770, p. 308. The variant account regarding 'single Combat' by Hicks comes from his log, which is held by the Alexander Turnbull Library, New Zealand, and cited by Beaglehole in *Cook*, p. 308, fn. 2. See also John Currey (ed.), *The Endeavour Journal of Zachary Hicks Lieutenant 13 April 1770-22 August 1770* (2006).

23   *Cook*, 3 May 1770, pp. 308-09.

appeared as if waiting for them to come close but 'as he was going up to them, he had a dart thrown at him out of tree which narrowly escaped him'. The thrower hastened down from the tree and fled with his companions. Banks gives a similar account of this episode and adds the observation that the spear was thrown at 'a signal by a word pronounced out loud' and that the youth who threw it 'had been stationed [in the tree] probably for that purpose'. In a somewhat supercilious tone he remarked that he went to the 'woods, botanizing as usual, now quite devoid of fear as our neighbours have turned out such rank cowards'. He also described the elderly couple met by the midshipman in greater detail than that in Cook's narrative. They were 'very old and grey headed, the children very young. The hair of the man was bushy about his head, his beard long and rough, the woman's was cropped short about her head; they were very dark coloured but not black nor was their hair woolly'.[24]

Banks had made an initial excursion inland on the south shore of the bay and described the soil, much as Cook had done, as either swampy or light sandy soil with 'very few species of trees'. It was probably on this occasion that he discovered the genus Banksia which included the well-known Banksia serrata or red honeysuckle. On the day before the *Endeavour* sailed from Botany Bay he spent the afternoon going further into the country on the north shore than he had previously done. He found it to be principally sandy and much like 'our moors in England'. No trees grew on it but 'everything is covered with a thin brush of plants about as high as our knees'. The surrounding hills were low and rose gradually in height for a good distance inland. Together with the meagre information on the soil contributed by Cook, these observations made by Banks seem flimsy evidence upon which the decision to select Botany Bay as a suitable site for a settlement, albeit of convicts, was eventually made.[25]

On Saturday 5 May, Cook took a party to the north shore and went four or five kilometres slightly inland, but near the coast. The land was mostly barren heath amongst marshes and morasses. Back aboard he was delighted to hear that a great haul of leather jackets had been made, as well as several stingrays, one of which weighed 180 kilograms cleaned. A further two stingrays were caught in shallow water and, according to Parkinson, even their innards 'had an agreeable flavour'. Cook had been anxious to depart from Botany Bay since Friday 4 May, but the wind was unfavourable until

24 *Cook*, 4 May 1770, pp. 309–10; *Banks*, vol. 2, pp. 59-60.
25 *Banks*, vol. 2, p. 60.

Sunday morning when, on 6 May, after a week's stay, the *Endeavour* set out to sea with a light breeze in its favour.

Another journal was written on the stay at Botany Bay, which has attracted little attention by scholars possibly because its authorship was disputed. Written by James Matra, and accepted as authentic by Beaglehole, although he did not make use of it, Matra's journal was published in London in 1771 and publicly known well before Cook's own journal was published. A copy of the original publication is held by several Australian libraries including the Mitchell Library, Sydney, and the National Library of Australia, Canberra. It was republished in 1975 by Antonio Giordano with a foreword by Professor G.M. Badger. The *Historical Records of New South Wales* has Matra's account pertaining to New Holland spanning from 31 March to 21 August 1770. The publisher declared that it was 'the production of a gentleman and scholar who made the voyage', which very probably accounted for the fact that it was generally attributed in France and England to Banks.[26]

The American-born Matra was of some education, as is proved by the clarity of his English and the correct spelling in his journal. He was signed on the *Endeavour* as a 'young gentleman' and promoted to full midshipman rank before the ship arrived home. He did not remain in the navy and, in 1787, he became the English Consul-General at Tangier and acted there as ambassador on several occasions, dying in 1806.[27] In his journal, Matra always referred to Cook with respect, despite the differences between them, which are recounted in Cook's journal, but omitted in Matra's. Matra was critical of his captain only once. It concerned the incident in New Zealand when Matra says that 'Cook, with several gentlemen, attended by a party of marines, landed on one of the islands, and incautiously suffered themselves to be surrounded by a great body of Indians'. Had it not been for 'several great shot fired a little over them', which 'greatly terrified' the Indians, Matra concluded that the Maori 'might with the greatest facility have destroyed

---

26 James Matra, *The Anonymous Journal (A Journal of a Voyage Round the World in his Majesty's Ship Endeavour)* (1975). See also Alan Frost, *The Precarious Life of James Mario Matra: Voyager with Cook, American Loyalist, Servant of Empire* (1995). In the *Historical Records of New South Wales* vol. 1, pt. 1 (1893, pp. 494-502 and fn. 1, p. 494) the section by Matra on the voyage up the east coast of Australia was recorded.

27 James Matra, *The Anonymous Journal (A Journal of a Voyage Round the World in his Majesty's Ship Endeavour)* (1975, pp. v to xv).

every one of our people on shore'.[28] The episode is also telling in its resemblance to Cook's final hours.

Matra also explained the background to the presence of Tupia on the *Endeavour*. Spelling his name as Tobia, he described him as he who 'had formerly been high priest of Otahitee, but being disgusted with the present regent, he voluntarily embarked on our voyage bringing with him an Indian lad named Tiato, an attendant'. Matra said of Tupia that he was man of 'great sagacity and judgement', an opinion with which Cook agreed.[29]

Matra recorded 19 April, a Thursday, as the day when they 'discovered the coast of new Holland'. Smoke was seen ashore on Saturday, Cape Dromedary was named and Bulli passed with the sighting of 'natives kindling fires along the shore'. On Saturday morning, 28 April, they came into Botany Bay and anchored at 1.30 that afternoon. He then gave a somewhat different account of the first encounter with the Aborigines, which, given its significance, deserves recording in full:

> But on attempting to land in our boats, a few of the natives advanced towards the shore, and two of them, armed with shields and spears, resolutely opposed our disembarkation. Until being wounded by our shot, and unsupported by any of their countrymen, they retreated slowly to their houses within the bushes, but constantly faced us the whole way. This they did to gain time for their wives to remove themselves with their children with their domestic and culinary utensils farther into the woods and when this was done they hastily retreated themselves.[30]

While relating this incident much as Cook and the others had done, Matra sees the behaviour of the people in an entirely different and more chivalrous light than that cast upon it by the other accounts. In this respect it would

---

[28] James Matra, *The Anonymous Journal (A Journal of a Voyage Round the World in his Majesty's Ship Endeavour)* (1975, pp. 88–89). Matra referred to the Maori always as Indians, but used 'natives' for the Aborigines except on pp. 115, 116. Given the ability of Tupia to converse with the Maori, Matra was astonished at the 'little difference' between the language spoken by the Maori and the Tahitians and concluded that 'one of these places was originally peopled by the other' (pp. 58, 105).

[29] James Matra, *The Anonymous Journal (A Journal of a Voyage Round the World in his Majesty's Ship Endeavour)* (1975, pp. 58, 64). Matra's attitude to the haka bears repeating: 'it is impossible to see, without astonishment, the degree of madness to which they will elevate themselves even in their harangues, that are preparatory to a feigned battle' (p. 107). Nonetheless, in summing up the Maori, he said they were 'habituated to the carnage of war from infancy, and of all mankind the most fearless and insensible of dangers' (p. 105).

[30] James Matra, *The Anonymous Journal (A Journal of a Voyage Round the World in his Majesty's Ship Endeavour)* (1975, p. 110). Despite being a member of the crew as a naval 'apprentice', Matra, unlike his captain, used the civilian method of dating.

seem that the Aborigines did all they could to protect their families and only departed once they believed them to be hidden safely from the men of the *Endeavour*.

Matra described the Aboriginal 'huts' as 'wretchedly built'. The people, however, though naked and black, 'differed from the negroes of Africa' in that their hair was long and straight, instead of having 'wool on their heads'. His description of their weapons and canoes was consistent with the others, as was his conclusion that the Aborigines lived 'chiefly on fish' but, unlike Cook, he specified 'ray-fish' as their main item of food. He also insisted, as did the other journal writers, that the Aborigines showed no interest whatever in any of the presents or trinkets given to them by Cook and the crew.[31]

There is a long account of a semi-warlike incident in which the Aborigines were prepared to 'challenge us to battle' by presenting themselves, armed, with the same number as the crew 'as they had counted in the boat' who had been sent ashore to fish. On being refused, they selected two only of their own 'and challenged as many of us to fight them' but, once this proposal was rejected 'they all retired'. Soon afterwards several came to the shore and an officer fired 'a musket loaded with a ball into a tree at some distance'. This feat evidently so delighted the Aborigines that they persuaded him to repeat the act 'which he did, and they soon after retired apparently well pleased'.[32]

In the immediate aftermath, 22 armed Aborigines followed the crew as they passed through the 'woods', stopping and starting as the crew did until they came to a further number of the *Endeavour* party. Someone suggested a 'scheme to entrap some of the Indians, which had near proved fatal'. The idea was to approach the Aborigines as closely as possible and then, 'feigning a fright' to run from them with the hope that by so doing they might entice them to a pursuit and thus afford the opportunity 'of surrounding and taking some of them'. The opposite happened in that, as soon as the crew began to run from the Aborigines, they were showered with a hail of spears none of which it seems met their intended mark. Matra says that 'After this attack, they all precipitately retired to the woods; and we, collecting their spears, returned with them to our ship'. With this incident behind them and

---

[31]   Matra's description of the soil, the birds and of 'a quadruped', clearly a kangaroo, is also of interest. James Matra, *The Anonymous Journal (A Journal of a Voyage Round the World in his Majesty's Ship Endeavour)* (1975, pp. 111-14).

[32]   James Matra, *The Anonymous Journal (A Journal of a Voyage Round the World in his Majesty's Ship Endeavour)* (1975, pp. 114-15).

'having procured a sufficient supply of wood and water, on Sunday the 6th of August [sic], in the morning, we sailed from the bay, which we named Sting-Ray Bay, from the great quantity of those fish which it contained'.[33]

If we are to accept the truth of Matra's account, we are forced to conclude that the summation of the Aborigines of Botany Bay by Banks was grossly wide of the mark in one respect at least. Banks said that he went 'botanizing' in the bush without any fear 'as our neighbours have turned out such rank cowards'. On the contrary, their behaviour in respect of armed combat bore a remarkable resemblance to that of the knights of feudal times. They were prepared to fight fairly and on equal terms without prejudice to the non-combatants. Furthermore, is it credible that on no occasion, and despite the numbers involved, no single spear thrown by the Aborigines at the newcomers whom they demanded to go away, met their mark? After centuries spent successfully hunting with spears and woomeras for game as small as fish and birds, as well as kangaroos and wallabies, did they now both individually and collectively, all lose their aim? Some months later at the Endeavour River both Cook and Banks were almost in awe of the accuracy of the Aborigines with their spears. Why should those of Botany Bay lack the same skill? Is it not more probable that their intention was to warn off the white men in the hope that so doing would prompt their hasty departure? Could it have been that, in order to avoid further conflict and deaths, they were deliberately inaccurate? In any event their behaviour marked them as a people of high civility.

In his journal, Banks made no précis of his observations of Botany Bay and its inhabitants. Cook, however, dwelt at some length on the matter in his journal of 6 May. He described the entrance and then the harbour which was 'capacious and commodious' with a safe place to anchor. Fresh water was available on the north shore in a 'very fine stream' while wood for fuel was 'everywhere'. While reflecting on the Aborigines, he came to a few, necessarily brief conclusions, given the paucity of information upon which he depended. They appeared to him to subsist solely on fish, remarking in a deleted passage in the original that 'none of us ever saw any provisions laid up in store so that I believe that they depend upon the present day

---

[33] James Matra, *The Anonymous Journal (A Journal of a Voyage Round the World in his Majesty's Ship Endeavour)* (1975, pp. 115–16). I find it difficult to understand how Matra could have mistaken May for August unless perhaps he wrote his account of the events which took place at Botany Bay in April and May of that year while the *Endeavour* was beached at the Endeavour River in August 1770. By Cook's account the *Endeavour* in fact sailed from Botany Bay on Sunday 6 May.

for their subsistence'. Their catch was principally of 'Oysters, Mussels, Cockles etc' and he observed that they sometimes roasted and ate them 'in the canoe, having often a fire for that purpose'. They did not seem to catch and eat the stingrays that abounded in the bay, although it seems possible on reflection that the large size of the stingrays and the frailty of the small canoes used by the Aborigines might have made catching them impossible, even dangerous. Although they were not numerous, the Aborigines did not live together in large groups but were 'dispersed in small parties along by the water side'. About as tall as Europeans, their bodies were not black, but very dark brown, and their hair was 'black and lank like ours' rather than woolly and frizzled. None wore clothing or ornaments, and none were found 'in or about their huts', from which Cook concluded that they 'never wear any', although some painted their face and bodies with 'a sort of white paint or Pigment'. He summed up the situation with, 'However we could know but very little of their customs as we were never able to form any connections with them, they had not so much touched the things we had left in their huts on purpose for them to take away'. Despite the paucity of the knowledge gained at Botany Bay, Cook was moved to cause 'the English Colours to be displayed ashore every day and an inscription to be cut out upon one of the trees near the watering place setting forth the Ship's name, date, etc'.[34]

Unlike Cook, who thought he had learnt very little from his week in Botany Bay, much can be learnt from the accounts that the authors of the journals left to posterity. Perhaps the most important fact is that the Aborigines made it plain from the very first moment that they wished to have no contact with their clearly unwanted visitors and that all they desired of them was that they would go away immediately. The initial response of two men to the landing is one of remarkable bravery and tenacity and can only be explained by their determination to resist at all costs. This was clear even before Cook had used arms, however harmlessly in the outcome, against them in response to their belligerence. That they would attempt to beguile his party to undertake an unsafe landing in their presence and thus open themselves to attack may well have been no more than a further working through of a response of determined resistance rather than of petty deception.

The Aborigines repeated their negative behaviour on every possible occasion until the *Endeavour* departed from Botany Bay. They refused to come close to the crew, they spurned every effort to communicate in any way, their belligerence was unwearied and they attempted to put small parties

---

[34]   *Cook*, 6 May 1770, p. 312.

into a position in which an attack by them may have proved to be successful. Even the request to lead crew members to water, which the Aborigines must have known was vital for life, was rejected. To conclude that their fear of the Europeans, or inherent hostility against strangers, were sufficient to cause the adult males to desert the elderly and children and thus leave them to the mercy of strangers can scarcely be put down to either neglect or cowardice. Sheer horror and desperation might explain it, provided it did in fact happen in the manner described by others, but not by Matra.

The seeming disinterest displayed in the presence in the bay of the *Endeavour* cannot be explained by ignorance, heedlessness or sheer stupidity. That the Aborigines of Botany Bay were forewarned of the arrival of the newcomers by the use of smoke signals is unquestionable. Because no landings had been made, those who warned them could not give more information than that a large vessel with strangers aboard was headed north and thus would inevitably pass by or enter Botany Bay. To run away from their home territory was not an alternative so they were forced to await the *Endeavour* with trepidation and hope that its people would not land, or if they did so, soon depart. Seeming disdain for the very presence of the ship and its crew, and the rejection of the useful objects pressed upon them, might well have been a futile attempt to convince the strangers that there was no value in their remaining at the bay. Above all the Aborigines had nothing to lose but their land — their beloved country. It was entwined with their heartstrings and the very essence of their being. Lose it and they lost all.

Nonetheless, much of this behaviour might point to the possibility that the Aborigines of Botany Bay had encountered vessels with strange crews on a previous occasion. Had such occurred in the recent past, it would be alive in memory and, if it had happened in the remote past, it could have been remembered in the Dreaming. The encounter might have been recalled as one entailing violence of a kind that induced the Aborigines to reject forcibly the presence of further strangers in their midst. It is particularly remarkable that, apart from a very elderly woman, not a single sighting of an adult or young woman was recorded. Experience might well have taught the Aborigines to conceal women from strangers.

Cook's behaviour and that of his crew at Botany Bay, as judged by the journals and the then prevailing standards of behaviour among many Europeans to Indigenous people, seems to have been exemplary. Unlike in New Zealand, there was no loss of life and Cook was careful to avoid wounding an Aboriginal person in any serious manner, despite what must have seemed to be to him repeated acts of provocation. Apart from taking a considerable number of spears, which was done in defence rather than scientific curiosity, nothing of real value to the Aborigines, such as a canoe, was taken from them. Fish and shellfish were abundant in the bay, as were stingrays. At the same time it would seem from Parkinson that the very presence of the *Endeavour* and its crew in the bay was enough to cause the Aborigines to be 'constrained by hunger' and thus forced to fish in the shallows away from the ship and to do so even before dawn. No evidence, such as animal or bird bones at camp fires or near the 'huts' was recorded, or of seeds used for meal. A bird carcass was refused. Even if fish alone formed their diet, however, a cursory examination of a midden would not suffice to conclude that it contained only shells.

The weaponry used by the Aborigines was described briefly by Cook in a passage that he subsequently deleted from his journal: 'The arms we saw among them were darts (some of which were barbed [altered from bearded] with fish bones stuck on with gum) and wooden swords, their defensive weapon is a "target" made of the bark of the gum tree.' By target he probably meant a shield. Thus the main offensive weapon was the spear, called variously a dart or a lance, while the wooden swords referred to were woomeras used to propel a spear. The fact that 'fish bones stuck on with gum' formed the main part of the spear clearly indicates that, given its frailty, it was used for fishing rather than hunting game such as kangaroos. It would also seem to be a somewhat ineffective weapon to use in human conflict. Some spears, however, lacked the bones that, together with the use of the 'target', must indicate that forms of hunting for larger game and conflict were entered into. Indeed Banks gives a lengthy description of the spear — he uses 'Pike or Lance' — which he said was 'most cruel' when used 'against men' as a weapon because it had a single sharp point and below it three or four barbs turned down so that once penetrated into the flesh the spear would do great damage on its withdrawal. The difficulty with this description, however, is its being interwoven with a long narrative that includes his impressions of the Aborigines and their customs at the Endeavour River without specifying differences. Perhaps the Aborigines of Botany Bay had no similar offensive weapon given that it is not mentioned by our journalists. That the boomerang was seen in the south but unremarked upon is curious given that it was in use there, but not in Cape York. The didgeridoo was not in use at the time in the south and probably not also at Cape York.[35]

---

[35] *Cook*, 6 May 1770, p. 312; *Banks*, vol. 2, August 1770, pp. 132-33.

Cook was constantly courteous, open and warm in his approach to the Aborigines and generous in offering so-called presents. They never showed any sign of a reciprocal gesture. There is no evidence that any member of the crew acted otherwise and Hicks did his best to approach unarmed. The Aborigines must have been aware that fresh water was essential for the survival of the men on the *Endeavour*, but their understanding of this common and basic need of humanity did not move them.

Banks remarked on the dwellings of the Aborigines, which both he and Parkinson called 'houses' regularly, while Parkinson said that they were also a 'kind of house or wigwarn [sic]'. This gives the impression that the dwellings were constructed in a manner pointing to their being at least semi-permanent, which, it appears, was not unusual on the coastline with its abundance of seafood. It is hard to understand what motive prompted the Aborigines so readily to desert their canoes and homes, which one must imagine were of some value to them.

The impressions made upon other, but earlier, Europeans when they first encountered a new people bears, in part, a striking similarity to that made upon Cook and his men on the Australian east coast. Pedro Álvares Cabral, in command of 13 ships with 1,200 men, left Lisbon in 1500 to go around Africa and thence to India. In so doing, he came upon the coast of Brazil and Pedro Vaz de Caminha, a Portuguese who sailed with Cabral, wrote an account for the king of their meeting the inhabitants. The complete nakedness of all they met struck the Portuguese forcibly: 'They were quite dark and naked', although some were in part painted. What struck de Caminha most forcibly was 'The innocence of this people', indeed it was 'such that that of Adam could not have been greater'. They had no iron tools but 'cut their wood and boards with stones … they do not till the soil or breed stock' and they seemed to subsist on manioc and 'the seeds and the fruits which the earth and trees produce'. Nonetheless, 'they are stronger and better fed than we are with all the wheat and vegetables we eat'.[36]

---

[36] The source for de Caminha's letter to the King of Portugal is William Brooks Greenlee (trans.), *The Voyages of Pedro Alvares Cabral to Brazil and India* (1937).

6

The Reef

At first light on the morning of 6 May the *Endeavour*, taking advantage of a mild breeze, sailed out of Botany Bay and turned north while remaining close to the shore.

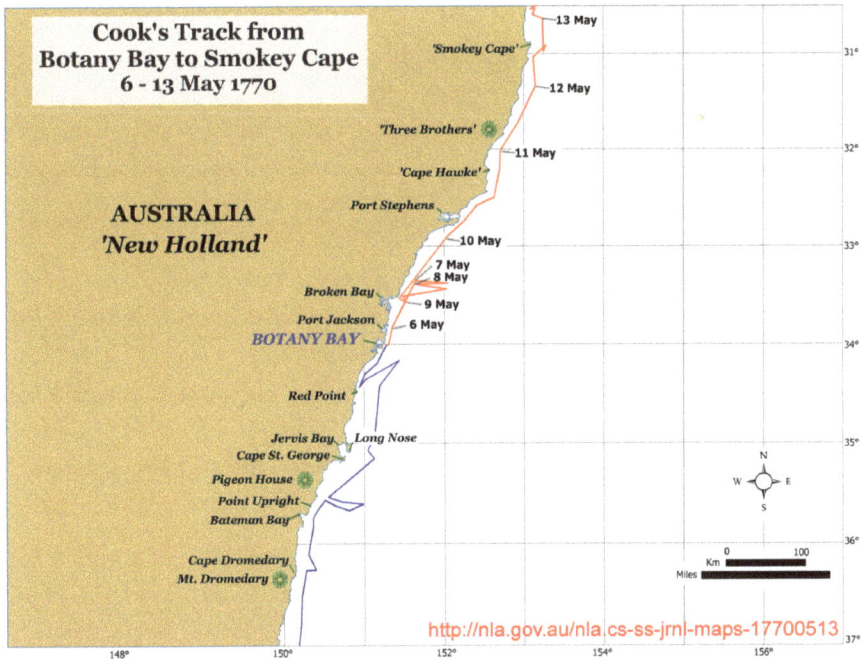

Cook's Track from Botany Bay to Smokey Cape 6 - 13 May 1770

There can be little doubt that the departure was a source of relief to both the Aborigines and their unwelcome visitors. Despite the fact that both Cook and Banks had written almost favourably of the physical attributes of Botany Bay, Arthur Phillip in 1788 arrived at an almost immediate conclusion that it was unsuitable for a settlement. He noted that the land was swampy and therefore a possible source of disease, while the bay itself was so open it could prove hazardous. Major Robert Ross, the military commandant, was straight to the point in his despatch to the secretary of the Admiralty, Lord Philip

Stephens, writing that the whole country appeared to be 'either sand, rock or swampy and, as far as we could judge, unfit for any kind of cultivation'. The result was a prompt exodus to Port Jackson. Botany Bay, however, refused to enter oblivion. Rather, while it became the butt of derision in song and legend, for many Australians it continued to be warmly remembered as the first site of settlement, albeit so briefly.[1]

Having spent a week at Botany Bay and stocked up with water and wood, as well as grass for the few animals aboard, time was precious and Cook had every good reason to hasten further on his journey to Batavia. By noon a bay or harbour was seen that Cook concluded 'appeared to be a safe anchorage'. He named it Port Jackson and thereby passed, without entering, one of the finest harbours in the world. There is no evidence that the name was given because a sailor of that name aboard the *Endeavour* was the first to see it. No such seaman was aboard. However the two secretaries of the Admiralty when Cook set forth were Sir George Jackson and Lord Stephens. Cook gave them a place in posterity with Point Jackson and Point Stephens, as he did likewise in New Zealand. In passing he mistook the Narrabeen Lagoon for a bay and named it Broken Bay. Noting that smoke was rising from flat land led him to 'suppose that there were lagoons which afforded subsistence to the natives such as shell fish, etc, for we as yet know nothing else they live upon'. Further north, he was interested to notice the smoke of several fires inland and one of them 'was upon the top of a hill which was the first we have seen upon elevated ground since we have been upon this coast' while, a little later 'three remarkable large hills lying contiguous to each other' took his fancy and he named them the Three Brothers. By night there were so many fires on a headland 'that caused a great quantity of smoke which occasioned my giving it the name of Smoky Cape'.[2]

Since Cook gave no description of the 'Country' since Botany Bay, he decided to do so on 14 May. The land beyond the shore had increased in height each day so that 'it may be called a hilly country [but] diversified with an agreeable variety of hills, ridges, valleys and large plains all clothed with wood'. His honesty forced him to concede that it was 'to all appearance as I have before mentioned' even to the extent that the soil near the shore was 'low and

---

[1]   Cook to Lord Sydney, 15 May 1788; and, Ross to Stephens, 10 July 1788, in *Historical Records of New South Wales: Phillip 1783–1792*, vol. 1, pt 2 (1893, pp. 121–36, 169–75). For a recent and valuable account of the *Endeavour* and the reef, see Chapter One of Iain McCalman, *The Reef: A Passionate History* (2013)

[2]   *Cook*, 6, 7, 11, 12, 13 May 1770, pp. 312, 313, 314, 315; 22 May 1770, p. 322; *Banks*, vol. 2, p. 62; *Historical Records*, vol. 1, pt 2, pp. 170-71.

sandy' which, in fairness, could not be unexpected. Banks was more optimistic. To him 'the country rose in gradual slopes carrying a great show of fertility … varying in appearance a good deal, generally however well clothed with good trees' and, later, 'beautiful as well as fertile'. At nine on the next morning they were about five kilometres from land and 'saw upon it people and smoke in several places'. Banks elaborated on this event and said that they were able for about an hour to observe through their glasses that there were about 20 of them 'each of which carried upon his back a large bundle of something which we conjectured to be palm leaves for covering their houses'. They 'walked upon the beach and then up a path over a gentle sloping hill behind which we lost sight of them'. He went on, 'Not one was once observed to stop and look towards the ship; they pursued their way in all appearance entirely unmoved by the neighbourhood of so remarkable an object as a ship must necessarily be to people who have never seen one'. Perhaps the Aborigines hoped that, were they to refuse to look, they would not be seen. In any case, while Banks and others on board the *Endeavour* could look at them with 'glasses', the Aborigines possessed no such means and carrying the palm leaves may have obscured their vision. On this day Parkinson only records that they 'saw six men, quite naked, walking upon a strait, white, sandy beach'.[3]

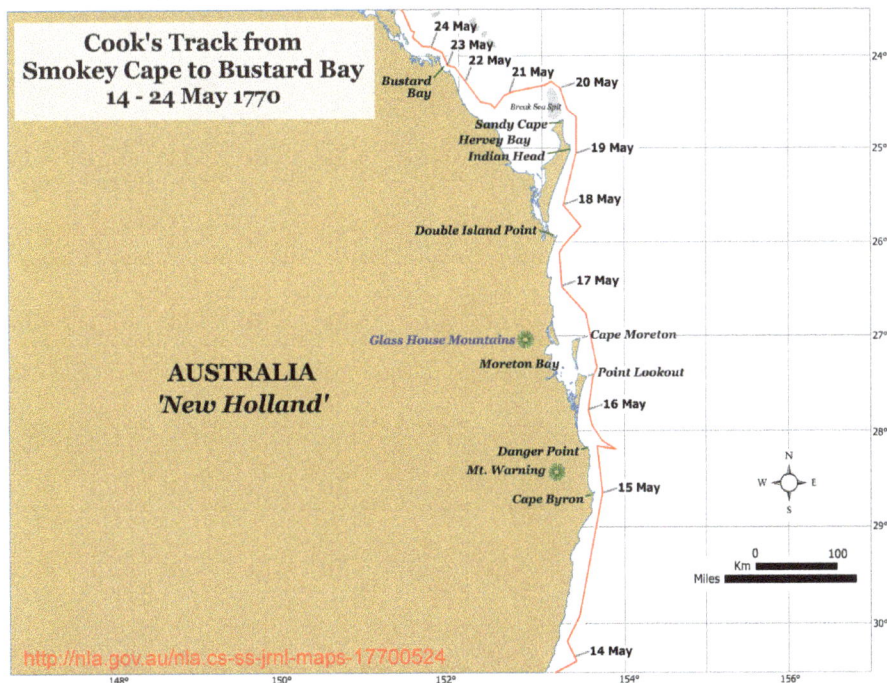

Cook's Track from Smokey Cape to Bustard Bay 14 - 24 May 1770

AUSTRALIA 'New Holland'

http://nla.gov.au/nla.cs-ss-jrnl-maps-17700524

3   *Cook*, 14, 15 May 1770, pp. 316–17; *Banks*, vol. 2, pp. 62-63; Sydney Parkinson, *Journal of a Voyage to South Seas* (1773, p. 182).

After naming Cape Bryon as they passed it, Cook for the first time sounded a note of caution, although he did not dwell on its full import, saying only that they 'discovered breakers ahead and on our larboard bow'. He simply named a Mount Warning, a Point Danger as well as a Point Lookout from which a bearing could be taken. Banks, however, made his own point with, 'We were fortunate just at this time to descry breakers ahead laying in the very direction in which the ship sailed', but it was brought to in time to avoid a disaster. Cook's next discovery was a 'wide open bay' that he named Morton Bay followed by Cape Morton. Both were named after the president of the Royal Society, James Douglas, 14th Earl of Morton, who, unbeknown to Cook, was already deceased by this time. In fact Moreton Bay, misspelt later, and ever since, lay behind the cape as did the Brisbane River. Slightly further on he could not fail to notice three hills inland 'very remarkable on account of their singular form of elevation' which to him bore a distinct resemblance to glasshouses. He duly named them as such.[4]

Having passed Indian Head in the night of 23 May 'a very extraordinary affair happened' to Cook's clerk Richard Orton. In drink taken and deeply asleep, all Orton's clothes were cut from him and, shortly afterwards, portions of both of his ears were also struck off. Cook said that Matra was 'The person whom he [Orton] suspected to have done this'. Initially, Cook decided that the charge was unfounded but, upon further consideration, he was induced 'to think that Matra was not altogether innocent'. He 'dismissed him the quarter deck and suspended him from doing any duty in the ship' judging that his services could well be spared and that he was 'good for nothing'. Understandably Cook's outrage at an event that was a flagrant violation of his authority caused him to take immediate, but potentially unjust, action. It seems that he did so without any convincing evidence, except Orton's suspicion that, if of any value, was nonetheless clouded by alcoholic fumes. Cook's own low opinion of Matra is surprising given that he nowhere explains it. The fact that Banks makes no mention of this act of violence must indicate that he felt unease, at least at the outcome, and probably stems from the friendship he had begun to form with Matra and which lasted throughout the latter's lifetime. Three weeks later Cook restored Matra 'to his duty as I did not find him guilty of the crimes laid to his charge'. This was done in the immediate aftermath of the almost fatal wrecking of the *Endeavour* on the Great Barrier Reef at which time Matra had made himself useful during the turmoil occasioned by the encounter. Finally, at Batavia, Cook and his officers offered a reward of 15 guineas, a very considerable sum, to anyone who would 'discover' the culprit

[4]   *Cook*, 15, 16, 17 May 1770, pp. 317, 318, 319; *Banks*, vol. 2, pp. 63, 64.

in the assault on Orton, and 'fifteen gallons of arrack', an Asian spirit distilled from coconut flowers, rice and other local sources — a generous amount of spirits indeed. Patrick Saunders, who had been demoted from midshipman to able seaman on the morning of the attack, promptly deserted the ship at Batavia which Beaglehole concluded stood badly against him given the chosen place was the 'least' inviting European settlement in the world at which to desert.[5]

Notwithstanding the overnight events Cook, accompanied by Banks and 'the other gentlemen', landed in order to examine the country. They came across '10 small fires' with cockle shells lying about, but 'the people were gone'. There were rudimentary bark shelters built near the fires, which were interpreted as being 'all the covering they had in the night'. Cook went further and avowed that many Aborigines did not even have that much covering, but slept naked in the open air although he did not wonder whether they used nearby fires or dogs to warm them. Tupia was with the party and he remarked that they were Taata Eno's 'that is bad or poor people', which was his way of expressing sorrow for their plight. The country thereabouts was much worse even than at Botany Bay, with dry and sandy soil and having no underwood about the trees. Banks noted 'several vessels of bark which we conceived were intended for water buckets' and concluded regarding the bark shelters that they were probably beds 'about the length and breadth of a man'. He also said that the locality was in 'a thicket of close trees', which would offer protection from the wind. Given that no houses, even ruined ones, were seen, and the fact that the ground was trodden down around the fire places, 'we concluded that they had for some time remained in this place'. They managed to shoot a fine bustard to consume at dinner the next day, which weighed six kilograms when dressed and was 'far the best we have eaten since we left England'. It was commemorated by naming the place Bustard Bay. Parkinson seemingly was not among the 'gentlemen' invited ashore, but he was able to relate that, from the ship, they saw about 20 people who stood 'gazing' out at them and that there was plentiful smoke 'arising out of the woods, which, perhaps, was only an artifice of theirs, to make us think they were numerous'.[6]

Having passed over the Tropic of Capricorn and named a cape after it, Keppel Bay was judged as a good anchorage, although Cook decided not to land there. It had been clear for some days that both the mainland and the

---

[5]   *Cook*, 23 May 1770, pp. 324-25, 324, fn. 1; Sydney Parkinson, *Journal of a Voyage to South Seas* (1773, p. 183). Cook omitted the event from his manuscripts A and G.

[6]   *Cook*, 23 May 1770, pp. 324-26; *Banks*, vol. 2, pp. 65–67; Sydney Parkinson, *Journal of a Voyage to South Seas* (1773, p. 183).

adjacent islands were inhabited because smoke and people were seen, which indicated that fresh water was available. Eventually, on 30 May, a landing was made but no water was found despite an extensive search, which explains the name given to an inlet — Thirsty Sound. Two 'people' were seen and they came across several 'fire places and saw smokes at a distance'. Banks said that near the fireplaces they saw 'grass laid together upon which 4 or 5 people had slept as I guessed about a fortnight before'. Others heard voices, but saw no one. Two men, however, followed a boat with Cook and Solander aboard but, as a strong tide was with them they did not stop and wait for the men to come to them. The country was judged as barren with no sign of fertility, while the mosquitoes were a positive curse as well as the burrs that stuck to the clothing of those who landed. The greater threat to their wellbeing, however, was not to be encountered on the land but in the sea. They were approaching the Great Barrier Reef.[7]

Ever optimistic about the condition of the land, and especially when seen from out to sea, Cook reported on 2 June that, near Cape Palmerston, it was, as had become the norm, 'pretty much diversified with mountains, hills, plains and valleys and seems to be tolerably clothed with wood and verdure' which he repeated on 4 June and was largely agreed upon by Banks, who even thought that it 'looked fertile and pleasant'. They were now, according to Pickersgill, 'running through a strait formed by a chain of very pleasant islands'. Because the passage was 'discovered on the day the Church commemorates the Festival' of Whitsunday, Cook was prompted to name it Whitsundays Passage while the islands became the Whitsundays. These matters possibly failed to impress Tupia who, complaining of very sore gums, which he had endured for almost two weeks, had to be put on an 'extract of lemon in all his drinks'. Remarkably, and entirely due to the sagacity of Cook and his ever watchfulness over the diet of his 'people', this was the first, but minor, onset of scurvy in the whole voyage.[8]

While among the Whitsundays, 'On a sandy beach upon one of the Islands we saw two people and a canoe with an outrigger that appeared to be larger and differently built to any we have seen upon the Coast'. Cook for the first time used the word 'people' of the Aborigines rather than 'natives', which might have been prompted by his realisation that these people had been in contact with an outside world that was closed to the people of the southern parts of the east coast. Banks confirms that impression of the Aborigines of

7   *Cook*, 29, 30 May 1770, pp. 330-33; *Banks*, pp. 70-73.
8   *Cook*, 2, 4 June 1770, pp. 335, 336; *Banks*, vol. 2, pp. 74, 75; Pickersgill, in *Cook*, p. 337, fn. 1.

the northern part as, potentially at least, more advanced than those of the south when he wrote, 'we saw with our glasses 2 men and a woman and a small canoe fitted with an outrigger, which made us hope that the people were something improved as their boat was far preferable to the bark canoes of Stingrays Bay'. Parkinson added that the canoe with outriggers was like those of Otaheite. It is also remarkable to note that Banks still used Stingrays Bay, a month after the name had allegedly been changed by Cook to Botany Bay. One would have thought that Banks would be the foremost to adopt the new name. In fact Cook was similarly undecided when he deleted a passage from his journal dated 7 June 1770, written when he was near Magnetic Island (Cook used 'Magnetical', 'because the compass would not travis [sic] well when near it') that stated 'we have had it frequently calm and been often at an anchor, we have caught no fish worth mentioning since we left Sting-Ray Harbour'.[9]

At Palm Isles on his chart, Cook noted people and canoes as well as some trees that were taken to be palms bearing coconuts. Cook thought that a few coconuts 'would be very acceptable to us at this time' and, to this end, Hicks was sent ashore with Banks and Solander, but the trees turned out to be 'no more than bad cabbage trees' although '14 or 15 new plants' were gathered by Banks. They were 'scarce … put off from the shore when an Indian came near it and shouted to us very loud'. It was dark and they could not see him so they faced back to the shore 'by way of seeing what he wanted of us', but he had disappeared. On the following day the *Endeavour* passed close to a small island on which were seen through the glasses 'about 30 men, women and children standing all together and looking attentively at us'. Banks remarked that they were 'the first people we have seen show any signs of curiosity at the sight of the ship' and Cook described them as 'quite naked and of a very dark colour with short hair'. Parkinson had one pleasant occurrence to remark upon saying that 'At night we saw a fire, which yielded a very grateful odour, not unlike that produced by burning the wood of gum benjamin'. Incense and perfume made from the Benzoin tree was used at the time.[10]

---

[9]   *Cook*, 4 June 1770, p. 337; *Banks*, vol. 2, pp. 74-75; Sydney Parkinson, *Journal of a Voyage to South Seas* (1773, p. 186). For the deleted passage, see *Cook*, 6 June 1770, fn. 1, p. 339.

[10]   *Cook*, 7, 8 June 1770, p. 339; *Banks*, p. 76; Sydney Parkinson, *Journal of a Voyage to South Seas* (1773, p. 186).

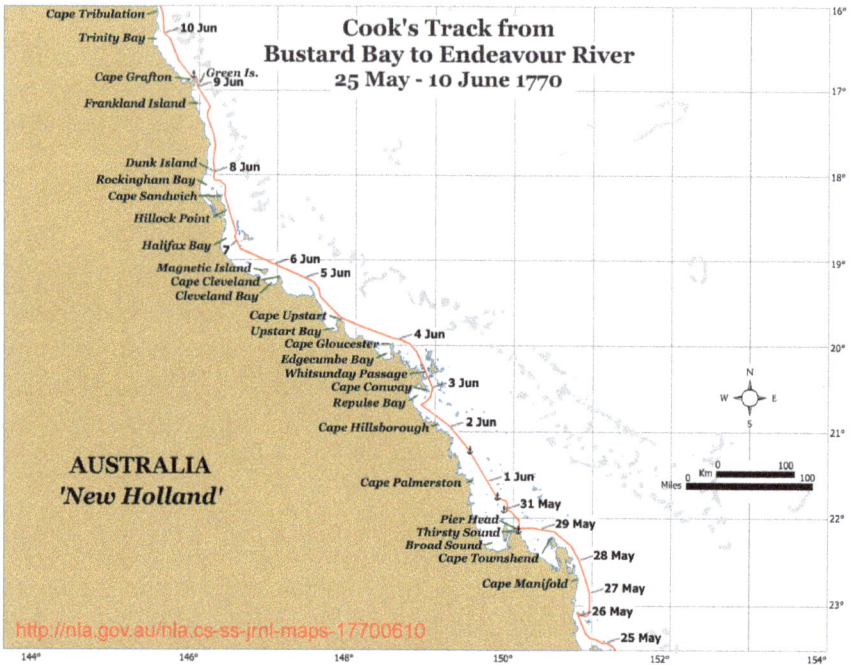

Cook's Track from
Bustard Bay to Endeavour River
25 May - 10 June 1770

As the voyage continued, Cook allowed himself the indulgence of a veritable outpouring of naming with, Point Hillock ('a round hillock or rock'), Iron Head, Rockingham Bay, Cape Sandwich and Halifax Bay. Whether intentional or not, the effect on the map reader is remarkable in that an unknown world immediately becomes intelligible, readily acceptable, and almost familiar. It is as if the new land has been baptised in the font of the old world and, thereby, welcomed not as a stranger but as a member of the family. Despite this and having noticed that Halifax Bay was 'well sheltered' with a good anchorage, he had no inclination to go ashore 'having hitherto met with so little encouragement' by which one assumes that, as well as the scarcity of fresh water, nothing of value or even of interest had been met since Botany Bay. The new land was not yet ready to surrender to the old.[11]

After Halifax Bay, Cook kept on busily naming features. Dunk Isle, the Frankland Isles, Cape Grafton and then Green Island followed, where Cook decided to land, principally in search of fresh water. Together with Banks and Solander he went searching, but failed to find a convenient position to enable the filling of barrels. Besides water, they found no trace of 'any other refreshment' so the party returned to the *Endeavour*, it being well into the evening. Cook admitted that he would have stayed for a day at least 'to have

---

[11]   *Cook*, 8 June, pp. 339-41.

looked into the country', but he decided against that step because he 'thought it would be only spending time and losing so much of a light moon to little purpose'. His haste to get on with the voyage was increasingly evident and it is this that prompted him to sail again at midnight. There is no indication that he saw any danger in so doing, even when only aided by the light of a pale moon along a perilous coast. Over the previous few days the presence of coral reefs had been evident in breakers on the sea and Banks described the new menace that would arise were an anchor to 'come home' or a cable break. Were that to happen they would go ashore on one of the shoals that surrounded them. Green Island was 'a small sandy island laying upon a large coral shoal … the first of the kind we had met with in this part of the South Sea'. It was now the Sunday after Whitsunday, the feast of the Holy Trinity, and they were passing a gentle indentation on the coast that scarcely warranted the title of a bay. Cook did not hesitate to name it Trinity Bay. At a later time, perhaps at Batavia, and in a different ink, he gave a name to the north point of Trinity Bay. He called it Cape Tribulation 'because here began all our troubles'.[12]

On Monday 11 June, with a wind from the east-south-east and within in sight of two small islands near the coast, probably the Hope Islands, which lay to the north-west, Cook shortened sail and hauled further off shore. He intended to sail through the night and to avoid any danger of running aground on an island. His concern about islands in his path was heightened by their obvious presence and because he realised that the islands discovered by Quiros were in about the same latitude of 20°, even though they were unaccountably transposed by 'some geographers' in roughly the same longitude to the coast Cook was now on.

What Cook did not know was that he had entered the Great Barrier Reef, which is about 2,400 kilometres long and, in extent, as large as Germany. At the point then reached by Cook, he was within 16 kilometres of the reef. In the event, 'having the advantage of a fine breeze and a clear moonlight night' at 9 pm the *Endeavour* suddenly fell from water of 14 to 21 fathom (about 27 metres) to 12, 10 and then eight fathom. Cook ordered all hands to 'their stations' in readiness to 'put about and come to an anchor' and the main anchor, called the best bower, was set for lowering. He was deceived, however, by coming into deeper water of 20 to 21 fathom at about 10 pm. Reassured as to the safety of the vessel Cook, Banks and others not directly involved

---

12 *Cook*, 9, 10 June 1770, pp. 342, 343, as also fn. 3, p. 343. In this and in many other instances I took note of the changes in pen, ink and additions to the handwritten text in Cook's journal at the National Library of Australia. When they were made is normally difficult to judge. See also *Banks*, vol. 2, pp. 74, 75, 76, 77.

in its sailing retired to their beds. Among those so engaged was a man at the lead taking the depth of the sea, which a few minutes before 11 pm was 17 fathoms. Before he could 'heave another cast the ship stuck and stuck fast'.[13]

Cook sprang from his bed half-clothed and took charge. He 'gave his orders with his wonted coolness and precision' while his officers 'behaved with inimitable coolness void of all hurry and confusion'. It was immediately apparent that the *Endeavour* was surrounded by shoal water, in places two and more metres in depth and her beating on the jagged coral bade fair to open her fully to the sea. Furthermore, she had struck at high tide, which offered less hope of her being refloated. All hands manned the pumps, including Cook and Banks, and about 40 to 50 tons of all manner of equipment, including six of the heavy guns, were cast overboard, but to no avail as the ship remained fast on the coral. At dawn the land was seen to lie about 45 kilometres distant with no islands visible between ship and coast. The weather remained fine and the sea calm, which served greatly to the advantage of all, but no progress was made throughout the day even at the return of high tide at about 11 am. In the evening, with a rising tide, the ship righted herself from heeling to starboard. The water kept defeating the pumps, however, and everyone aboard, including Cook, rightly feared that once completely afloat and in deep water the damage to her hull would fully expose the *Endeavour* and she would go down with all hands, there being no hope of fewer than a handful reaching the land in the available boats. Fears were heightened to despair when, now in high water adjacent to the reef, a mistaken estimate of the water level in the hold was made and gave the crew a more drastic impression of their immediate peril. Banks, who earlier on had ceased to hope and prepared for the worst now decided that 'most of us, must be drowned: a better fate maybe than those would have who should get ashore without arms to defend themselves from the Indians or provide themselves with food … so barren had we always found' the land. Furthermore, he imagined what prospect would those face who managed to survive given they would be 'debarred from a hope of ever again seeing their native country or conversing with any but the most uncivilised savages perhaps in the world'? Parkinson echoed the same sentiments: 'We were, at this period, many thousand leagues from our native land … and on a barbarous coast, where, if the ship had been wrecked, and we had escaped the perils of the sea, we should have fallen into the rapacious hands of savages.' Later, however, Parkinson was more circumspect in recording his memory of the event: 'We ran upon a rock on the coast of New-Holland, and should inevitably have all perished, had not the kind providence of God, interposed in our favour. We

---

[13]   *Cook*, 11 June 1770, pp. 343-44.

had many hair-breadth escapes on this coast, that I am of the opinion our account of it will deter any from going that way again.'[14]

The gross sentiments expressed in these passages in respect of the Aborigines need to be put in the context of men who had been separated from their friends and family and their homeland for almost two years. Since Rio de Janeiro, no communication of any nature had been possible either to or from England. Furthermore, their supplies were running short and their immediate destination, Batavia, must have seemed almost beyond attainment even were they to survive their immediate peril. The remarkable thing is that everyone involved seemed to have retained their composure throughout the protracted episode.

When the mistake regarding the water level was recognised, a communal sense of relief was experienced by all, but further action was undertaken in the form of fothering that entailed lowering a sail on which bundles of chopped oakum and wool were placed and hauled under the vessel to cover the hole made in the hull of the ship. Unbeknown at the time, a large segment of coral had broken off and remained fixed in the hole, which, together with the fothering, ensured that the *Endeavour* could sail safely, at least as far as an anchorage ashore, were one to be found. No depth of water was found at Hope Islands as was the case at Weary Bay. Cook decided to dispatch the pinnace to seek a suitable harbour. On the evening of Thursday 14 June, the pinnace returned with the good tidings that such had been found lying about 11 kilometres distant to the north. Had Cook been aware that no other harbour that would meet the needs of his ship lay along the remainder of the coastline to the north, he would have been even more greatly relieved.[15]

The weather had turned and the wind was such that, had the ship still been on the coral, she would have been ground by its teeth into a wreck. Cook and Banks went into the harbour, which proved to have a narrow and shallow entrance and although small, it was 'very convenient for our purpose' wrote Cook. Two days passed before the weather permitted an entry, which entailed running aground twice because the entrance was sanded up. Nonetheless, by Monday 18 June, the *Endeavour* was snug within the harbour and lay resting close to the water's edge. Cook was much pleased with his crew whom he praised with almost military phraseology saying, 'no men ever behaved better than they have done on this occasion, animated by the behaviour of every

[14] *Cook*, 11 June 1770, pp. 343–45; *Banks*, vol. 2, pp. 77–79; Sydney Parkinson, *Journal of a Voyage to South Seas* (1773, p. 186), and Parkinson to his cousin, Mrs Gomeldon, from Batavia, 16 October 1770, in *Banks*, vol. 2, p. 323.

[15] *Cook*, 13, 14 June 1770, pp. 347-48.

gentleman aboard'. He had no words to praise the ship or give thanks for the width of her bottom, which, despite all her ungainliness, had caused her to remain steadfast on the coral where many a ship with a narrow keel would have perished.[16]

---

[16]   *Cook*, 13, 14, 15, 16, 17, 18 June, pp. 347–49; *Banks*, vol. 2, pp. 77–83.

7

The Guugu Yimithirr

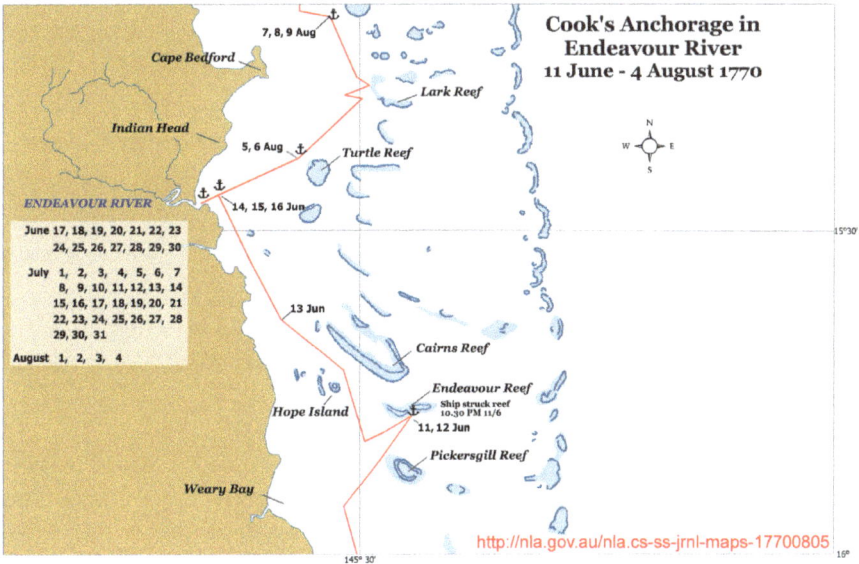

Cook's Anchorage in
Endeavour River
11 June - 4 August 1770

7, 8, 9 Aug

Cape Bedford

Lark Reef

Indian Head

5, 6 Aug   Turtle Reef

ENDEAVOUR RIVER   14, 15, 16 Jun

June 17, 18, 19, 20, 21, 22, 23
24, 25, 26, 27, 28, 29, 30

July 1, 2, 3, 4, 5, 6, 7
8, 9, 10, 11, 12, 13, 14
15, 16, 17, 18, 19, 20, 21
22, 23, 24, 25, 26, 27, 28
29, 30, 31

August 1, 2, 3, 4

13 Jun

Cairns Reef

Endeavour Reef
Ship struck reef
10.30 PM 11/6

Hope Island   11, 12 Jun

Pickersgill Reef

Weary Bay

http://nla.gov.au/nla.cs-ss-jrnl-maps-17700805

145° 30'   16°

The local Aboriginal people at the time of Cook's visit were the Guugu
Yimithirr, whose land lay to the north of the Annan River, which runs below
present day Cooktown. This means that the people met by Cook and his men
on the south and north sides of the Endeavour River, known to the Aborigines
as Wahalumbaal, were Guugu Yimithirr people. While still offshore waiting for
favourable weather to effect a landing, Cook wrote, 'Some people were seen
ashore today'. He makes no reference to seeing or speaking to the Aborigines
for the next two weeks. The probable reason for this is that he was deeply
preoccupied with repairing the *Endeavour*. Exhausted at night having expended
all his energies during the day, he sometimes left it to others to record their
impressions. When he sailed out of the harbour on 4 August he named the
Endeavour River 'after the ship', which was his way of recognising how much
was owed to the river for its role in the virtual salvation of his vessel. Otherwise
he was not impressed by its size being 'a small bar harbour or creek' only about

20 kilometres in length and rising from a small freshwater brook. It would not be suitable for shipping beyond less than two kilometres from the entrance, but it had one precious quality in that, on its south side for about 250 metres, the bank was so steep that ships at low water could erect a stage to it and 'lay afloat' there. Thus it was 'extremely convenient for heaving a ship down' to repair and clean the *Endeavour*, which was badly needed.[1]

While awaiting the landing, Banks remarked that 'At night we observed a fire ashore near where we were to lay, which made us hope that the necessary length of our stay would give us an opportunity of being acquainted with the Indians who made it'. He was surprised to see that 'Fires were made upon the hills and we saw 4 Indians through our glasses who went away along shore, in going along which they made two more fires for what purpose we could not guess'. In a footnote, Beaglehole surmised that the fires were 'for signalling' and that Aborigines up and down the coast 'were well apprised of the *Endeavour*'s arrival'. There can be little doubt that the Aborigines along the coast from the first days of the arrival of the *Endeavour* had been well advised of its presence and signalled ahead to others as it progressed. In fact, when close to the coast, the ship could have been detected at night by its lantern, which was kept alight throughout. The fires in question, however, were more than likely to have been lit for burning off grasslands than as a signal and, furthermore, there was no need to engage in signalling while the *Endeavour* remained stationary.[2]

The first, rapidly completed, task for the skilled workmen aboard was the erection of a ramp from the ship to the shore. Two tents were set up, one for provisions and the other for the sick. Eight or nine crew members were ill, but quickly recovered. Tupia, however, was by now seriously ill and no medicine served to make him well, while Charles Green was 'in a very poor way'. Tupia forced himself to go fishing and ate nothing but his catch, which quickly restored him, while Green lingered longer in bad health.

Cook went up a nearby hill from which he had a good view of his surroundings. He was met with a 'very indifferent prospect'. The low land about the river was covered by mangroves while the higher land 'appeared to be barren and stony'. He quickly turned to practical matters by having a forge set up and the armourer and his mate turned to making nails while the carpenters began to repair the ship. He had the ship moved to a better situation slightly further along the edge of the river and was appalled when

---

[1]   *Cook*, 16 June, 4 August 1770, pp. 328, 365.
[2]   *Banks*, vol. 2, p. 82 and fn. 1.

this revealed how great a portion of the hull had been damaged by the coral. Work on it proved difficult because it could only be done every 24 hours at low tide.[3]

Unlike Cook, Banks had no responsibility for the repair of the ship. He was botanising with Solander even before the ship was moored and, on the next day, he went walking on the south shore where he saw the old 'frames' of Indian houses and 'places where they had dressed shellfish in the same manner as the Islanders, but no signs that they had been at the place for six months at least'. Why he compared the preparation of the shellfish to that witnessed among the Pacific Islands, rather than to that observed at Botany Bay, is unclear. Other dwellings that had been lived in more recently were seen on the north shore and the first sighting of a kangaroo was made and remarked on by Cook who first saw it himself on 24 June, after it had been reported on by others, including Banks who claimed to have seen it. The animal seen by Cook was very close to the ship, in size about that of greyhound, of a mouse colour and swift of foot. He said that he would have taken it for a wild dog 'but for its walking or running in which it jumped like a hare or a deer'. Banks saw it again soon afterwards and was able to remark on its long tail, but admitted that 'what to liken him to I could not tell, nothing certainly that I have seen at all resembles him'. The other animal seen was the dingo, which Matra took to be a wolf. From the beginning it was clear that Banks, Solander and others roamed about freely, thereby indicating that they felt no fear whatever of the Aborigines. Cook made no move to prevent their doing so and even encouraged it by giving leave readily to all 'to go into the Country knowing that there was no danger from the natives'. As for the Aborigines, they seemed determined to ensure that, if it came to the point at which a meeting took place it would be on their terms. Signs of their presence, however, abounded and Banks saw 'one tree and only one notched in the same manner as those at Botany Bay', which indicated that a portion of bark sufficient to make a canoe had been removed.[4]

Banks remained busy with Solander collecting a wide variety of new plants. He also attempted to revive others collected earlier in the voyage and stored in the bread room, where they had suffered badly from seawater damage. He remarked with a note of forbearance that 'many were saved, but some entirely lost and spoiled'. Meanwhile John Gore went eight or nine kilometres inland and 'saw the footsteps of men', while others crossed over to the north shore

---

3   *Cook*, 19 June 1770, p. 349; 22 June 1770, and fn. 4, pp. 350-51; *Banks*, vol. 2, p. 83.

4   *Banks*, vol. 2, pp. 83, 84, 85, 86; *Cook*, 24 June 1770, pp. 351-52.

of the river and came across still burning fireplaces, 'but they saw nobody nor have we seen one since we have been in port'. Food supplies had turned for the better with a few wild vegetables, including yams, being discovered and were boiled with the peas, a sufficient quantity of which remained available. Fish, caught with nets, abounded to the degree that Cook could issue a plentiful supply to everyone. The moderate ease of living could not remove everyone's desire to depart once the repair of the *Endeavour* had been satisfactorily achieved. To that end Cook went up the small rise straight above the landing place and known as Grassy Hill. From it, 'I saw what gave me no small uneasiness which were a number of sand banks or shoals laying all along the coast'. They lay only six or seven kilometres from the shore and the outermost stretched as far as he could see with his glasses. He concluded that it would be 'difficult if not impractical' to return by a southern route, given the prevailing wind from the south-east, and the problem suffered by all vessels like the *Endeavour* of struggling to run into the wind. That the temperature had risen to 30° C 'in the shade', which was two or three degrees higher than previously recorded 'in this place', served to dampen his spirits even further.[5]

Cook then decided that further investigation had to be made offshore before a decision was taken to depart the harbour, to which end he sent the master, Robert Molyneux, in the pinnace 'to look for a channel to the northward'. On his return, Molyneux reported that there was a 'passage out to sea' about 30 kilometres from the harbour and judged that the passage led beyond the reef, 'which I very much doubted' said Cook. Molyneux had also landed on a dry reef where he took aboard a large quantity of giant clams and the coxswain of the boat, a small man, said that he was able to completely conceal himself in an empty shell. Because the Aborigines had 'no boats that they dare venture so far out at sea in', Cook surmised that they were unable to visit the shoals off the coast where sea life abounded as, otherwise, they would have seen large shells about their fire places. Molyneux also landed on a bay slightly north of the harbour where 'he disturbed some of the natives whom he supposed to be at supper; they all fled upon his approach and left him some fresh sea eggs and a fire ready lighted behind them, but there was neither house or hut near'. Banks reported this event and also that Tupia had seen two 'people who were digging in the ground for some kind of roots; on seeing him they ran away with great precipitation'. Tupia did not assert that the diggers were women as he surely would have done were such have been the case.[6]

---

[5]   *Banks*, vol. 2, pp. 85–86; *Cook*, 29 June, 1 July 1770, pp. 353, 354.

[6]   *Cook*, 2, 3 July 1770, pp. 354, 355; *Banks*, vol. 2, pp. 87, 88, 90.

Cook, uneasy about the alleged passage seen by Molyneux, told him to go further out to sea. Molyneux confirmed Cook's doubts when he realised that the reef was still about him and that 'there was no getting out to sea that way'. As a form of recompense for the disappointment caused by his news, he was able to produce three turtles that had been caught with the boat hook on a reef almost 40 kilometres out to sea. 'This day all hands feasted upon turtle for the first time', said Cook.[7] Banks expressed the reaction of many in a more explicit manner:

> The promise of plenty of good provisions made our situation appear much less dreadful; were we obliged to wait here another season of the year when the winds might alter we could do it without fear of wanting provisions: this thought alone put everybody in vast spirits.[8]

Banks and Gore, with three others, had set out on 6 July to go up the river and penetrate inland to ascertain the condition of the country, during which they passed beyond the headwaters of the river. They returned after three days and Cook remarked that they had 'met with nothing remarkable' as well as that there was no real variation in the soil and its produce. Banks, however, reported that they passed over land 'covered thick with long grass, and seemed to promise great fertility were these people to plant and improve it'. When they reached a point where the river contracted into 'a fresh water brook' they saw smoke close by which convinced them that 'the natives, who we had so long had a curiosity to see well, were there'. Accompanied by two others, Banks approached the fire 'hoping that the smallness of our numbers would induce them not to be afraid of us' but they had already fled. There were 'houses' and fresh 'branches of trees broken down with which the children had been playing'. Near the fire lay the shells of a kind of clam and 'roots of a wild yam that had been cooked in it'. Banks then remarked with clear sincerity, 'Thus we were disappointed of the only good chance we have had of seeing the people since we came here by their unaccountable timidity'. Overnight the party slept well, being free from mosquito bites, and 'had the Indians come they would certainly have caught us all napping but that was the least in our thoughts'. Had Banks been aware of the proclivities of the two-metre-long 'alligator' seen in the river, he might not have slept so well. Only one other crocodile had been seen. It was swimming in the river near the ship.[9]

In the afternoon of 10 July, three weeks since the *Endeavour* entered the harbour, seven or eight people were seen on the south side of the river, two

---

7   *Cook*, 9 July 1770, pp. 356-57.

8   *Banks*, vol. 2, p. 90.

9   *Cook*, 9 July 1770, pp. 356–57; *Banks*, vol. 2, pp. 88-90.

of whom walked out on a sandy point opposite the ship but, as soon as Cook put out in a boat to go and speak with them, they ran away 'as fast as they could'. During the following morning, four more were seen 'striking fish' on the north side of the harbour from a small canoe fitted with outriggers. Cook would not permit any of the crew to approach them. Rather he wanted to 'let them alone without seeming to take any Notice of them'. Eventually two in a canoe came 'so near the ship as to take some things we throwed at them' including cloth, paper and nails. These items failed to arouse their interest but a small fish, accidentally thrown at them, caused them to express 'the greatest joy imaginable'. They left and returned with the two others taking 'such trifles as we gave them'. All four, one of middle age and the rest 'young' were carrying arms and landed close by on the shore where 'Tupia soon prevailed upon them, to lay down their arms, and come and set down by him' on the ground. Cook, Banks and others went with presents to them, which they received happily. Banks said that they 'soon became very easy, only jealous if any one attempted to go between them and their arms'. They refused an invitation to dine and retired to the north side of the river where, it appears, they were all living at that time.[10]

Cook gave a detailed description of the Aborigines. They were all less than 171 centimetres tall and their limbs were proportionally small. Wholly naked, their skin was the colour of wood soot or dark chocolate and their hair was 'black, lank and cropped short and neither wooly nor drizzled'. Unlike those met by Dampier on the west coast, these lacked no front teeth. In fact their teeth were even and good, and their eyes were 'lively' and all were 'clean limbed, active and nimble', which was readily evident given they were totally unclothed. Parts of their bodies were painted either red or white and 'their features were far from being disagreeable'. Finally, Cook declared that their voices were 'soft and tunable' and, while they were able to repeat with ease many of words used by the whites, 'neither us nor Tupia could understand one word they said'. On the next day two men who were in the original group of visitors came across the river with two others and again landed ashore near the ship. The newcomers were introduced by name, one of which was recorded by Banks as Yaparico, and they brought a fish with them as a present in response to the one given to them the day before. It was observed that each had a hole bored through the septum of the nose and one had a fishbone through it. They departed with some haste when 'some of our gentlemen' began examining their canoe rather too closely for their comfort.[11]

---

10   *Cook*, 10, 11 July 1770, pp. 357–58; *Banks*, vol. 2, pp. 90-93.
11   *Cook*, 10, 11 July 1770, pp. 357, 358; *Banks*, vol. 2, pp. 92-98.

Again, the Aborigines returned, this time making up a party of five men. A woman and a boy remained on the other shore, but close enough to be easily seen through glasses. Cook said that 'the Woman was as naked as ever she was born, even those parts which I always before now thought nature would have taught a woman to conceal were uncovered'. The men remained all morning with the ship's company, seemingly completely at ease although they stayed close to their canoe. Banks gave a long description of the Aborigines. He remarked that newcomers were always introduced by name and that they were delighted with their reception at Tupia's tent. Presented with fish they indicated that it be cooked, which, when done, they ate parts and gave the rest to Banks's 'Bitch'. They were generally short in stature and only one among them reached 174 centimetres in height. They had few ornaments, which were made up of shells and strings worn as necklaces and bracelets. Although naked, they contrived to cover those parts of their bodies the Europeans were accustomed to hide by using their hand or something they happened to be holding in it. They did so 'as if by instinct'. He also said that only one had a pierced ear. Their canoes were much 'inferior' to those seen in the islands and they were only able to convey four people. Their 'lances' were like those seen in Botany Bay with bone-tipped ends, thus affording them with 'a terrible weapon'.[12]

Gore, the best marksman on board, shot a young kangaroo of about 17 kilograms when cleaned. Both Banks and Cook described it in detail, but their main point was that neither could compare it to any European animal known to them. In the event 'dressed for our dinners' it proved to be excellent meat. One assumes that Cook observed his usual custom of insisting that all food be shared equally, even if the kangaroo had to serve as an entrée to the turtles, which were now customary at the table. It might seem strange that two other icons of Australian fauna, the emu and the koala, were never sighted. But the emu was normally a bird of the inland, into which no meaningful penetration was made, while it was scarcely to be expected that the people of the *Endeavour* spent much time gazing up into the habitat of the koala. In any case the men of the *Endeavour* did not go about at night, when koalas were more likely to be seen. Snakes, 'both of the venomous and other sorts' were seen but the dingo remained elusive. Cook remarked that they only ever saw one tame animal on the whole east coast, a dog, 'who frequently came about our tents to pick up bones etc'. Cook used his own spelling for the kangaroo as variously 'kangooroo', 'kanguru' and 'kangura', and said that here, where they were clearly identified for the first time, they 'are in the greatest number for

---

12   *Cook*, 12 July 1770, pp. 359; *Banks*, vol. 2, pp. 92-93.

we seldom went into the Country without seeing some'. The plentiful turtles, some 100 to 130 kilograms in weight, whose fresh meat was a delight to all, made up for other deficiencies, although there were some few barrels of both beef and pork still available for consumption, as was there wheat, which was served ground at breakfast.[13]

Tupia had soon reached friendly terms with the Aborigines, with whom he attempted to communicate despite the language barrier and who gave him 'longish roots' which proved to be of 'a very good taste'. Cook, who was grateful for the assistance that he received from Tupia in establishing relations with the people of Tahiti and New Zealand, failed to notice the role he played in the same manner with the Aborigines, although it assuredly helped to establish good relations with them. In any case, unlike at Botany Bay, Cook, Banks and others were able to foster that relationship themselves. Cook, with Banks and Solander, visited the north shore and met five Aborigines whom they had not seen before and who came towards them showing no sign of fear. Two wore necklaces made of shells, which they valued and refused to part with. Cook and the others wanted to follow them in the hope, as Banks explained, that they 'might have an opportunity of seeing their women'. However, 'by signs [they] made us understand that they did not desire our company'. On returning to the *Endeavour* they found several Aborigines on board who had shown a deep interest in the 12 turtles lying on the deck 'which they took more notice of than anything else on the ship'. Nonetheless they soon departed, peacefully. Banks said that many 'Indians were over with us today and seemed to have lost all fear of us and became quite familiar'. One proved his dexterity with his two-metre-long 'lance' by throwing it 'swiftly and steadily about four feet above the ground for a distance of 50 paces' while others came on board 'and soon became our very good friends'. Cook had already gone inland and climbed a hill on the north shore from where he was able to look over the 'inland country', which he described with his now familiar 'hills, valleys and large plains diversified with woods and lawns'. With Banks, he also took a longish walk of about 10 kilometres along the north shore and ascended a hill — 'Indian Head', according to Beaglehole — from where they could look out to sea. The view was daunting because it 'afforded us a melancholy prospect of the difficulties we are to encounter, for in whatever direction we turned our eyes shoals innumerable were to be seen'.[14]

Ten or 11 Aborigines came to the *Endeavour* on 19 July, having put 'a larger

---

[13] *Cook*, 14, 15 July, 4 August 1770, pp. 359-60, 367; *Banks*, vol. 2, pp. 93-94.
[14] *Cook*, 16, 18 July 1770, pp. 360-61; *Banks*, vol. 2, p. 95.

quantity of lances than they had ever done before' in a nearby tree. A man and a boy remained near the tree to guard the weapons. The purpose of the visit was soon evident in a request made for a share of the eight or nine live turtles still lying on the deck. A refusal was met with a blend of bewilderment, resentment and anger, all of which was understandable in a people to whom turtles were clearly highly regarded as food and as their rightful possession. They made no claim to all the turtles and would assuredly have been appeased had they been given even an unequal share. When it became obvious that any share would not be offered they attempted to take two turtles 'to put over the side'. Banks asserted that one Aborigine had stamped with his foot and 'pushed me from him with a countenance full of distain'. Cook expressed the situation in milder terms saying that the Aborigines, having been thwarted in their attempt to procure a turtle, were disappointed and 'they grew a little troublesome and were for throwing everything over board they could lay their hands upon'. No cooked food was available except some bread which 'they rejected with scorn' when he offered it to them 'as I believe they would have done [with] anything else excepting turtle'. Their refusal of the bread was also understandable in that it was stale, being all that remained of the large quantity that had to be disposed of as worthless because it had been spoilt by seawater while the *Endeavour* was on the coral. Ill-disposed at the whole episode, the Aborigines leaped into their canoe, however, they remained close by.[15]

Clearly thinking that the episode was over, Cook, accompanied by Banks — who was bent on returning to his 'plant gathering' — and five or six others went ashore. They were joined by the Aborigines who took fire from one already lit near the shore and set it to the grass in a circle around the landing place with 'surprising dexterity and quickness', causing it to burn 'with vast fury'. Banks's tent, loaned by him to Tupia who had convalesced in it, was saved, but a piglet of the sow's litter was 'scorched to death'. The Aborigines then went nearby where 'all our nets and a good deal of linen were laid out to dry', and 'with the greatest obstinacy they again set fire to the grass'. Cook was forced to fire small shot at their ringleader, which wounded him slightly and caused all of them to retreat. To ensure that the superiority of his arms was recognised, Cook fired a musket ball over them. Notwithstanding, they returned with their spears in readiness, but they were soon repulsed without violence. A 'little old man' appeared from behind some rocks by the river's edge and approached with a headless spear thereby making it plain that a peaceful resolution was desirable. This was rapidly achieved when the other

---

15   *Cook*, 19 July 1770, p. 361-62; *Banks*, vol. 2, pp. 95-97.

Aborigines joined the little old man and together they 'came to us in a very friendly manner'. Cook and his party immediately gave back the spears that had been aimlessly thrown at them and Cook said that everything was reconciled. Four newcomers were among the Aborigines who were introduced by name and, although no inclination was shown to again board the *Endeavour*, they all remained abreast of her for two hours. While departing they 'set the woods on fire' at a distance of a mile or two from the landing place, and thus in no wise threatening the ship and her crew. In concluding, Banks offered an opinion of lasting value to those intrepid souls who wish to camp in the Australian bush. He wrote: 'I had little idea of the fury which the grass burnt in this hot climate, nor of the difficulty of extinguishing it when once lighted: this accident will however be a sufficient warning for us if ever we should again pitch tents in such a climate to burn everything round us before we begin.' Although its purpose was not understood, it had become clear that the Aborigines were engaged in widespread burning off on the land. Banks reported 'all the hills about us for many miles were on fire and at night made the most beautiful appearance imaginable'.[16]

After the episode with the turtles, and despite the act of reconciliation, the Aborigines did not visit the ship again. The obvious cessation of activity on repairing the ship, the removal of all their possessions, as well as the storing aboard of large quantities of water in barrels and the presence of live turtles on the deck, were all clear signs that the departure of the *Endeavour* and its people was imminent. That some contact with other peoples had been made by the Guugu Yimithirr before the arrival of the *Endeavour* seems probable. The structure of their canoes being fitted with outriggers indicates this, unless such an innovation had evolved there separately. The people of the Torres Strait islands certainly went to sea with canoes fitted with outriggers and also sails. The same applied to the people of the East Indies, at least for coastal fishing. There is no evidence that canoes with sails were seen at the Endeavour River, and Cook was clear in his own mind that the local canoes were incapable of true sea-going ventures.

How peaceful that earlier contact had proved to be there is no way of knowing, but the repeated and determined protection of the women perhaps indicates that the conduct of any previous visitors had been unacceptable. But over a period of seven weeks, after a cautious, indeed prudent, period of close observation of Cook and his people, friendly contact had been made and maintained, which was temporarily marred in only the one instance. To the Aborigines, despite their rejection of trinkets, these new people were

---

[16]   *Cook*, 19 July 1770, pp. 361-62; *Banks*, vol. 2, pp. 96-97.

assuredly of great interest, perhaps even fascination, although they were careful to control their emotions. Above all it was clear that their visitors were not a warlike people. They had come in peace and remained in peace. The turtles excepted, they had not plundered or stolen anything. They had tried to learn from the Aborigines and to teach them some of their language. In not a single instance had it been intimated to the Europeans that their presence was undesirable and that they should depart forthwith, which was in marked contrast to their rejection at Botany Bay. It is surely not improbable that, to them, sheltered perhaps for vast eons of time from contact with other people, the huge and wondrous *Endeavour*, its people and their leader of noble bearing had become welcome among and reconciled with the Guugu Yimmithir.

Their presence, nonetheless, was continued to be felt and remarked upon. A turtle caught on the islands had a lengthy 'Indian turtle peg' embedded in its flesh and the wound had healed over it. This made Cook sure that the Aborigines could only take turtles when they came ashore to lay their eggs, or when they encountered them on the nearby islands, 'for they certainly have no boat fit to do this at sea or that will carry a turtle'. On this same day a sailor straggled away from his companions who had been sent out by Cook 'into the Country to gather greens'. Clearly word of the act of reconciliation had been passed around because he came across four men who were 'broiling a fowl and the hind leg of one of the animals before spoken of' (a kangaroo) and, although he was armed only with his cutting knife, he had the good sense not to run away, but sat down with them. After a while they 'felt his hands and other parts of his body' and then allowed him 'to go away without offering the least insult, and perceiving that he did not go right for the ship they directed him which way he should go'. Banks repeats this episode, but diverges from Cook in some details. He was astonished that the Aborigines were able to take the game and especially the cockatoos, which were 'most shy'. Finally, when Banks found a bundle of clothes given as presents to the Aborigines, he imagined that they had discarded all they had received, including the various 'trinkets', 'for they seemed to set no value upon anything we had except our turtle, which of all things we were the least able to spare them'. Cook reinforced that remark with perhaps a note of regret when he said that, given they had to go five leagues out to sea to capture turtles and, at that, in 'blowing weather', they were not 'overstocked in this article'. Indeed within 10 days he was forced to send the yawl out to the islands for more turtles given that 'those we had got before were nearly all expended'.[17]

---

[17] *Cook*, 22, 23, 29 July 1770, pp. 362–63, 364; *Banks*, vol. 2, p. 98.

In the meantime, the days were fast slipping by, but the wind 'would not permit us to sail' despite 'everything [being] on board the ship' with all hands ready to resume the voyage. On a day 'dedicated to hunting the wild animal', a kangaroo was shot by Gore that weighed 36 kilograms, but it proved poor fare at the table being, as Banks judged, 'too old' and 'certainly the most insipid meat' he had eaten. On Friday 3 August, a suitable wind arose and Cook decided to sail out, but immediately ran twice on the sand banks on the north side of the river, exactly as he had done on his entry into the harbour on 17 June, over seven weeks before. Having finished botanising, all this delay made Banks irritable, but Cook had good reason to feel uneasy. Further delay with no means of increasing provisions, during which time was spent to no good purpose with his people nonetheless needing daily food, made him very anxious to get to sea. Finally, on 4 August, at seven in the morning the *Endeavour* 'stood off to sea' with the pinnace ahead of her sounding for hidden shoals. No farewells to or from their erstwhile Aboriginal friends took place. The *Endeavour* departed the place of her salvation in silence.[18]

Matra passed rapidly over the passage from Botany Bay to the Endeavour River and gave scant attention to the encounter with the reef. Equally, his treatment of the time spent at the Endeavour River was brief. He noted on 18 July that 'the natives of the country' began to visit, but his description of them was clearly written in haste, probably well after they had occurred, and lacked both the 'sagacity and judgement' he ascribed to Tupia. He is the only journal writer to regard the Aborigines as in any respect like indigenous people of other continents. They were 'low of stature', 'small and slender in shape, but very active' with 'flat noses, thick lips, and bandy legs, like the negroes of Guinea'. They were also 'ignorant, poor, and destitute'; 'strangers' to bread which they would not eat, 'naked and slovenly'. He admitted that 'we saw none of their women'. Matra also skimmed over the conflict concerning the turtles and concentrated on the attempt by the Aborigines to burn the fishing nets and linen. Clearly still affronted by Cook's treatment of him after Orton was assaulted, he accused the captain of wounding 'several of them ... but a few hours after they returned peacefully'. Neither Cook nor any other writer recorded several Aborigines being wounded, although small shot was used and 'one must have been a little hurt because we saw a few drops of blood on some of the linen' lying out to dry.[19]

[18]   *Cook*, 22, 27 July, 3, 4 August 1770, pp. 362, 363, 365; *Banks*, vol. 2, pp. 100, 101.
[19]   James Matra, *The Anonymous Journal (A Journal of a Voyage Round the World in his Majesty's Ship Endeavour)* (1975, pp. 122-23).

8

Torres Strait

When leaving the country of the Guugu Yimithirr, Cook knew that he had a long stretch still ahead of him before he reached the hoped-for strait between New Guinea and the mainland. But, for the first time throughout the voyage, he was tortured as to a decision. Was it truly worthwhile to risk his vessel and crew by sailing north when he knew that to go out to sea through the shoals in unknown waters was to expose them to very high danger. A grave and almost constant state of unease, which was an unusual state of mind for the captain, made him 'quite at a loss which way to steer'. His diligent study of the charts he had aboard was of no help as to whether he should 'beat back to the southward around all the shoals or seek a passage out to the eastward or to the north, all of which appeared to be equally dangerous'.[1]

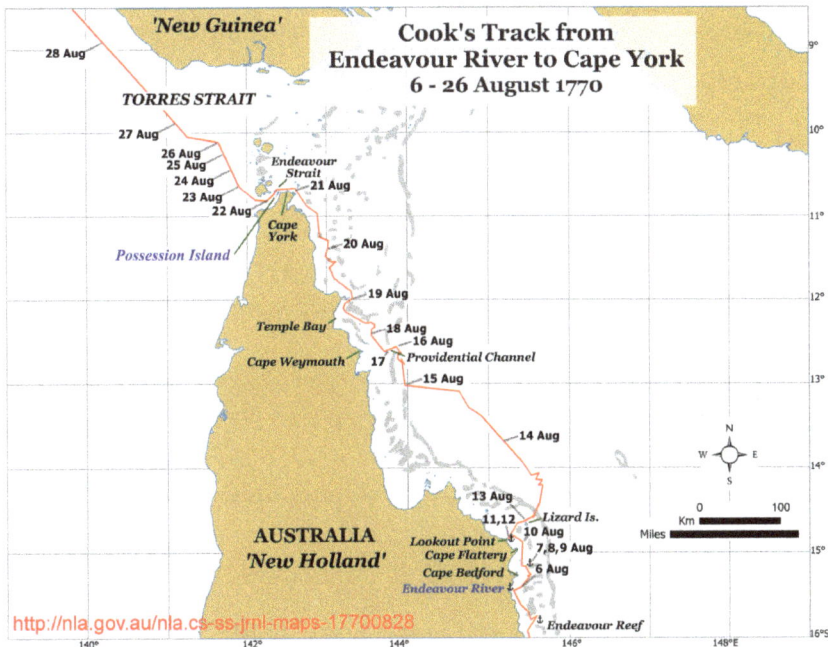

Cook's Track from Endeavour River to Cape York
6 - 26 August 1770

http://nla.gov.au/nla.cs-ss-jrnl-maps-17700828

---

[1]   *Cook*, 4, 7 August 1770, pp. 365, 70.

More importantly, in light of his determination to clear up the still-vexed question as to whether there was a strait between New Holland and New Guinea, he, with Banks and other officers, had studied several charts before entering the strait itself. They included a map by the Robert de Vaugondy family and published in Charles de Brosses's *Histoire des navigations aux Terres Australes* (1756). Cook remarked that, given the place names, the charts clearly showed the Dutch and the Spaniards had circumnavigated New Guinea. He acknowledged the general accuracy of the maps, but he seems to have given undue recognition to the Dutch when, of the 47 names, 40 were in Spanish and only seven in Dutch. Another chart comes from an earlier atlas based on charts drawn up at the order of the King of Portugal. Entitled *Suite du Neptune Francois, ou Atlas nouveau des cartes Marine* (1700), it has Portuguese or Spanish names of saints with the exception of the Portuguese name Los Abrolhos, which is on both maps and on the Vaugondy as a reef on the southern coast of Papua and therefore to be avoided. The lack of accuracy in calculating longitude, in the *Suite* in particular, is evident in that the Gulf of Carpentaria lies south of the western border of New Guinea. Nonetheless, in these charts, Torres Strait is clearly marked lying above Cape York and below the eastern portion of New Guinea, and thus intended to designate the voyage that Luís Vaz de Torres had taken through the strait. Despite the evidence presented to him, Cook continued to argue that the question was unsettled and he would hold to that until he had passed through the strait himself.[2]

Master Molyneux had very probably and with good reason despaired of sailing further north. He thus advised Cook to give up any hope of so doing and recommended that he go back on his tracks to the south. In that way they could go home by sailing south of Van Diemen's Land and from there across the southern Indian Ocean to the Cape of Good Hope. Cook was hesitant to accept this advice, because it 'would be an endless piece of work, as the winds now blow constantly strong from that quarter'. Furthermore, it was decidedly risky to his vessel and his people to sail south on a lengthy voyage knowing that almost no worthwhile provisions would be available until they reached the Cape. Furthermore he knew that, despite the work done at the Endeavour River, his trusty vessel was seriously in need of a thorough overhaul, which demanded attention as soon as possible. In his heart he remained determined to chart the remainder of the coast and settle the question as to the existence of Torres Strait so that, despite all his misgivings, Batavia, where he could

---

2   The question is discussed at length by Beaglehole in *Cook*, pp. clvii–clxv. See also *Cook*, 3 September 1770, pp. 410–11 and the three charts from de Vaugondy, the *Suite du Neptune François* and Dalrymple reproduced in *Cook*, pp. clviii, clix and clxiii.

undertake repairs to the ship, and sail from there to home, remained his fixed goal. In the event all his fears were realised when, on 7 August, the ship was almost driven onto the reef and, although Cook described the event in temperate terms, Banks was certain that they had very narrowly escaped disaster. Three days later, after much manoeuvring, Cook was confident that they were safe with a 'clear open sea before us', but he was quickly disabused of his optimism, which later prompted him to name a nearby headland Cape Flattery.[3]

Unlike during the days before the ship was almost lost on the coral, great care was now taken with a boat constantly sounding the depth of water ahead. Cook revealed his own acute anxiety by climbing up the main mast to ascertain whether the report by Molyneux and others who 'all asserted ... that they saw breakers in a manner all around us' was true. He could not deny the evidence and immediately decided to make in close to the land, probably wanting to be in a position to make land readily were the *Endeavour* again cast upon the reef. He went ashore and climbed a high hill, which he named Point Lookout. From there he noticed that the land was 'low and chequered white sand and green bushes etc for 10 or 12 miles inland, beyond which is high land'. He could also see the Howick group of small islands. Returning aboard he resolved to visit one of several larger islands nearby from where he hoped to ascertain whether there was a clear passage out into the safer waters in the ocean beyond the reef.[4]

On 12 August 1770, a landing was made on Lizard Island, which lay about five leagues from the mainland. The ruins of several huts were noticed and nearby there were 'heaps of shells', which indicated that 'at some seasons of the year' the Aborigines visited the island by canoe. Banks also remarked that Master Molyneux, who, having spent the night on a low island in the Turtle group where he saw vast numbers of turtle shells as well as still edible fins hanging from trees to dry, concluded that the Aborigines had been there a short while beforehand. The sailors ate the fins 'heartily'. He also saw 'two spots clear of grass which had lately been dug up'. Their shape and length of about two metres indicated that they might well have been recently dug graves. In any event Molyneux took them to be such. Banks, who also landed, gathered a few new plants as well as some large lizards that abounded in a small woodland. They also saw seven or eight 'frames of their huts', built 'upon the tops of eminences exposed entirely to the SE, contrary to those

---

[3]   *Cook*, 7, 10 August 1770, pp. 370, 371; *Banks*, vol. 2, p. 101.
[4]   *Cook*, 11, 12 August 1770, pp. 371-72.

of the main which are commonly placed under the shelter of some bushes or hill sides to break off the wind'. One explanation for the difference could have been that other Aborigines visiting the islands would have also come from the south-east and a constant vigilance might have been kept by the local inhabitants to ensure that they were unable to do so unexpectedly. An 'enormous' bird's nest of about seven metres in circumference and a height of a metre built entirely of sticks was come across, which Banks concluded had to be a pelican's nest, but Beaglehole supposed was that of an osprey. Among the Cockburn Islands they passed a small island on which they saw five people of whom two carried 'lances'.[5]

Whether the two areas of freshly dug earth seen by Molyneux were gravesites raises the question of burial practises among the Aborigines both at Botany Bay and at the Endeavour River. At each place no evidence of such practises was seen, unlike in the Society Islands and New Zealand where they were carefully noticed and commented upon. Had they been graves on the island, the similarity to European practise was remarkable. On the reasonable assumption that the deceased in question had died recently and in a short time of each other, the question arises as to the cause of death. The elderly or infirm would be unlikely to travel out to the islands, so that death by misfortune or in conflict seems more likely. The fact that none of our journal writers gave any further consideration to the matter is a peculiar omission.

Cook became increasingly anxious with the added delays hindering progress. He knew that they had to be clear of the coast of New Holland before the south-east trade wind changed to the north-west in November when they 'would infallibly lose our passage to the East Indies this season'. Furthermore, that they had only three months of provisions left while they were running down on some of them already, meant that they had to be off and away as quickly as possible. All his officers agreed with his decision but, for Cook, it was clear that to go further out to sea would inevitably mean being unable to chart the coast, which would be too distant, yet that sacrifice had to be made for the greater good of survival. Although he was presumably unaware that he would be forced thereby to leave only about 240 kilometres of coastline from Cape Melville to Cape Direction 'pricked in' on his chart, he was prepared to do so in order also to avoid the 'continual danger' of being locked in on the coast and waste more time. A day later

---

[5]   *Cook*, 12, 20 August 1770, pp. 373-74, 383; *Banks*, vol. 2, pp. 103-04; Beaglehole in *Cook*, p. 104, fn. 2.

he could at last feel comfortable because they had 'got safe out' and he felt free to look back and give thought to the recent past. Since 26 May they had travelled 360 leagues during which a man had never ceased heaving 'the lead' to ascertain the depth of water, which was absolutely necessary even though, as Cook with good reason imagined, it was an occurrence of a magnitude that had 'never happened to any ship before'. He deeply regretted leaving the coast unexplored even though he felt sure that its northern point was close. Surprisingly, he now said, 'I believe that it doth not join to New Guinea', which perhaps was an admission, in some measure at least, that he finally accepted the authenticity of the ancient charts.[6]

About the beaches, at the Endeavour River and on repeated occasions, bamboo, coconuts, plant seeds and pumice stones had been seen, none of which were native to New Holland and very probably had been carried by the easterly trade wind from the New Hebrides (Vanuatu), which Quiros had named Australia del Espiritu Santo. From his charts, Cook was uncertain how far east those islands lay given that on most charts they were set down adjacent to, or were part of, the coast of New Holland. Nonetheless he was 'morally certain that he [Quiros] never was upon any part of this coast'. He gave no proof of his assertion except to say that the position of the New Hebrides had been calculated as being 'about 22° to the East of the coast of New Holland'. How was that calculation arrived at before Cook had charted the coast? Indeed, when deciding to chart that coast before leaving New Zealand, Cook said that he would do so 'until we arrive at its northern extremity, and if this should be found impractical then to endeavour to fall in with the land or islands discovered by Quiros'. This surely indicates that he expected to find them much closer than 1,600 kilometres further east. The explanation can only lie in his acceptance of Dalrymple's 1767 *Chart of the South Pacifick Ocean*, a copy of which Dalrymple gave to Banks before the *Endeavour* sailed and which Banks showed to Cook. On this chart the New Hebrides lie in roughly that distant position far off from the east coast of New Holland. Even had that coast been extended further east, as was done on some old charts, the New Hebrides could never be rightly depicted as lying anywhere adjacent to the coastline Cook was charting.[7]

Anxious lest he lose sight of the coast altogether and thus miss Torres Strait, Cook decided to sail westward and, by the afternoon of 16 August, land was sighted but, between it and the ship, breakers were beating onto

---

[6] *Cook*, 13 August 1770, pp. 374-46.

[7] *Cook*, 31 March, 14 August 1770, pp. 273, 376. For de Vaugondy see *Cook*, Figure 9, p. lxxx; Dalrymple's chart is Figure 18, p. clxiii.

the reef. The night passed in trepidation and 'the roaring of the surf was plainly heard and at day break the vast foaming breakers were too plainly to be seen not a mile from us towards which we found the ship was carried surprisingly fast'. Cook finally turned for help from a source he had hitherto been inclined to disregard and wrote 'in this distressed situation we had nothing but Providence and the small assistance our boats could give us to trust to … [because] between us and destruction was only a dismal valley the breadth of one wave'. On the other side of that valley stood a wall of coral rock which rose up above them and on which 'the ship must be dashed to pieces in a moment' because the distance between them, and thus life and death for most if not all of them, was about 25 metres. At that same moment 'a small air of wind sprung up', which quickly died down, but it freshened again, though feebly. Cook called it 'our friendly breeze', which, added to the towing by the boats, enabled the *Endeavour* to broach a narrow channel and arrive safely within the reef. He named it Providential Channel. Pickersgill put down their deliverance directly to 'the immediate help of Providence', without which they 'must inevitably have perished', while Banks remarked that 'no man I believe but who gave himself entirely over' and 'a speedy death was all we had to hope for'. Cook, ever as faithful to his crew as they were to him, wrote that 'in this truly terrible situation, not one man ceased to do his utmost, and that with as much calmness as if no danger had been near'. Remarkably, throughout the whole time since dawn, the astronomer, Charles Green, assisted by two others, Masters Mate Charles Clarke and Gunner Stephen Forwood, continued to take observations, although Green later admitted that they did so aware they were close to the reef upon which 'we expected the ship to strike every minute'.[8]

Banks has a lengthy account of this perilous episode, which was either written jointly with that of Cook or, at the least, both versions concur so remarkably in composition and phraseology that close dependence of one to the other is indisputable. That aside, only the captain could feel obliged to dwell upon its implications in respect of his responsibility. He acknowledged that 'the pleasure which naturally results to a man from being the first discoverer' could prompt anyone to undertake such a hazardous venture. To come upon a coast and leave it unexplored because of danger would be well nigh inexcusable and expose him, justly, to a charge of 'Timorousness'. Yet, if he embarked on the venture despite the danger and failed in his objective, he would be charged with 'Temerity'. While absolving himself of either charge, he had to admit that a lack of prudence might more justly be laid against him in that he had

---

[8] *Cook*, 16 August 1770, pp. 377-81; *Banks*, vol. 2, p. 106; Pickersgill and Greene, in *Cook*, pp. 380 and 378.

continued to sail 'with a single ship' among countless and often submerged reefs. He did not admit that to do so at night might justifiably result in a higher charge than mere prudence. His justification for such rashness lay in the fact that thereby he had been able to chart the northern half of the east coast and say something of its 'produce'. Otherwise he would have departed not having established whether the mainland was continuous or merely composed of chains of islands. He would also remain ignorant in regard to its produce, although it would be difficult to argue that his account had added anything of significance to the hitherto unknown produce of New Holland. The wise men of the Admiralty would ponder Cook's words on the dangers inherent in sending a single ship on long and dangerous voyages. Cook would never sail unaccompanied again. But yet again, in the midst of the great danger to which his vessel and its crew were exposed, Cook appears to have never once lost his head or showed the slightest sign of despair. To a man his crew followed his example.[9]

Louise Antoine de Bougainville preceded Cook in these same waters while searching for the east coast of New Holland, and it is of some relevance to set down the reason why he turned away from this exact area on 6 June 1776:

> The sea was breaking at intervals on these reefs, and several heads of rock rose from the water. This last encounter was the voice of God which we heard with docility. Prudence did not permit us to follow an uncertain route during the night amidst such dangerous places.

Unlike the brave, but slightly impetuous Cook, Bougainville's prudence would not permit him to sail at night and he lacked the potentially uncertain benefit of a good moon. Furthermore, and again unlike Cook who had made a point of being able to say something about the 'produce' of New Holland, Bougainville was under no illusions. Why then risk disaster on a coast which offered no useful prospects to anyone.[10]

From then on, Cook stuck firmly to his intention of hugging the coast and Beaglehole whimsically described the voyage as, 'wriggling (if an undignified non-nautical word may be used) between shoals and reefs and sandbanks'. Turtles had become scarce and were sorely missed, given that a good-sized specimen proved sufficient to serve all aboard with one decent meal. Cockles, some so large that it took two men to move them, became an acceptable substitute. On one island several Aborigines came out on a point 'and looked at the ship for a little while and then retired'. This seeming lack of interest

---

9   *Cook*, 17 August 1770, pp. 379–80; *Banks*, vol. 2, pp. 105-08.
10   J.C. Beaglehole, *The Exploration of the Pacific* (1966, pp. 222, 223).

probably further proved that the word of the *Endeavour* passing by had been sent ahead regularly so that sighting it was by now an accepted occurrence. The weather was both 'charming' and 'moderate', which gave Cook the freedom to indulge in another welter of naming features on the coast. Cape Weymouth, Forbes's Isles, Bolt Head, Cape Granville, Temple Bay, Sir Charles Hardy's Isles, Cockburn Isles and Bird Isles were all named, in the main after dignitaries and similar worthies of the Admiralty and government. Thus the new land became daily increasingly wedded to the old. New Holland was destined to become irrevocably British, in nomenclature at least.[11]

As they proceeded carefully on 21 August, Cook, still careful to stay close in, gave a lengthy description of the islands and the shoals. By 1 pm a small passage opened before them, which they entered with caution and anchored overnight there. Meanwhile Banks recorded the sighting of 10 Aborigines standing on a hill. Nine were armed with the normal lances while the tenth had a bow and arrows. Two wore large mother of pearl ornaments 'hung round their necks' and three broke away from the main group to follow the *Endeavour* with the 'bow man' among them. They stood as if waiting to resist, or assist in a landing, but they walked away 'leisurely' when the ship came in close to them. Beaglehole concluded that 'it seems unlikely that these "Indians" were Australian aborigines, who did not use the bow and arrow or have mother of pearl shell ornaments of this kind. They must have been Melanesians.' His argument, based on exclusion, is peculiar because it ignores the fact that the use of the weapons and ornaments could have been adopted from the nearby New Guineans. Next day in the morning, three or four women were seen gathering shellfish on the beach. Through his field glasses Banks thought that they appeared in the customary manner except that they were 'more naked than our mother Eve', which was unlikely unless he was acknowledging the use of the fig leaf by Eve.[12]

At dawn 'we got again under sail, having first sent the yawl ahead to sound' but, now confident of a safe passage, the yawl was put in tow until shoals were again seen, when it joined the long boat and the pinnace in patrolling and sounding the waters ahead. By noon they could see islands far to the west, probably Horn and Thursday islands, and Cook realised that the land to his south was 'the Northern Promontory of this country. I have named it York Cape in honour of His Late Royal Highness the Duke of York.' He gave its latitude and longitude almost exactly and described the

---

[11]   *Cook*, fn. 5, p. 381; 18 August 1770, p. 381; *Banks*, vol. 2, p. 109. For the naming see *Cook*, pp. 381-83.

[12]   *Cook*, 21 August 1770, pp. 384-85; *Banks*, vol. 2, p. 110.

cape as 'rather low and very flat as far inland as the eye could reach and looks barren to the southward of the Cape' which he modified by admitting that the valleys between the distant hills 'appeared to be tolerably well clothed with wood'. By four o'clock he was hopeful 'that we had at last found a passage into the Indian Seas' but to be certain he decided to land on an island and achieve satisfaction.[13]

---

[13]   *Cook*, 21, 22 August 1770, pp. 385-87.

9

Creating New South Wales

On this small island, which he inevitably named Possession Island, at about 6 pm on 22 August 1770, Cook decided to reassert his earlier acts of taking possession of that portion of New Holland that he had charted for his king. It is true that the inability of Tupia or anyone else aboard the *Endeavour* to communicate with the Aborigines made a meaningful interaction unrealistic. Nevertheless, the fact remains that at New Holland, as at New Zealand, Cook made no attempt to negotiate with the people who had lived with and on their land for long ages before it was claimed in the name of a distant monarch and a nation unknown to all of them. He never claimed that New Holland was terra nullius, which, given his amicable contact with its inhabitants at the Endeavour River, would have been a manifest absurdity in its implications, even though the term was foreign to him and everyone else at the time.

The following account of this ceremony is exactly as it was set down by Cook in the holograph held by the National Library of Australia with its deletions, additions and spelling. He wrote,

> with a party of Men accompan'd by Mr Banks and Dr Solander upon the Island which lies at the SE point of the Passage: before and after we anchor'd we saw a number of People upon this Island arm'd in the same — manner as all the others we have seen except one man who had a bow and a bundle of Arrows, the first we have seen on this coast. from the appearence of these People we expected they would have opposed our landing but as we approached the Shore they all made off and left us in peaceable posession of as much of the Island as served our purpose. After landing I went upon the highest hill which however was of no great height, yet not less than twice or thrice the height of the Ships Mast heads but I could see from it no land between SW and WSW so that I did not doubt but there was a passage, I could see plainly that the Lands laying to the NW of this passage were composed of a number of Islands of various extent both for height and circuit rainged one be hind a nother as far to the Northward and Westward as I could see which could

not be less than 12 or 14 Leagues. Having satisfied myself of the great Probabillity of a Passage, thro' which I intend going with the Ship and therefore may land no more upon this Eastern coast of New Holland and on the Western side I can make no new discovery the honour of which belongs to the Dutch Navigators but the Eastern Coast from the Latitude of 38° South down to this place I am confident was never seen or viseted by any European before us and notwithstand I had in the Name of his Majesty taken posession of several places upon this coast I now once more hoisted English Coulers and in the Name of His Majesty King George the Third took posession of the whole Eastern Coast from the above Latitude down to this place by the Name of New South Wales together with all the Bays, Harbours Rivers and Islands situate upon the said coast after which we fired three Volleys of small Arms which were Answerd by the like number from the Ship.[1]

Given that the Dutch saw no value accruing to their empire by claiming possession of New Holland, it is ironical that, close to the monument commemorating Cook's taking possession, there are remains of shafts where 155 kilograms of gold were extracted in the late nineteenth century. The ancient continent had its own treasures but they lay hidden for a time.

What portion of New Holland did Cook effectively claim? His longitude at 'this place' (Possession Island) was 142.4° east. Its latitude was 10.73° south, while the latitude he referred to, 38° south, had been calculated on 19 April 1770, the day on which the east coast of New Holland was first sighted. He said 'down to this place' because at 10.73° it was clearly much lower than 38°. Taken literally this means that he claimed for the Crown all the land, with its rivers and the Great Dividing Range from the tip of Cape York down to just below the Victorian border with New South Wales. Had he used his longitude also, it practically bisects Cape York and then runs down Queensland west of Winton, crosses Cooper Creek several times, enters New South Wales east of Mount Bygrave and Tibooburra, runs almost equally between Broken Hill and Wilcannia and then enters Victoria near Mildura on the Murray. Running through the Mallee and Wimmera and crossing the Grampians near Mount William, it ends on 38° latitude at about 50 kilometres in from the coastal city of Warrnambool. Cook's eastern claim commences at that point and ends on a line running east above Geelong, over Port Phillip Bay and through Dandenong just south-east of Melbourne. It ends when entering the Tasman Sea about 16 kilometres south of Bairnsdale. In both cases the southern and western parts of Victoria

---

[1]   Cook, James, *Journal of the HMS Endeavour, 1768-1771*, National Library of Australia, Manuscripts Collection, MS 1, 22 August 1770.

as well as Tasmania were not included, but the area he claimed eventually became the most populated and highly regarded segment of the continent.

Cook was well aware that the Dutch had chartered the western coast of the Gulf of Carpentaria and his words in the act of possession imply that he was thereby leaving it open to them to claim any part of the continent west of Possession Island. Clearly he respected, even admired, those 'Navigators' who had gone out before him in search of hitherto unknown lands and he had no hesitation in recognising the primary role of the Dutch to the British in regard to most of New Holland. Thus he would have had no reason to change his wording, which makes it clear that his original version was amended at the demand of the Admiralty in London. High officers of the government were not about to concede, in an offhanded manner, especially when expressed by a minor officer of the navy, that the Dutch had any rightful claim in the matter, despite the fact that the Dutch East India Company had never made any pretension to do so. On the other hand both Cook and the Admiralty were well aware that Van Diemen's Land had been claimed for the Dutch by Tasman in 1642, but neither knew of there being a strait separating it from the mainland. Given, however, that Tasman had claimed possession at latitude 43° south it was thought reasonable to assume that any land above 38° south could be safely claimed.

Despite Cook's scruples in acknowledging the rights of the Dutch, no such tendency was shown by his king and government in 1787 when appointing Arthur Phillip as the Governor of New South Wales. The carefully delineated area of Cook's claim had grown immensely in a short 16 years. What was deemed now to be 'our territory' and, therefore, Phillip's responsibility, extended from the top of Cape York at 10°37' down to 43°39' south, which was where Tasman had taken possession of Van Diemen's Land on 3 December 1642. Even more adventuresome was the claim made to 'all the country inland to the westward as far as the one hundred and thirty-fifth degree of longitude', which ran down the line decreed by Pope Alexander VI in 1493 and encompassed almost exactly one half of the continent. Not content with this 'all the islands adjacent in the Pacific' within the same latitudes were claimed, which included New Zealand except for its southern extremity below 43°39' south.[2]

The naming of this newly-claimed land proved to be a slight obstacle.

---

[2]   For the land claims in 1786 see *Historical Records of New South Wales: Phillip 1783-1792*, vol. 1, pt. 2 (1893), George III's Commission to Arthur Phillip, 12 October 1786 and repeated on 2 April 1787 and again in the Instructions to Phillip by the King on 25 April 1787, pp. 24-25, 61-68, 85-92.

In the original version of Cook's claim there was no space for the three words 'New South Wales' and only one word was used, but it was erased and cannot be identified with certainty. Furthermore in none of the journals and logs of the voyage is the name New South Wales used. That being the case, the only conclusion can be that the full name was added later. Again it is possible that the Admiralty had a final hand in the matter because an officer of the Royal Navy, Sir Thomas Button, later admiral, had given the name New South Wales in 1612 to the whole western shore of Hudson's Bay in Canada. By Cook's time that name had fallen into disuse and he might even have been unaware of its previous use. The same cannot be said of the Admiralty, where old charts were held and distant memories remained fresh. In any event, it is exceedingly odd that Cook, unprompted, would have bestowed the name on a huge area of land that is, admittedly, south of the Equator but, at that time, was not south of any other noted territory. What possible reason was there for Cook to have come up with the name New South Wales? Beaglehole was able to identify name after name on Cook's charts to explain their relevance, but he made no attempt to do so with this almost outlandish name. Perhaps there was a high official of the Admiralty who was an ardent Welshman and remembered that Button was of the same origin. After all the Dutch had never attempted to do anything useful with New Holland and neither at the Admiralty nor elsewhere in London were suggestions forthcoming as to what use this new land might be put. Why not revive the use of New South Wales? Did it matter?

In his journal entry, Banks made no mention of the act of taking possession, as if to him it was an irrelevant distraction from his scientific purposes. Parkinson ran his narrative covering two days into the one and garbled the facts. He saw the Aborigines 'gazing at us' who then fled when the ship's company landed. He mentioned the act of possession briefly as the hoisting 'of a jack' followed by the firing of a 'volley' answered by volleys from the marines on the shore of the island, as well as those on the ship 'and three cheers from the main shrouds'. He follows this account with: 'The natives were armed with lances, and one of them had a bow in his hand. In other respects they were much like the people we saw last, being quite naked, and of a dark colour.'[3]

On the next island on which they landed, Cook and Banks shot birds for the table 'till our ammunition was quite expended'. In honour of the birds, the island was named Booby Island, although it was no more than a 'barren

---

[3]   *Banks*, vol. 2, pp. 110, 111; Sydney Parkinson, *Journal of a Voyage to South Seas* (1773, p. 198).

rock'. Banks remarks, 'I myself botanized and found some plants which I had not before seen'. Cook now decided that, being west of 'Carpentaria or the northern extremity of New Holland' with 'an open sea to the westward', proved that there was a strait between New Holland and New Guinea which 'until this day has been a doubtful point among geographers'. He had swung to and fro on this question for so long that it must have afforded him great relief to be rid of it and he was assuredly happy to have come safely through such a dangerous passage. Indeed he had no wish to know more about that whole shoal and reef-ridden area 'having been already sufficiently harassed with dangers without going to look for more'. He named the passage Endeavour's Strait, despite being aware from Dalrymple that Torres, whose name Cook never mentioned, had preceded him. He willingly admitted that he had been unable to do more in charting the abundant reefs of the Strait than he had been able to 'on the eastern coast of New Wales'. Here again the change from New Holland to New Wales had to be interlinear. Clearly it was added later, but before South had been decided upon. Neither Banks nor Parkinson make any mention of New Wales or New South Wales and Cook only does so twice.[4]

Cook was justifiably proud of his charts, which he considered equal to any others that had not 'undergone a thorough correction'. In this respect he was conscious of his debt to Green who was 'indefatigable' in making the calculations necessary to establish their location daily by measuring latitude and longitude by observing the sun and moon. Cook was well aware that a great deal of his own much-needed time would have been spent in so doing 'which I could not at all times very well spare' and he generously expressed his gratitude while also applauding Green for having taught several petty officers to undertake the task, which they succeeded in doing 'almost as well' as Green himself. Cook also highly recommended the use of *The Nautical Almanac and Astronomical Ephemeris* (1767), edited by Nevil Maskelyne, which gave lunar distances to help mariners calculate longitude by observation of the moon. Cook thought that without the *Almanac* 'the calculations are laborious and discouraging to beginners' and he hoped that all officers would use them at sea.[5]

---

[4] *Banks*, vol. 2, pp. 110-11; *Cook*, 23 August 1770, pp. 390, 391, 392.
[5] *Cook*, p. 392.

10

The Land and its Owners

After writing his journal entry for 23 August 1770, Cook embarked on a lengthy and conscientious summary of various aspects of the whole east coast which he called New South Wales, although its extent was ultimately restricted somewhat with the naming of Victoria and Queensland as well. He began with observations on the land itself, which he found 'indifferently fertile', which stricture also applied to water, as illustrated by the difficulty Cook's men often experienced in finding it fresh and in a good supply. Although there were small brooks and springs there were no 'great rivers', which is a surprising conclusion given the several rivers of a considerable size that he had passed south of the Endeavour River, the last river mouth able to provide a suitable anchorage. It became even more so when he later said that the coast north of latitude 25° (near to today's Bundaberg) 'abounds with a great number of fine bays and harbours which are sheltered of all winds'. In places devoid in large measure of trees, the land was rocky and barren, which was especially so in the north of the country. For that reason the land in general 'naturally produces hardly anything fit for man to eat and the natives know nothing of cultivation', which explained why 'we never saw one inch of cultivated land in the whole country'. To sum matters up, while he rejected the harsh judgement on the land as 'barren and miserable', which was made by Dampier and the Dutch, he thought that it 'doth not produce any one thing that can become an article in trade to invite Europeans to fix a settlement upon it'. Notwithstanding the above, Cook remained optimistic and wrote, 'In this extensive country it can never be doubted but what most sorts of grain, fruits, roots etc. of every kind would flourish here once brought hither, planted and cultivated by the hand of industry, and here are provender for more cattle at all seasons of the year than ever be brought into this country'.[1]

He also wrote at length on the inhabitants of New Holland, but admitted that 'none of us were ever very near any of their women, one gentleman

---

[1]   *Cook*, pp. 395-97.

excepted', which must refer to the seaman's encounter with the elderly woman at Botany Bay. He then explained that the men, 'whether through jealousy or disregard … never brought any of their women along to the ship, but always left them on the other side of the river where we had frequent opportunities of viewing them through our glasses' and later remarked almost unwearyingly on their nudity. Although the men never went about without carrying their throwing sticks and spears, it was not necessarily because they were 'in fear of their enemies', but to use the weapons to kill game. Thus, to him, the Aborigines were not 'a war like people, on the contrary I think them a timorous and inoffensive race, no ways inclinable to cruelty'. He was impressed, nonetheless, with their use of spears, which were helped in their trajectory by a 'throwing stick' that allowed them to 'hit a mark at a distance of 40 or 50 yards with almost, if not as much certainty as we can do with a musket'. They were not 'very numerous' and lived 'in small parties along by the sea coast, the banks of lakes, rivers, creeks' while,

> their houses are mean small hovels, not much bigger than an oven, made of pieces of sticks, bark, grass, etc. And even these are seldom used but in the wet season for in the dry times we know that they as often sleep in the open air as anywhere else. We have seen many of their sleeping places where there has been only some branches, or pieces of bark raised about a foot from the ground on the windward side. They seem to have no fixed habitation but move about from place to place like wild beasts in search of food, and I believe depend wholly upon the success of the present day for their substance.

Furthermore they never ate anything raw but roasted or boiled everything on 'slow, small fires'. While decrying the structure of their frail canoes, despite which they could venture over 30 kilometres out to the local islands for turtles, he admitted that because 'they draw but little water', their canoes were admirably suited for fishing on mud banks. He remarked, however, that the people of the Endeavour River area had only one canoe between them, seemingly without giving thought to the possibility that this could well have been the result of a deliberate act of concealment of other canoes, given how vital the use of a vessel, no matter how humble, was to their daily existence.[2]

After giving a short vocabulary, the generous captain launched into a remarkable eulogy of the 'Natives of New Holland ', which deserves to be recorded in full:

> From what I have said of the Natives of New-Holland they may appear to some to be the most wretched people upon Earth, but in reality they

---

[2]   *Cook*, p. 395.

are far more happier than we Europeans; being wholly unacquainted not only with the superfluous but the necessary Conveniences so much sought after in Europe, they are happy in not knowing the use of them. They live in a Tranquillity which is not disturbed by the Inequality of Condition: The Earth and sea of their own accord furnishes them with all things necessary for life; they covet not Magnificent Houses, Household-stuff &C². they live in a warm and fine Climate and enjoy a very wholesome Air, so that they have very little need of Clothing and this they seem to ˏᵇᵉ fully sensible of, for many to whom we gave Cloth &C². to, left it carelessly upon the Sea beach and in the woods as a thing they had no manner of use for. In short they seem'd to set no Value upon any thing we gave them, nor would they ever part with any thing of their own for any one article we could offer them; this, in my opinion argues that they think themselves provided with all the necessarys of Life and that they have no superfluities.[3]

Cook obviously thought at length about this passage, which Beaglehole dismissed as 'nonsense'. Indeed, its contents almost persuaded him that Cook 'had spent the voyage reading Rousseau' on the 'noble savage', even though the fact is that Jean-Jacques Rousseau never used that expression which has done nothing to overturn the belief that he had. This, however, led the eminent scholar — which Beaglehole unquestionably was — to remark that Cook must have been 'rather taken' with his judgement of the Aborigines because he had repeated a good deal of it in a letter to his friend, John Walker, on 13 September 1771. The letter was thus written well after his return home, when he had ample time to revise his original thoughts had he deemed it necessary to do so. Not content with those strictures, Beaglehole commented further on Cook's text with, 'There are simplicities still in this sailor' and wondered whether he 'had been listening to some oration of Banks' or read something 'adorned with the Banks version of the fashionable intellectual indiscretions'. The true point at issue is whether Cook reported what he had seen and experienced or whether he embellished his account with imaginary details inconsistent with his observations. Far from being 'nonsense', Cook wrote justly and generously on the Aborigines he had met, especially over a period of five weeks at the Endeavour River, so that 'nonsense' more aptly describes Beaglehole's conclusion that voices the jaundiced and biased judgement still widespread in his own day on the Aborigines. As for Cook reading Rousseau, it is more than likely that he had never looked at a line written by him.[4]

In his second letter to John Walker from his home in London and dated

---

[3]   *Cook*, pp. 398-99.
[4]   J.C. Beaglehole, *The Life of Captain James Cook* (1974, fns 1 & 2, p. 252); Cook to Walker in *Cook*, pp. 506-09.

13 September 1770, Cook wrote that the Aborigines of New Holland 'may be truly be said to be in the pure state of nature'. Irrespective of the meaning given to this expression, whether by Thomas Hobbes or others, Cook's use of it places him in the invidious position of an explorer delving into fantasy land. Cook did not know what is now known of the Aborigines. Those he met at the Endeavour River had their origins on this continent at least 60,000 years BC and, thus, 53,000 years before one of the most ancient cities of the so-called civilised world, Jericho in Palestine, was founded about 7,000 BC. They lived harmoniously in a highly developed relationship of respectful use and conservation with the world of which they formed an integral part. They communicated in rich and complex languages; their art depicted their world in ways gracious and pleasing as well as immediately intelligible to and treasured by those honoured to behold it. Through their Dreaming, and in song and dance, they conserved and passed on the long and bountiful story of their relationship with the earth and all on and in it, of the celestial world and the spirit moving through every element of creation and giving life even to the seemingly lifeless. War, the waging of which is a final yardstick in the measure of a civilisation, was unknown to them at least in its expression of evil in a total war when the innocent also die. To the degree that the way of life of the Aborigines was bedded in the pure state of nature, Cook both experienced and affirmed it.

Banks follows his entry of 26 August 1770 with a heading, 'Some account of that part of New Holland now called New South Wales'. This heading was very probably written after Banks returned home because, in his text, he always used New Holland rather than New South Wales. Incidentally, and curiously, he continued to use Sting Rays Bay rather than Botany Bay, which surely indicates that the former was used aboard the *Endeavour* well after it was supposedly changed into the latter on 6 May 1770. Unlike the journals written by Cook and his officers, Banks was not obliged to surrender his journal to Cook to be sent home to the Admiralty from Batavia, so it would be unreasonable to argue that his additions and corrections were made to that end there. This makes it more than likely that Banks only used New South Wales rather than New Holland once that name had finally been adopted by the Admiralty. The same applies to Botany Bay.[5]

Banks wanted to give a better account of his 'Indians' than Dampier, who was 'the only man I know of who has seen them besides us'. To Banks, Dampier 'either was very much mistaken in his account or else that he saw

---

[5]   *Banks*, vol. 2, p. 111; Beaglehole in *Cook*, p. 388, fn. 1.

a very different race of people from those we have seen'. Nevertheless his account has considerable value, at least in a comparative sense and especially when Banks admitted, when first sighting Aborigines on the east coast on 22 April 1770, that through their glasses they appeared to be 'enormously black', indeed to the degree that 'the prejudices we had built on Dampier's account influence us that we fancied we could see their colour when we could scarce distinguish whether or not they were men'. With that in mind, an examination of Dampier's impressions of the Aborigines of the north-west of the continent is needed.[6]

On his first visit in 1688, Dampier spent five weeks on the west coast in King Sound from 4 January to 12 February. He returned in 1699, landed at Shark Bay on the central west coast of Western Australia on 7 August, sailed north to Roebuck Bay and departed from New Holland on 1 September. He had intended to go much further and chart the east coast of New Holland, but the unseaworthiness of his vessel prevented him from doing so.[7] On that initial visit Dampier came ashore to speak with the 'natives' but they would 'not abide our coming', as had happened at Botany Bay with Cook. Dampier explained that, running short of provisions, he hoped to obtain some by exchanging 'toys' for any food that they had to offer. He was disappointed, whether in respect of those people encountered near the shore or those slightly further inland, all of whom lacked grain and vegetables, fowls — whether tame or wild — cattle, cats and dogs. Dampier remarked that 'they have no occasion of such creatures unless to eat them for, of that food which they have, they leave no fragments'. Very few birds were seen, unlike on the east coast, although an animal track was seen, probably that of a kangaroo. Finally they had 'no houses or anything like a house' but, like the Aborigines of the Endeavour River, they lay at night behind 'a few boughs stuck up to keep the wind from them'. He found the soil dry and sandy as well as 'destitute of water'.

Dampier, like Cook, Banks and others, concluded that the Aborigines of the east coast deliberately lived close to the sea. The marked difference was that, although they lacked canoes, 'they get their living out of the sea without net or hook, but they build weirs across the bays and every low water. Whether

---

6   *Banks*, vol. 2, pp. 111-12, 50.

7   All quotes from Dampier are taken from 2005 Gutenberg Australia editions of his *A New Voyage Round the World* (1697) and *A Voyage to New Holland* (1703). Both are unpaginated. Dampier's manuscript of his first visit is in the British Library (Sloan MS 3236). The often quoted, negative description by Dampier of the Aborigines as the 'miserablest people in the world' is only found in the printed version. Perhaps the manuscript was touched up later for added effect.

night or day they search those weirs for what the sea hath left behind which is all that they have to depend on for a livelihood.' This meant that sometimes they ate well, but at other times 'providence seemed to be niggardly, giving them a taste instead of a bellyfull'. While the men fished, the sick, the old and the children remained behind preparing a fire to cook the food, which was eaten 'without salt or bread'. They lived close to the weirs and moved easily from place to place 'for they are not troubled with household goods nor clothes'. They nonetheless attempted to cover their private parts, unlike those met by Cook in the east, if one accepts the minimal attempts by some men to do so at the Endeavour River. In fact it is true that the feature of the east coast Aborigines most remarked upon was their nudity. Of the westerners, Dampier wrote, 'all that they wear is only a piece of vine about their wastes under which they thrust either a hand full of long grass or some small boughs before to cover their privities'.

The physical description of the Aborigines is much as that given by Cook and others, except for Dampier's description of the removal of two fore teeth, apparently in infancy. Another difference is that Dampier was able to come close to the women; otherwise how would he be able to comment on their teeth? He does not appear to refer only to elderly women. He wrote:

> They are people of good stature, but very thin and lean. I judge for want of food. They are black yet I believe their hair would be long if it was combed out but for want of combs it is matted up like a negro's hair. They have all that I saw two fore teeth of their upper jaw wanting [in] both men women and children.

He asserted that they had 'not one graceful feature in their faces'. Although they had nothing resembling a woomera, he said that they had 'for arms a lance sharpened at one end and burned in the fire to harden it and a sword made with wood which is sharp on one side'. In short their main weapon was without the barbs that were customary in the east. His assertion regarding the use of stone hatchets to make spears and swords is not supported by any evidence and he simply states that they were 'cut with stone hatchets as I have seen in the West India'.

While on the coast Dampier and his crew were well supplied by their own men with turtles and fish so, after the initial attempt to barter for food, it became unnecessary to do so. On one occasion the fishermen 'met some of the natives swimming from one island to the other' and brought back four of them to the ship. They 'took no notice of anything that we had, no more than a brute would' but, given some victuals they ate them with relish and, once ashore, 'ran away as fast as their legs would carry them'. When they met others on the islands where they could not run away they did not attempt to escape 'but the women and children would be frightened at our approach'. Apparently the male, adult Aborigines were not so afraid of the Europeans that they refused to go aboard their ship and there is no evidence that they were forced to do so. Exactly as had occurred at Botany Bay and at the Endeavour River, the people of the west had no interest in any of the possessions of the Europeans except their food. Dampier saw no evidence of religious belief among them, but he approvingly noticed that they shared their food equally among all and that they lived in companies of 20 or 30 people and thus supported each other.

On his second visit in 1699 Dampier wrote, 'all of them have the most unpleasant looks and the worst features of any people that ever I saw'. Because he was only about 120 kilometres south of where he had landed at King Sound in 1681, he concluded that they were 'probably the same sort of people'. Their eyesight was poor and thus they were 'much the same blinking creatures (here being also abundance of the same kind of flesh-flies teasing them)'. Black of skin, they were both tall and thin 'but we had not the opportunity to see whether these, as the former, wanted two of their foreteeth'. He concluded that these people, like those seen on his first visit, did not erect dwelling places of any kind, rather they threw together three or four boughs 'stuck up to windward' before which they sheltered. At the adjacent fireplaces there were always 'great heaps of fish-shells, of several sorts; and it is probable that these poor creatures here lived chiefly on the shellfish' as distinct from the small fish caught in fish pens by the Aborigines further north. The lances or spears, however, were of the same kind in both places. Again there was no direct tendency to aggression even though some of the males waved their spears and shouted.

In his summary, Banks firmly stated that this immense land, larger than Europe, was 'Barren it may justly be called and in a very high degree', and again, 'in every respect the most barren country I have seen', while, finally, even 'the whole fertile soil bears no kind of proportion to that which seems by nature doomed to everlasting barrenness'. This makes more than passing strange his own 'enthusiastic recommendation in 1799 of Botany Bay as a site for a convict settlement' to the House of Commons. He stated that the extent of rich soil was small but 'sufficient to support a very large number of people' and that 'the country was well supplied with water'. In fairness to Banks, it must be noted that Parkinson had also said about Botany Bay that

'The country is very level and fertile; the soil, a kind of grey sand; and the climate mild: and though it was the beginning of winter when we arrived, everything seemed in perfection'. Furthermore, Banks admitted in 1770 that they only saw the coastal strip 'as you sail along it' and therefore inland only 'as far as our situation would allow us to do'. That naturally meant they were able to speak of an inland perhaps only five or six kilometres from the coast, and thus they knew almost nothing of it. Cook later admitted this, stating 'the interior of this immense tract of land is not at all known'. It is as well that such an admission of the situation was made because an accusation summing it up passed later into the folk language of Australians. In rhyming slang, they used 'Captain Cook' or, more simply, 'Cook' instead of 'look' when describing Cook's charting of the coast. An example taken from the Sydney paper *Truth* in 1899 sums up this opinion succinctly: 'The Cap'en, he merely squinted around, cursory-like, and I'm hanged if his name don't stick to that job, too. How do I mean? Why, if a chap just glances at a thing, don't we still say he has a "Cook" at it?' Clearly those using the expression were unaware that Cook, in charting an unknown coast and in waters laced in large measure with grave dangers, was going beyond the call of duty with a single vessel already precariously battered at a time when his supplies of food and other necessities were lacking.[8]

Banks concluded that the land was 'thinly inhabited and they only once saw as many as thirty inhabitants gathered together who made up a family of men, women and children gathered on a rock to watch the ship pass by'. At the Endeavour River the people they met or saw at a distance 'consisted of 21 people, 12 men, 7 women a boy and a girl, so many at least we saw and there might be more, especially women whom we did not see'. They were, however, 'a very small people ... in general about 5 feet 6 in height and very slender; one we measured 5 feet 2 and another 5 feet 9, but he was far taller than any of his fellows'. Women were only seen from afar through glasses and, when seen, 'they were generally employed in some laborious occupation as fetching wood, gathering shell fish etc'. Despite the difficulty in making a judgement, Banks wrote, 'That their customs were nearly the same throughout the whole length of the coast ... I should think very probable', although the canoes made by the northern Aborigines he considered 'far superior' to those made in the south. Furthermore, in every place they were apparently 'ignorant of the arts of cultivation', but the reason for the alleged

---

[8]   *Banks*, vol. 2, pp. 112, 113; Beaglehole in *Cook*, p. 113, fn. 2; Cook to Walker, in *Cook*, 13 September 1771, p. 508; *Truth*, 14 May 1899 in W.S. Ramson (ed.), *The Australian National Dictionary* (1988, p. 167); Sydney Parkinson, *Journal of a Voyage to South Seas* (1773, p. 181).

ignorance was never explained and it was assumed, as a consequence, that the inland, lacking marine life and hence food for humans, must be uninhabited. He considered the houses built by the Aborigines at 'Sting-Rays Bay' better than those at the Endeavour River, although in both cases they were all 'framed with less art or rather less industry than any habitations of human beings probably that the world can show'.[9]

Perhaps the isolation of the coastal Aborigines from those inland beyond the Great Divide, and the fact that goods available in one place on the coast did not differ markedly from those available in similar localities, explains Banks next remark: 'These people seemed to have no idea of traffic, nor could we teach them', and that they received willingly what they were given but returned little in exchange with the exception of one small fish 'that they brought us as kind of token of peace'. It is also possible that the Aborigines saw nothing belonging to the Europeans that they regarded as worthy of barter. They were not prepared to barter for the turtles, some of which, at least, they obviously believed belonged rightly to them. In a noteworthy difference to the people encountered in the Society Islands, however, the Aborigines 'whatever opportunities they had they never once attempted to take anything in a clandestine manner; whatever they wanted they openly asked for and in almost all cases bore the refusal if they met one with much indifference, except turtles'. With clear approval, Banks also remarked on the fact, to him, 'rarely observed among the most cleanly Indians', that they seemed 'to be entirely free from lice' which he hinted could be because they never used oil or grease on their hair nor oiled their bodies, which at that time was 'so common among most uncivilized nations'. Finally he thought their 'spare, thin bodies' indicated a 'temperance in eating', which, whether done through 'necessity or inclination' was 'equally productive of health.'[10]

Banks wrote a great deal more of descriptive material on the Aborigines than Cook and the other journal writers. He somewhat laboriously decided that the colour of their skin was 'chocolate'; their hair was 'in none of them at all resembling the wool of negroes'; the bone that men wore through their nostrils gave them 'a most ludicrous appearance' and the red (ochre) and white (uncertain as to its origin) paint they lay on their bodies were decorations, as were their necklaces and bracelets of shells. The scars he deemed to be 'marks of their lamentations for the deceased'. Awed, at both landings, by the 'equally dexterity' with which the Aborigines threw their

---

9   *Banks*, vol. 2, pp. 122-23, 128, 129, 135.
10   *Banks*, vol. 2, pp. 125, 126.

spears, especially when aimed at fish, he also praised their fish hooks and lines. He was startled at the manner in which they made fire in 'less than 2 minutes' and started grass fires with ease, which brought him close to the mark when he concluded that the widespread practise might have had something to do with their hunting the kangaroo. In the end he composed his own eulogy to the people of New Holland and their existence which is slightly more restrained than that of Cook. The two passages do not rely on each other, but both firmly assert a positive judgement of the Aborigines and, thus, diverge widely from Dampier's dirge-like account. In Dampier's favour, it must be acknowledged that he did not have the same opportunity to come close to the people of the west coast as Cook and Banks had done on the east, a meeting that was especially rich at the Endeavour River. In his concluding passage Banks wrote, 'Thus live these I had almost said happy people, content with little, nay almost nothing', and thus, 'From them appears how small are the wants of human nature, which we Europeans have increased to an excess which would certainly appear incredible to these people could they be told of it'. As examples of these excesses he instances the 'Luxuries' that, in his eyes, had degenerated into necessities, such as 'strong liquors, tobacco, spices, tea, etc, etc'.[11]

Parkinson did not write a journal in the formal sense but, perhaps, his lack of time at night, so well spent on illustrations of plants, animals, coastal views and much else, precluded his doing so. Furthermore he often gave an account of whatever he deemed worthy of mention up to days, even weeks, after the event occurred, which might have made it less trustworthy. After describing the plants, birds, animals and fish in and around the Endeavour River, he dealt with the 'natives' who were 'naked', of a 'diminutive size, ran very swiftly and were very merry and facetious', which probably meant that they were happy and fun making. They had small bones so that he 'could more than span their ankles; and their arms too, above the elbow joint'. The rest of his description is much the same as that in the other journals, but he adds that they had 'regular well-set large teeth, tinged with yellow' and mostly 'cut off the hair from their heads' while some 'wore their hair, which was curled and bushy', which latter description did not fit that of the other journalists. He dwelt on the marks on their 'breasts and hips', which were like 'ridges, or seams, raised above the rest of the flesh, which look like the cicatrices of ill-healed wounds'. Some of them were 'painted with red streaks across the body' while others were 'streaked over the face with white, which

---

[11]   *Banks*, vol. 2, pp. 124, 125, 126, 130, 131.

they call carbanda'. On the appearance of the women he was justifiably brief because they 'did not approach nearer to us than the opposite shore, had feathers stuck on the crown of their heads, fastened, we were informed, to a piece of gum', which surely indicates that some member of the crew must have been able to get closer to them.[12]

The Aborigines made their presence clear only 'by degrees' and initially only on the north shore. After fish had been thrown to them they came close, landed and 'came forward to meet us showing signs of amity as they came along'. He then remarked that 'they were so much abashed at first, that they took but little notice of us, or any thing about us, though they did not seem to be apprehensive of danger'. He used 'abashed' to mean 'embarrassed', without attempting to spell out what caused them to be embarrassed. He also remarked that they showed 'a great antipathy to our tame birds, and attempted to throw one of them over-board', which might have been their way to indicate their pity for the birds and thus their attempt to set them free. The brief description of the impasse reached over the turtles was remarkable only in that it omitted to mention its cause — the refusal to give them a turtle. As was the case in Botany Bay, the general opinion was that the Aborigines lived 'mostly on shell-fish, the remains of which we saw frequently about their fires'.[13]

While Banks only recorded 38 words, Parkinson dwelt at some length on the language of the Guugu Yimithirr, which was not harsh but distinctly articulated and 'made with a great motion of their lips'. The only word that 'we could distinguish, to accord with the Otaheitean language' was 'aipa', which they seemed to repeat as 'a mark of dissent'. Clearly uncertain as to its meaning, however, he omitted it from his list, which included over 200 words dealing with parts of the human body, the birds, animals, plants, natural features, utensils and weapons, human acts and names — but only, for an obvious reason, male names and then only nine of them.[14]

Matra passes over the passage north rapidly with a short account of the encounter with the reef. Equally brief is his treatment of the time spent at the Endeavour River. He skimmed over the conflict caused by the refusal to share the turtles and concentrated on the attempt by the Aborigines to burn the fishing nets and linen: 'Captain Cooke [sic] wounded several of them …

---

[12] Sydney Parkinson, *Journal of a Voyage to South Seas* (1773, p. 189).

[13] Sydney Parkinson, *Journal of a Voyage to South Seas* (1773, p. 195).

[14] Sydney Parkinson, *Journal of a Voyage to South Seas* (1773, pp. 188–95); *Banks*, pp. 136-37.

but a few hours after they returned peacefully.'[15]

Likewise, Matra gave a cursory treatment to the passage inside the reef and into Torres Strait. Matra seems to have considered Cook's observation from 'a small eminence' on Possession Island as the moment when they 'discovered' the 'Indian sea'; although the word might not mean any more than that they now knew where they were. Having taken 'possession of the country, etc, in the name of his Britannic Majesty' they then 'sailed through the Strait, which separates New Holland from New Guinea; and which we now discovered to be parts of the same continent'. Perhaps by 'same continent' he meant that, being separated by such a narrow strait, both landmasses belonged to each other. Otherwise the remark is inexplicable.[16]

Based on Dampier and the journals written on the *Endeavour*, to draw the conclusion that there was a gulf between the level of human development on the east and west coasts of the continent is unavoidable. Dampier's account of the consumption of only one kind of food in the form of fish and other products of the sea in the west is possibly inconclusive because it was drawn only from the lack of visual evidence and a cursory examination of the contents of the middens. In the east, Parkinson noticed that, besides a modest array of fruits, vegetables and seeds, even poisonous plants such as the cycas media were treated to make them safe for humans. But, on both his visits, Dampier noted the absence of water-going craft or canoes, of fish hooks or fishing lines. Local rock art, both ancient and in more recent times, strongly indicates that knowledge of seagoing vessels was that gained by observing those sailed off the coast by overseas visitors. Given the proximity of the west to Timor, and the fact that the spread of human habitation throughout the Pacific depended on suitable vessels, makes it exceedingly strange that the Aboriginal people of the west of the continent have left no evidence of attempts to construct even rudimentary vessels.

The unwelcoming and unsympathetic way in which Dampier was greeted by the Aborigines in the west bears some slight resemblance to the welcome extended to Cook at Botany Bay, but it is markedly different to the peaceful and even welcoming experience at the Endeavour River. It is surely not mere fantasy to speculate on the possibility of previous visitors to both coasts, possibly including Europeans. Yet there is a remarkable difference in that,

[15] James Matra, *The Anonymous Journal (A Journal of a Voyage Round the World in his Majesty's Ship Endeavour)* (1975, pp. 122-23).

[16] James Matra, *The Anonymous Journal (A Journal of a Voyage Round the World in his Majesty's Ship Endeavour)* (1975, p. 127). The date of taking possession is given as 21 August 1770 and sailing through Torres Strait takes place on 'the next morning', 22 August 1770.

in the west, no precautions were taken to protect women while, in the east, the repeated and determined protection of the women by the men perhaps indicates an unwillingness to trust foreign adult males from other parties.

The differences between the Aborigines of the Endeavour River and those of Botany Bay need further consideration. In the south, it is possible that three separate groups were encountered, while there was known contact only with the Guugu Yimithirr in the north. One factor in particular, however, again draws attention to the development of the canoe. The Aborigines of the north-east of the continent were constructing dugout canoes with outriggers from at least the seventeenth century. While suggestions have been made that the Maori people of New Zealand, or others from distant Pacific Islands, might have visited the east coast of Australia, it is difficult to sustain the argument. The Maoris voyaged in double hulled vessels rather than in those fitted with outriggers. Had they come to New Holland the double hull, perhaps, would have come into use there also.

In many respects Cook and those with him regarded the Guugu Yimithirr people as more technologically advanced than the southerners, despite the minor differences between them. The weapons used by both were much the same, although those in the north might have been more effective. While neither built 'huts' or 'houses' that were structurally sound, which suggests that they were not intended to be permanent residences, it does seem that in the south the Aborigines made constant use of such structures while in the north there is no evidence of their living in them at the time of Cook's visit. The difference in the winter and early spring temperatures possibly accounts for this variation and it may have been the case that, in mid-winter, some use was made of structures in the north.

None of the journal writers remarks on marked physical differences between the two groups so that, essentially, they were regarded as the one people. Both painted their bodies in somewhat the same manner while, in the south, less use was made of bodily scarring. Their teeth were the same, but there was widespread nasal piercing in the north. No comparison can be made between the languages given nothing was learnt at Botany Bay of the local language or languages. In the north, clearing the land by fire was much in evidence and understandable given the proximity of spring and the promise of growth in that season. Clearing by fire in the south with the approach of winter was scarcely to be expected.

While the absence of contact with women was the same, the most notable difference was that, while children were met regularly in the south, there is not a single instance of a child even having been seen in the north, although it was obvious at one camp that the children had been playing there shortly before the arrival of Banks and two other of the ship's crew. This perhaps might be explained by the much longer time gap between the first sightings of the Europeans by the Aborigines at each place. If it can be assumed that a warning had been sent ahead to the people at Botany Bay, it does not appear to have registered negatively among them and first contact was initiated directly by Cook. When he and his men landed they found the people engaged in their normal day-to-day activities in and among their dwellings, as well as fishing close by. In the north the Aborigines do not seem to have had dwelling places on the south side of the river, or at least near to where the *Endeavour* was moored, so that close contact was less likely. Over two weeks passed before first contact was made and, at that, by the Aborigines who came from the north side during which time plans could have been made to hide the women and children. Yet this does not fully explain why no woman, except one elderly lady, was ever seen at a close pass and it is difficult to accept that the women were always occupied gathering seeds and plants in the bush when the Europeans were in the vicinity.

The Aborigines treasured turtles as an item of food and, given the impossibility of carrying them home alive from the islands in frail canoes, it is likely that only the men could partake of them. The Aborigines must have been astonished to see how they were caught in largish numbers by Cook's crew. This occurred once a period of mutual understanding and trust had been arrived at, which makes it more difficult to comprehend why Cook, especially, could not bring himself to share even one turtle with them. Banks's explanation that the turtle was the one thing 'we were the least able to spare them' rings hollow. Banks had referred to them as 'our good friends' before the incident and, even afterwards, he calls them 'our friends'. To share a foodstuff so prized as the turtle would seem to have been a way of demonstrating friendship.

Nonetheless, the remarkable and most pleasing fact is that, despite the short period of hostility, amicable relations were resumed almost immediately after the 'little old man' came in peace to Cook and his men. In the aftermath of this experience the episode of one of the crew straying from his companions, being amicably treated by the Aborigines and assisted to walk in the correct direction back to the *Endeavour* testifies further to the genuine character of a relationship that enriched those involved.

Throughout the whole period of the stay at the Endeavour River, there is no evidence that Cook and his crew acted in any way contrary to the high dictates of civility among fellow human beings. Yet it is impossible to compare the richness of the relations with the people of the Endeavour River to those of a generally sterile and negative nature experienced at Botany Bay. Nonetheless, the Guugu Yimithirr of the Endeavour River area and the people of the *Endeavour* set down a pattern of dignified and precious human relations that could serve as a guidepost in the consciousness of all Australians. This relationship was formed at and about modern day Cooktown, rather than at Botany Bay. Justice and history demand that this fact be recognised and made known.

11

New Guinea to Savu

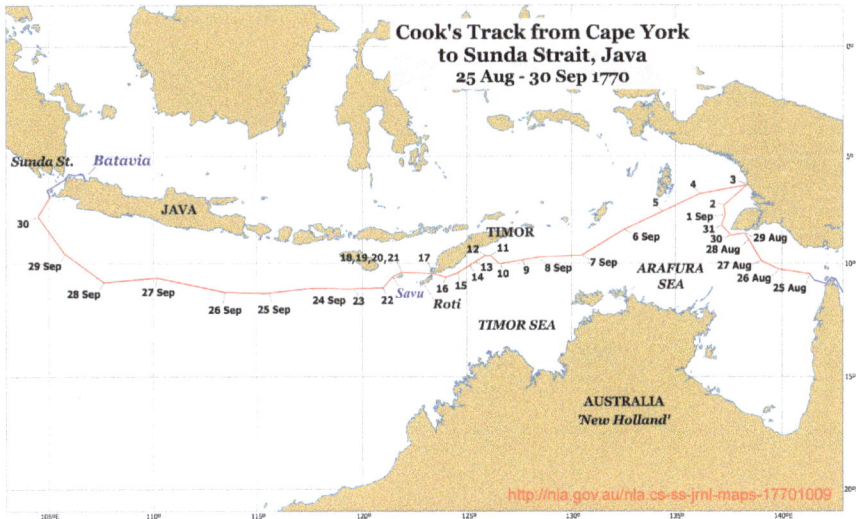

Cook's Track from Cape York
to Sunda Strait, Java
25 Aug - 30 Sep 1770

http://nla.gov.au/nla.cs-ss-jrnl-maps-17701009

Having passed through Torres Strait, Cook intended to sail north-west and thus come upon the south coast of New Guinea, but the quantity of dangerous shoals that he encountered prompted him to sail west until, on 29 August 1770, he came close to the shore in water Banks declared 'as muddy as the River Thames' and smoke indicated that the country was inhabited. A few days later they were on the east coast of New Guinea and Cook, with Banks, Solander and 10 marines, landed at about 10 am. They came across a structure described by Cook as 'a small shade [shed?] or hut' and by Banks as a 'house or shed' that he described: 'It consisted of 4 stakes drove into the ground, 2 being longer than the other two; over these were laid cocoa nut leaves loose but not half enough to cover it.' This indicates that, when Banks spoke of a 'house', he meant a building or structure — even though primitive. He used 'house' or 'hut' for those he saw on the east coast of New Guinea, but 'shed' had not been previously used by either. Cook's 'shade' might be merely a matter of pronunciation rather than spelling.[1]

Very soon after landing they were attacked by a small body of men who 'rushed out of the woods with a hideous shout', and threw spears at them. Cook also said, as did Banks but in different words, that the natives of New Guinea used an odd weapon 'more extraordinary to us ... which caused a flash of fire or smoke'. Small shot was directed at them, they ran away and the landing party, given that they 'could not search the Country with any degree of Safety', returned to the *Endeavour*. Banks enlarged on the matter. Arrived at the decision 'that nothing was to be got here but by force, which would of course be attended with the destruction of many of these poor people, whose territories we had certainly no right to invade either as discoverers or people in real want of provisions; we therefore resolved to go into our boat'. The fact that, once safely aboard, they noticed up to 100 people coming together on the shore made the decision a wise one. Cook decided that they had landed near a place named the Cabo de la Costa de Santa Bonaventura (the Cape of the Coast of Saint Bonaventure). That name was marked on the French charts and the location lay south of Keer Weer, which had been probably named by Jan Carstensz in 1623. Capo (cape) and costa (coast) are the correct spelling in both Spanish and Portuguese, whose navigators had charted New Guinea before the Dutch. Cook decided that 'no new discovery can be expected to be made in these seas, which the Dutch have, I believe, long ago narrowly examined'. Curiously, he concluded that the French maps must 'by some means have been got from the Dutch', while granting that 'the Spaniards and the Dutch have at one time or another circumnavigated the whole of the Island of New Guinea, as the most of the names are in these two languages'. As for the part of the coast he was on, he found the old chart to be 'tolerably good' and thus felt obliged 'to give some credit to all the rest notwithstanding we neither know or by whom or when they were taken'. He also claimed to have always thought that there was no strait between New Guinea and New Holland before he sighted four of the old maps on which it was clearly marked: 'We have now put this wholly out of dispute; but, as I believe, it was known before, tho' not publicly, I claim no other merit than the clearing up of a doubtful point.'[2]

---

[1]   *Cook*, 26, 28, 29 August, 3 September 1770, pp. 404, 405, 408; *Banks*, vol. 2, pp. 141, 145.

[2]   Cook had access to Charles de Brosses, *Histoire des navigations aux terres Australes* (1756) and Robert de Vaugondy, *Carte Générale qui représente Les Mers des Indes, Pacifique, et Atlantique et principalement le Monde Austral divisé en Australasie, Polynésie et Magellanie. Pour servir à L'Histoire des Terres Australes* (1756). De Vaugondy's volume is the first to use the terms Polynesia and Australasia. See also Beaglehole in *Cook*, fn. 1, p. 410; fn. 1, p. 411. For Cook on the land, see his journal for 3 September 1770, pp. 408, 409; *Banks*, pp. 142-43.

Cook need not have so underplayed his achievement. The Dutch had not circumnavigated New Guinea and Tasman, sent expressly to do so, had not been able to pass through Torres Strait from the west, while Cook, though doubtful as to whether it existed, did so from the east even though, in so doing, many difficulties had to be surmounted. The more perplexing aspect of this matter is why the Dutch had not persisted in opening a more convenient passage into the Pacific from the west than that above New Guinea. It is difficult to avoid the conclusion that they had quickly decided New Holland offered no prospect of establishing financially worthy trading connections and thus avoided any further losses by pursuing them. In 1606 Willem Janszoon had sailed into the western end of Torres Strait shortly before Torres did so from the east. He found the lands he saw 'inhabited by savage cruel, black barbarians who slew some of our sailors'. In 1623 Carstensz revisited the Gulf of Carpentaria. To him it was 'the most arid and barren region that could be found anywhere on earth; the inhabitants too, are the most wretched and poorest creatures that I have ever seen in my age and time'. By 1644 the Dutch had made up their minds about the inhabitants of New Holland. The presumption was that they were 'rude, wild, fierce barbarians' in whose presence it was advisable to be well armed because 'barbarians are nowise to be trusted'. There is a huge gulf between this manner of thinking by the Dutch and that clearly expressed by Cook and Banks.[3]

Indeed, when Tasman returned to Holland from his voyage in 1644, he was congratulated by the governor-general and councillors for the fact that the 'vast and hitherto unknown South-land had by Tasman been sailed round in two voyages', which was untrue and left the most important question unanswered. Had Tasman and his companions discovered anything that would make a profit for the Dutch East India Company? The answer was emphatic in its acerbic expectation that Tasman and his men would have been able to explore the inland. The company stated that the seaman

> had found nothing that could be turned to profit, but had only come across naked beach-roving wretches, destitute even of rice, and not possessed of any fruits worth mentioning, miserably poor, and in many places of a very bad disposition ... We are left quite ignorant what the soil of this South-land produces or contains, since the men have done nothing but sail along the coast; he who wants to find out what the land yields, must walk over it in every direction; the voyagers pretend this to have been out of their power, which may to some extent be true.

---

[3] The quotes in this paragraph are taken from the excellent article by John Mulvaney, 'The Australian Aborigines 1606–1929: Opinion and fieldwork', part 1, in *Historical Studies Australia and New Zealand*, vol. 8, no. 30, Nov. 1957, pp. 131-51.

As a result it was decided 'to have everything more closely investigated by more vigilant and courageous persons than had hitherto been employed on this service; for the exploration of unknown regions can by no means be entrusted to the first comer'. So much then for the Dutch explorers, but the same in respect of aspirations for profit could be said of Cook. He also, but with equally and good reason had only sailed 'along the coast'.[4]

Cook also wrote at some length speculating, sensibly, on whether the natives of New Guinea and New Holland 'are or were originally one people, which one might well suppose as these two countries lay so near to each other and the intermediate space filled with islands'. Yet, if there had ever been 'friendly communication' between them, it was odd that coconuts, bread fruit, plantains and such like had never been transplanted to New Holland, where they would have been precious 'for the support of man'. Cook noted that Jacob le Maire had 'given us a vocabulary of words spoken by the people of New Britain which, before Dampier's time was taken to be a part of New Guinea, by which it appears that the people of New Britain speak a very different language from those of New Holland'. Thus, if the people of New Britain and New Guinea were of one origin and spoke the same language, then it follows that the New Hollanders are 'a different people from both'. Parkinson concluded that the New Guineans were not negroes, 'but are much like the natives of New Holland, having shock hair, and being entirely naked'. He also thought that the land was 'very fertile, having a great number of different sorts of trees, which formed very thick woods. The soil is very rich, and produces much larger plants than grow on the islands'.[5]

Before leaving New Guinea, Cook showed his great common sense and humanity when, once on board and having rejected the inclination of some of his officers to send men ashore to cut down trees to obtain coconuts, he wrote:

> … a thing that I think no man living could have justified, for as the natives had attacked us for mere landing without taking any one thing, certainly they would have made a vigorous effort to defend their property, in which case many of them must have been killed, and perhaps some of our own people too, and all of this for 2 or 300 green cocoa nuts, which, when we had got them, would have done us little service; besides nothing but the utmost necessity would have obliged me to have taken this method to come at refreshments.

---

[4] See J.E. Heeres, *Abel Janszoon Tasman's Journal* (2006, p. 118).

[5] *Cook*, 3 September 1770, p. 411; Sydney Parkinson, *Journal of a Voyage to South Seas* (1773, p. 201).

Cook always shared the available food equally among the ship's company, irrespective of rank. On 4 August 1770, while at the Endeavour River, he wrote:

> Whatever refreshments that were got that would bear a division I caused to be equally divided amongst the whole company generally by weight, the meanest person in the ship had an equal share with myself or anyone on board, and this method every commander of a ship on such a voyage as this ought ever to observe.

In any event, and without the coconuts, Cook's crew were happy to be on their way from New Guinea so much so that 'the sick became well and the melancholy looked gay'. Banks explained that most of the crew were stricken with 'nostalgia' because they 'were now pretty far gone with the longing for home'. The exceptions were Cook, Solander and himself who were too busy to be so afflicted.[6]

By 7 September, Cook accepted that some of the charts were wrongly 'laid down' because he expected to sight 'Wessels Isle' stretching out from the coast of New Holland but failed to do so. In fact, his route was at least 160 kilometres from the Wessel Islands, so that the old charts were much in error at this point. To Cook,

> this is not to be wondered at when we consider that not only these islands, but the lands which bound this sea have been discovered and explored by different people and at different times, and compiled and put together by others, perhaps some ages after the first discoveries were made.

It is difficult to judge what he encompassed by 'the lands that bound this sea' but, on one matter, he was clear. He lamented at length the inefficiency of previous navigators, even though they were deprived of the aids to navigation available in his own day, but he came down hard upon the publishers who put out 'rude sketches' as accurate ones and the seamen 'who lay down the line of a coast that they have never seen and put down soundings where they have never sounded'. Disaster had to result from these practises but, even when a modest navigator admitted that his charts were in some measure 'defective', the publishers and sellers would omit his confession 'because they say it hurts the sale of the work'. The consequence was that 'we can hardly tell when we

---

are possessed of a good sea chart until we ourselves have proved it'.[7]

After Matthew Flinders, who was a great navigator in his own right, had circumnavigated the Australian coast in the course of 1802–03, he made a thoughtful and accurate estimate of Cook's earlier contribution:

> This voyage of Captain Cook, whether considered in the extent of his discoveries and the accuracy with which they were traced, or in the labours of his scientific associates, far surpassed all that had gone before. The general plan of the voyage did not, however, permit Captain Cook to enter minutely in the details of every part; and had it been otherwise, the very extent of his discoveries would have rendered it impossible. Thus, some portions of the east coast of Terra Australis were passed in the night, many openings were seen and left unexamined, and the islands and the reefs lying at a distance from the shore, could, generally, be no more than indicated; he reaped the harvest of discovery, but the gleanings of the field remained to be gathered.[8]

Flinders did not claim that Cook was the first 'discoverer' of Australia; merely that what he did 'far surpassed all that had gone before', which seems to imply that Flinders had seen other, less accurate charts than those done by Cook. In fact, Flinders had seen some of the Dieppe charts and he remarked that those charts, at least insofar as the north and north-west coasts were concerned, made 'the coincidence of form ... most striking'.[9]

The voyage continued with a moderate south-east wind, but gradually it lessened and the 'croakers' (prophets of doom) aboard moaned that the western monsoon was about to spring up, which would impede the passage to Batavia. That was the same wind of which Cook, after leaving the Endeavour River, was afraid might prevent their discovery of Torres Strait. Two days later the favourable wind increased slightly 'and left our melancholy ones to search for some new occasion of sorrow'. By this time rations were being maintained reasonably well, remarkably so, given over two years had passed since their departure in August 1768. It was still possible to open a barrel of pork, which was short by only two of the 308 pieces it was expected to contain. Coasting along the south coast of Timor they passed through Roti Strait at the south-west end of Timor and that night, 16 September, they witnessed a remarkable

---

[7] *Cook*, 7 September 1770, p. 413. Beaglehole explained that the Admiralty made no provision for the 'compilation and issue of charts to ships' leaving the matter to the seaman to make them and the masters of vessels to acquire them. Once made, the publication of the charts was left entirely to free enterprise, which engaged too frequently in profit before putting probity as its yardstick and especially by making further additions even when the errors remained uncorrected though well known to be such. See Beaglehole in *Cook*, fn. 4, pp. 413-14.

[8] Matthew Flinders, *A Voyage to Terra Australis* (1814, vol. 1, pp. lxxxii-iii).

[9] Matthew Flinders, *A Voyage to Terra Australis* (1814, vol. 1, pp. lxxxii-iii).

display of aurora borealis that lasted until midnight. Some of his officers strenuously argued that they land at Concordia, the main fort of the Dutch on Timor, for 'refreshments'. Cook refused to do so 'knowing that the Dutch look upon all Europeans with a jealous eye that come among these islands'. In any event they were not so much in need of 'necessities' as to force them to land 'at a place where I might expect to be but indifferently treated'.[10]

The Portuguese, having got as far south as Timor in 1515, had set up a trading post there in 1566 but, in the mid-1600s, they had been defeated by the Dutch who concluded a treaty with the five provinces of Savu in 1756. Savu was about 50 kilometres long and, at Cook's arrival, held roughly 9,000 inhabitants. Among them a German named Johan Christopher Lange, who acted as a kind of governor of the island in the name of the Dutch East India Company and his assistant, born on the island of Portuguese parents, were not of local stock, as was a 'Dutch Indian' who served as schoolmaster. Whatever else he taught it was not Dutch, of which the locals had none. Initially the prospect of obtaining provisions seemed dismal, but things improved once Lange and the local king, or raja, had been suitably refreshed with 'plenty of good liquor' to the point of stupefying drunkenness at dinner aboard the *Endeavour*. Mutton was served at the meal and the king asked for 'an English sheep'. Although only a single sheep remained at this stage it was nonetheless presented to him, with Banks contributing one of his greyhounds, which indicates that some gravity was beginning to be felt about the remaining supplies. Cook was told that the island had an abundance of sheep, buffaloes, hogs and fowl, which resulted in much pointless skirmishing, both verbal and mildly threatening, as to sales, but of no effective consequence. Cook concluded that the governor, but not his assistant henchman, was only out to line his own pockets by charging extortionate prices. It seemed possible, however, that the locals would be happy to trade at reasonable prices provided no spices were involved, the control of which trade was entirely in the hands of the Dutch and jealously guarded to the degree that none of the major islands of spice production sold any. Rather, spices were conveyed in small measures to other islands where they were not grown but from which they were traded. On the next day Cook, with a party, landed again and visited the 'town' which was of Catholic Portuguese origin. Given that the Portuguese had long-since departed, however, the locals had returned to their individual gods and forms of worship described by Lange as 'a most absurd kind of paganism', although high

---

[10]   *Banks*, vol. 2, pp. 147, 148, 149; *Cook*, 16 September 1770, p. 417.

standards of moral behaviour prevailed. The women were chaste, marriage was a lifelong contract, polygamy was prohibited and stealing was unknown, although it seems that an attempt was made to steal an axe from the *Endeavour*. Eventually Cook bought nine buffaloes for a musket each, 30 dozen fowl, six sheep and some hundred of gallons of syrup made from the juice of the palm tree. The buffaloes proved to be disappointing, weighing only an average of 90 kilograms each.[11]

Banks discoursed at great length on the customs of the people and the general conditions of the island but Cook, perhaps imagining that Dutch scholars had studied these matters sufficiently well, wrote much less and always to the point. The great continent lay in close proximity to Savu; so close that in leaving that island Cook decided that the constant swell of the sea from the south was not due to the wind 'but to the sea being so determined by the position of the coast of New Holland'. Furthermore, Savu was dry a good part of the year because of the hot winds that blew from the same quarter. According to Banks all agreed that nonetheless the island of Savu was 'equal in beauty if not excel; anything we had seen even parched as it was by a drought'. Words failed him and he confessed that it 'requires a poetical imagination to describe and a mind not unacquainted with such sights to conceive'. The distance of Savu to Darwin (1,000 kilometres) makes it remarkable that neither Cook nor Banks, both greatly impressed by the richness of Savu and hence Timor in practically every material aspect, made a comparison between New Holland, with its alleged barrenness, and Savu. At Savu, the hills had been cleared and planted under thick groves of palms and coconut trees 'a circumstance seldom seen in any perfection so near the line [Equator]. The sap of the palms was used to make abundant wine that, according to Cook, was a

> very sweet agreeable cooling liquor. Besides the animals mentioned earlier, the people raised horses, asses and goats and grew any manner of fruits, including oranges and mangoes, as well as maize, millet, corn and rice, European herbs such as celery, majoram, fennel and garlic with an abundance of betel nut, tobacco, cotton and indigo.

Dogs, cats, rats, and pigeons also abounded and were eaten except for the rats. Much animal flesh was either exported alive or killed and salted to be sent to the capital, Concordia, or to other islands controlled by the Dutch. In fact at the time that the *Endeavour* was in port at Savu, much meat was

---

[11] *Cook*, 17-20 September, pp. 417-21; *Banks*, vol. 2, pp. 150-77. For a scholarly account of the history and ecology of Savu as well as the early relations between the Portuguese and the Dutch, see James J. Fox, *Out of the Ashes: Destruction and Reconstruction of East Timor* (2003) and *Harvest of the Palm: Ecological Change in Eastern Indonesia* (1977).

being exported to Timor where the Dutch had behaved so badly to the local population that they were in dire need of provisions.

For an undiscovered reason, fish was not eaten except by the 'common or poor people' who were allowed to eat little, if any, meat. Although Cook was informed that Concordia was a free port where ships of any nation could call for supplies and naval stores, he was happy not to have done so because 'King's ships, I am persuaded, would be looked upon as spies'. He went so far as to state that he would 'prefer going to a Portuguese settlement before any of the Dutch' and that 'my falling in with Savu was mere chance and not design'. The women dressed with 'the strictest decency', both sexes wore ornaments, some made of gold, and in the sturdy houses built on stilts 'the loft was appropriated to the women'. Slaves were bought and sold for 'a good, large fat hog, horse etc', but only within the same island and they could not be punished without the approval of the raja. Peace prevailed among the five sections of the island, but the Dutch were often at war with the people of Cupang on Timor, but not it seems with the Portuguese, who still held control of eastern Timor. It was Dutch policy to prevent the islanders learning their neighbours' languages, and even Dutch itself, so as to ensure that they were unable to communicate with each other and thus pose no threat either by force or trade. In general, Banks seems to have been much reserved in respect of the Dutch for their personal qualities rather than for political reasons. In Banks's eyes the Dutch Company and its agents were mere mercenaries plundering the islands for profit and using their men to fight the Timorese because their lives were not 'near so valuable as those of Dutchmen'.[12]

Three days after landing at Savu, sail was set on 22 September for Batavia, confident of good winds based on Lange's assurance that the eastern monsoon would last until December. Before arriving off Java Head on the west end of Java, Cook took possession of 'the Officer's, Petty Officer's and Seamen's Log Books and Journals, at least all that I could find, and enjoined everyone not to divulge where they had been', meaning the places that they had seen and or visited. Banks, having no role in the Royal Navy, was not expected to hand over his journal. Because Green was in the employ of the Crown, although not an officer on the ship, his journal, in which he wrote his last entry on 2 October, was included in Cook's collection. Some grave anxiety was felt because it seemed possible that they had passed the Sunda Strait and thus the

---

[12] Sydney Parkinson, *Journal of a Voyage to South Seas* (1773, p. 204); *Cook*, 21 September 1770, pp. 422, 423, 425, 427; *Banks*, vol. 2, pp. 158–60, 161, 165, 167, 169, 170, 171, 172, 175, 172.

passage to Batavia, which proved to be due to an error in longitude, the first of any consequence on the voyage. Cook knew that 'either our Longitude must be erroneous or the Straits of Sunda must be faultily laid down in all books and charts'. He had made allowance in his reckoning for the 'westerly current' after leaving Savu, which did not eventuate, and he had not been able to take lunar readings. These factors left him out by almost 3° in his reckoning.[13]

Having passed Krakatoa, which was dormant, they were close enough to the shore of Java to send a crew for fruits for Tupia, who was 'very ill', and grass for the remaining buffaloes. The returns were meagre indeed. They now had to pass through Sunda Strait between Java and Sumatra and come up to Batavia on the north-eastern side of Java. The passage, though only about 190 kilometres in length, was notoriously difficult. Shortly they saw an anchored Dutch vessel to which Cook sent Hicks to get news from home. There were two ships, both 'Dutch East India men' from Batavia, and Banks gave his version of the news Hicks brought back. England was in turmoil with people running up and down the London streets crying 'Down with King George, King Wilkes for ever'. The Americans were likewise disturbed and refusing to pay taxes while the Poles and Russians were about to go to war. Hicks also brought back some London newspapers, which were enthusiastically received even though much outdated. Cook ignored trifles based on possible rumours and concentrated on more pressing matters, although he was delighted to learn that the *Swallow* under Philip Carteret had been at Batavia two years previously.[14]

---

[13]   *Banks*, vol. 2, pp. 177, 178, 179; *Cook*, 30 September, 1, 2 October, pp. 426, 427.
[14]   *Cook*, 1, 2, 3 October 1770, pp. 427, 428; *Banks*, vol. 2, pp. 179–80.

12

Fatal Batavia

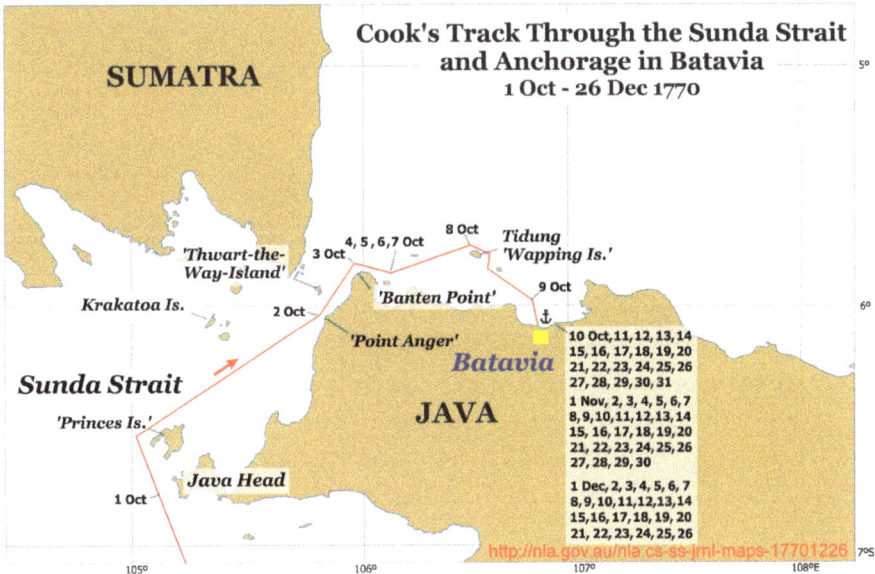

Cook's Track Through the Sunda Strait and Anchorage in Batavia
1 Oct - 26 Dec 1770

Maintaining his suspicion of the Dutch, Cook was almost sure that a smallish Dutch packet, 'stationed here' to carry Dutch mail to Batavia, was in fact engaged in examining 'all ships that pass and repass these Straits'. He meant the Sunda Strait and he was not surprised when the packet followed the *Endeavour* but bore away until, on the following afternoon of 4 October, its captain came aboard anxious to sell various foodstuffs, but at exorbitant prices. The captain also produced a set of questions about the *Endeavour* and its personnel. Cook sent Hicks, 'as I would not see him myself', with instructions to write down the name of the *Endeavour* and put down 'from Europe' in answer to where they came from. The captain 'expressed some surprise', as indeed he might, given the direction from which the *Endeavour* had arrived, but said that 'we might write down what we pleased' as it was only intended to use it to give information to other English ships that might pass through. This was followed up by a visit from a Dutch officer who came aboard from a prau with a document signed by the governor's secretary. It contained nine questions. Cook answered number one, 'To what nation the ship belongs?' and number four, 'Where unto designed to go?'. The officer responded in the manner of the previous visitor and the episode closed without recriminations, although Cook was certain that serious matters were afoot given that the papers were to be delivered immediately to the governor and his council at Batavia. Nevertheless he sailed on in at times tempestuous waters, buying from a small boat three turtles weighing in all 66 kilograms for a dollar, and 26 pumpkins, for which the owner demanded 'we cut a dollar and give him a part' but finally accepted a Portuguese peça 'shining and well coined'. No indication was ever given in the journals as to the origin of the various forms of currency available to Cook although, apart from the Spanish dollars that were in widespread use, it is unlikely that lesser used currencies were aboard at the outset of the voyage.[1]

Cook's entry for the afternoon of 11 October records that the *Endeavour* 'anchored in Batavia Road' although, inexplicably, Banks dated it the ninth and Parkinson the tenth. Parkinson counted the number of large ships in the road as 16, three of which were British. A boat came alongside with a Dutch officer and crew and asked 'who we were and immediately returned' to the town. Banks remarked that the officer and crew 'were almost as Spectres, no good omen of the healthiness of the country we were arrived at; our people however who truly might be called rosy and plump, for we had not a sick man among us, jeered and flouted much at their brother sea men's white faces'. In light of the appalling loss of life suffered on the *Endeavour* shortly afterwards, these remarks are especially poignant. Hicks was despatched to inform the governor of their arrival 'who told him he should be glad to see Captain Cook'. Hicks returned laden down with fruit and 'a bundle of London newspapers, which were very acceptable presents' even though much out of date. In the meantime the ship's carpenter gave Cook a grave account of the state of the vessel, which clearly necessitated heaving her down and repairing as much as possible of her bottom at Batavia before attempting to return home.[2]

Promptly on the next day, the governor received Cook 'very politely' and told him that he would be given all the help that he needed. That night a wild electrical storm struck vessels in the harbour and a bolt of lightning all but wrecked a Dutch vessel with an iron spindle on its main mast and lying

---

[1]   *Cook*, 2, 3, 4, 5 October 1770, pp. 427, 428, 429, 430; *Banks*, vol. 2, pp. 179-80, 181.
[2]   *Cook*, 11 October 1770, pp. 422-23; Sydney Parkinson, *Journal of a Voyage to South Seas* (1773, p. 214); *Banks*, vol. 2, p. 184.

adjacent to the *Endeavour*. Cook was grateful that an 'electrical chain' had been set up on his ship before sailing from home, which saved his vessel when it was also struck. He was now convinced that every ship ought to have a similar device and he also gave sensible advice to the Dutch that they should warn their seamen never to have iron spindles on their masts. He then met with the governor and council by whom he was officially informed he would 'have everything that he wanted'. Although he refrained from remarking upon it, the behaviour of both the governor and his council was such that it must have gone far to dispel any negative ideas he had entertained previously. The warmth of their welcome combined with their tolerant, humane and generous behaviour to override the previous impressions engendered by the lesser individuals encountered in the islands whose semi-ignorant and devious use of authority was a simple reflection of their utter dependence on that of the Dutch East India Company, whose rule was final.[3]

A Dutch vessel sailed for Holland on 14 October carrying a brief letter to the secretary of the Admiralty notifying him of their arrival at Batavia. In it, Cook explained that because his ship was 'leaky' he was obliged to 'heave her down at this place' and that he already had leave to do so. He did not explain his main and gravest problem. In short, though he had sufficient funds to pay for 'a few naval stores' and for daily provisions while in port, as well as on the voyage home, he lacked the larger sum needed to pay for the repair of the *Endeavour*, which was increased by the refusal of the authorities to allow any but local labour to engage in same. Cook was convinced that his own men could have done this as efficiently as any other artisans, but he was in no position to press the point. His request to the governor 'to be supplied with such sum or sums of money as he may want towards such ends' was granted, which indicates the trust reposed by the Dutch in both the integrity of the British Government and its ability to honour debts promptly.[4]

With considerable justification, Cook was proud of the condition of his men and told his superiors that, 'upon our arrival here I had not one man upon the sick list'. What lay ahead eluded him. Batavia, after the burning down of Djakarta in 1619 by the Dutch, was laid out on canals with the houses closely aligned along them in the manner of Holland. The city's situation on a swamp, which was caused by an earthquake, proved to be an ideal breeding ground for mosquitoes, as well as a cesspit due to the lack of sanitation. This led to constant outbreaks of malaria from the mosquitoes and dysentery from the

---

[3]   *Cook*, 12 October 1770, p. 433.
[4]   *Cook*, 14, 16, 23 October, pp. 433, 434, 435; Beaglehole in *Cook*, fn. 1, p. 433; Cook to Stephens, in *Cook*, 14 October 1770, p. 499.

water, which caused up to 50,000 deaths annually. Banks stated that 'everyone on shore and many on board were ill ... occasioned no doubt by the lowness of the country and the numberless dirty canals which intersected the town in all directions'. Cook summed up the tragedy later in his letter to his mentor and friend, John Walker, who had sent him to sea on his first voyage in 1747. Something of the religion of his master came through in his letter when he spoke for only the third time of the possible influence of a power beyond his control. He wrote:

> We arrived at Batavia in October all in good health and high spirits ... [and] we thought all our hardships at an end, but Providence thought proper to order it otherwise ... [and] we contracted sicknesses that here and on our passage to the Cape of Good Hope carried off above thirty of my people.

Seven were lost at Batavia, 24 more between there and the Cape of Good Hope as well as others at the Cape itself. Hicks died on the last section of the voyage to home. Tupia and his servant Tiata died at Batavia, bewailing their miserable fate, while, among the others, were many of those most needed on the ship including Robert Molyneux, the master; William Monkhouse, the surgeon; John Thompson, the carpenter; John Satterly, the one-handed cook; Charles Green, the astronomer; Sydney Parkinson, the botanical artist; Herman Spöring, naturalist; and John Gathrey, the boatswain. The tailor, barber, butcher and poulterer all perished. Banks went down badly ill, Solander came close to death and, although he did not mention it in his journal, 'the Captain also was taken ill on board' before departure. He, like many of the others, was stricken down by the same ailment called 'flux' by him and 'intermittents' by Banks, which referred to dysentery, the continuation of which was probably caused by drinking the water taken aboard at Batavia. The overall effect of disease reduced the number able to work to about 20, on some days less. To replace the dead, 19 men were taken on at Batavia and 10 more at the Cape of Good Hope. Cook gave his final account at sea two weeks after leaving Batavia:

> In the course of this 24 hours we have had four men died of the flux ... A melancholy proof of the situation we are at present in, having hardly well men enough to tend the sails and look after the sick, many of the latter are so ill that we have not the least hopes of their recovery.[5]

On 24 October Cook said that he 'went up to Town in order to put on board the first Dutch ship that sails, a packet for the Admiralty containing

5   *Cook*, 15 November 1770, p. 434; 31 January 1771, p. 448; and Cook to Walker, 13 September 1771, in *Cook*, p. 509; *Banks*, vol. 2, pp. 187-88, 192; Ray Parkin, *H.M. Bark Endeavour: Her Place in Australian History* (2006, pp. 96-98).

a copy of my Journal, a chart of the South Sea, another of New Zealand, and one of the East Coast of New Holland'. The copy of his journal was done for Cook, often in a careless manner, by his clerk, Richard Orton. It ends on 23 October and is signed 'James Cook' in his own hand. No mention is made of also sending aboard the *Kronenburg*, which was about to sail immediately to the Cape of Good Hope, the journals that he had collected from others on his ship perhaps because, prudently, he thought he had better have a read of them before submitting them to the Admiralty. He included another letter to Philip Stephen at the Admiralty giving a brief account of his voyage in which 'I have with undisguised truth and without gloss inserted the whole transactions of the voyage'. He was confident that his charts laid down longitude as accurately as was then possible and he warmly acknowledged the unfailing assistance of the astronomer, Green, in that work. Unstintingly he praised his officers and crew who 'have gone through the fatigues and dangers of the whole voyage with that cheerfulness and alertness that will always do honour to British seamen'. With admirable modesty he said that 'Altho the discoveries made in this voyage are not great, yet I flatter myself that they are such as may merit the attention of their Lordships'. Finally he remarked that 'altho I have failed in discovering the so much talked of southern continent (which perhaps does not exist) and which I myself had much at heart, yet I am confident that no part of the failure of such discovery can be laid to my charge'. In his last paragraph he added a somewhat strange sentence: 'Had we been so fortunate not to have run ashore [on the coral], much more would have been done in the latter part of the voyage than what was'. He might have been referring to the fact that his chart lacked a section of the coast that, being forced to sail well out to sea, he was unable to achieve. He might also have been referring to his previously stated hope of reaching the islands discovered by Quiros, for whose seamanship he had much admiration. Apart from these possibilities it is unlikely that he could have done 'much more' even had the *Endeavour* been in first-rate condition.[6]

As to his reference to the search for the southern continent, perhaps Cook was subtly suggesting that no one would ever find it because it didn't exist. Nevertheless he was slightly disarming when he alleged that he had the search 'much at heart'. Surely he meant no more than that he had obeyed his orders and at least made a genuine attempt to prove either the impossible or at least the highly unprovable. Thus he had no difficulty in claiming that

---

6   *Cook*, 24, 25 October 1771, pp. 435, 436; Cook to Stephens, from Onrust, near Batavia, 23 October 1770, in *Cook*, pp. 499-501.

'this voyage will be found as complete as any before made to the South Seas on the same account', although the original words 'this voyage will be thought as great and as complete as any before made to the South Seas' were amended, or toned down in the final version, possibly at the suggestion of the Admiralty. It is more likely, however, that Cook, given his reticence about his own achievements, did so unprompted.[7]

A huge question, however, remains unanswered. Why did Cook omit making detailed reference to his charting of the east coast, as well as stressing the fact that, in his estimation, he had cleared up the doubtful point of the existence of Torres Strait? Indeed in writing to Walker later, and with greater freedom, he claimed that he had 'got into the India sea by a passage entirely new', which was a large and unfounded claim. Yet, even before Cook's charting of the east coast, it was already clear that New Holland was huge and Cook himself was prepared to concede that, 'if New Holland can be called an Island it is by far the greatest in the known world', while admitting that he knew nothing of its inland. Why, however, was this vast territory not accepted as the still sought-after great southern continent? The answer must be that it had not lived up to the expectations held of it as being a place inhabited by welcoming and engaging people, rich in gold and silver and all manner of other products, thus holding out prospects to those who exploited it of an economic future perhaps unequalled in history. Dampier and the Dutch had put those hopes at an end and the ardent money men of the Dutch East India Company were confirmed in their rejection of New Holland, which Cook, by his own experience, could add nothing to alter. As Tasman had found in respect of Van Diemen's Land, Cook could scarcely expect any applause for charting its remaining coast or claiming access to the Pacific through a strait. In short, nothing Cook had done would enhance New Holland one iota in the judgement of the men in London, or elsewhere. It is scarcely to be wondered at that the high authorities who ruled the seas waited for 15 years before agreeing on a proposal to make something of their ownership of eastern New Holland, and were drawn to acquiesce only when a prison was mooted.[8]

The repair of the *Endeavour* took only five days, although it was painfully obvious that the ship had been more seriously damaged on the reef than anyone had imagined to be the case, including Cook who said, 'and yet in this condition we had sailed some hundreds of leagues in as dangerous a navigation as in any part of the world, happy in being ignorant of the continual danger

---

[7]   Cook to Stephens in *Cook*, 23 October 1771, p. 501.
[8]   Cook to Walker, in *Cook*, 13 September 1771, pp. 508-09.

we were in'. As he keenly watched the local workmen, including some slaves, undertake the needed repairs he admitted that his own crew of invalids could never have managed to undertake the task given that more than 40 were sick and the rest were in 'a weakly condition', except for the 70-to-80-year-old sail maker who was 'generally more or less drunk each day', which clearly accounted for his health given that he did not need to drink the local water.[9]

It would be unworthy not to recognise the great captain and his valiant crew without including Cook's last words on men who sent others to sea in safety. They so admirably substantiate his thorough sense of his own nationality, his generous recognition of the expertise of the Dutch and his consummate common sense:

> In justice to the officers and workmen of this yard, I must say that I do not believe that there is a Marine Yard in the world where work is done with more alertness than here, or where there are better conveniences for heaving ships down both in point of safety and dispatch. Here they heave down by two masts, which is not now practised by the English. But I hold it to be much safer and more expeditious than by heaving down by one mast; a man must be not only bigoted to his own customs, but in some measure divested of reason, that will not allow this, after seeing with how much ease and safety the Dutch at Onrust heave down their largest ships.[10]

In those same days, Banks recorded that 'the Captain also was taken ill on board' without explaining the nature of his illness. Cook never mentioned it, or remarked on its gravity. Seemingly he recovered rapidly, which led Beaglehole to conclude that, like Banks, he suffered from malaria rather than dysentery because 'the full force of dysentery was only felt after the ship had left Batavia'. The preparations for departure went on daily from 17 November until 24 December, during which provisions were taken aboard, as well as about 45,000 litres of fresh water brought from Batavia to Onrust. This explains the dysentery experienced fatefully by so many on the voyage to the cape. The official of the Dutch company responsible for the water, and who charged an exorbitant price for it, 'takes care to tell you that the water is very good and will keep sweet at sea, whereas everybody else tells you that it is not so'. This prompted Cook to advise his potential seagoing readers not to put in at Batavia unless bound by necessity to do so and to pause there for the briefest possible time because it was the source of the 'death of more Europeans than any other place upon the Globe'. He explained that all the Dutch captains to

---

[9]   *Cook*, 9, 26 December 1770, pp. 437-38, 441.
[10]   *Cook*, 14 November 1770, pp. 438.

whom he had spoken said that, with only seven deaths (Beaglehole counts six and Banks eight), 'we had been very lucky and wondered that we had not lost half our people in that time'.[11]

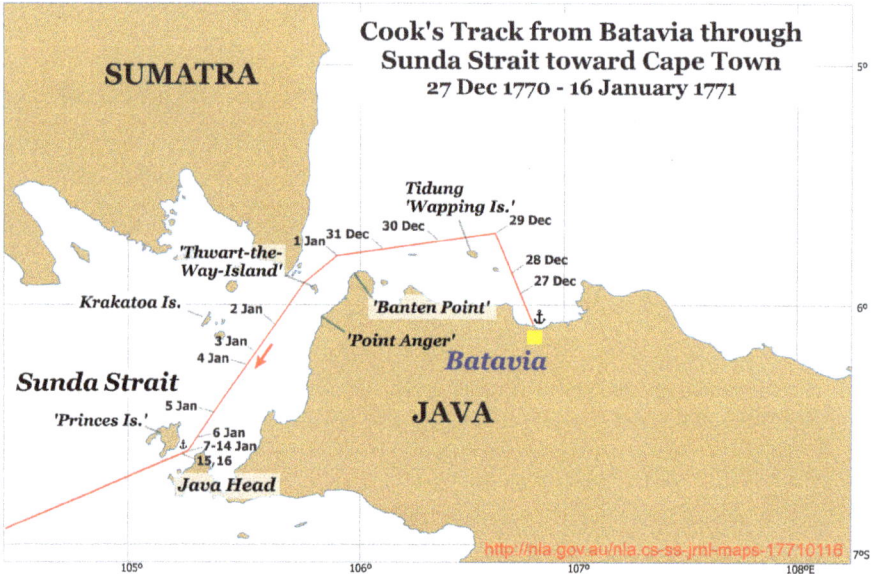

Cook's Track from Batavia through Sunda Strait toward Cape Town
27 Dec 1770 - 16 January 1771

SUMATRA

Tidung
'Wapping Is.'
30 Dec   29 Dec
1 Jan 31 Dec
'Thwart-the-
Way-Island'   28 Dec
                           27 Dec
Krakatoa Is.   2 Jan   'Banten Point'
          3 Jan   'Point Anger'
          4 Jan   *Batavia*
Sunda Strait
          5 Jan   JAVA
'Princes Is.'
          6 Jan
          7-14 Jan
          15,16
Java Head

http://nla.gov.au/nla.cs-ss-jrnl-maps-17710116

Christmas Day was set down for departure and, unlike on previous occasions, seems not to have been celebrated or even mentioned by Cook and Banks. One happy note was struck by the recovery of Solander. His life had been despaired of, but he survived due to the ministration of Doctor Jaggi, a local physician, to whom much praise was due because 'at this juncture especially [it] was indefatigable'. Cook was particularly moved by the death of Tupia. He put it down to the almost total lack of a vegetable diet, to which the islander had been accustomed throughout his life, and described him as 'a shrewd, sensible, ingenious man, but proud and obstinate'. Poor Tupia might well have vexed his Captain by refusing to eat some of the vegetables put before him because Cook said that his obstinacy 'tended much to promote the diseases which put a period to his life'.[12]

---

[11] *Banks*, pp. 191-93, 232; Beaglehole in *Banks*, vol. 2, fn. 1, pp. 232; and Beaglehole in *Cook*, fn. 3, pp. 441; *Cook*, 17-24, 26 December 1770, pp. 435-40, 443-44.

[12] Banks, pp. 193, 194, 232; Cook, 25, 26 December 1770, pp. 440, 441, 442.

13

Cape Town and Home

With all in readiness, the *Endeavour* put to sea on 26 December 1770. In Cook's eyes the human tragedies undergone at Batavia could never be erased from memory, compounded as they were by the deaths that were still to follow and directly connected by the weeks they had spent there. But the main objective had been achieved. The *Endeavour* was again seaworthy and, after a lengthy absence, her home port was the objective.

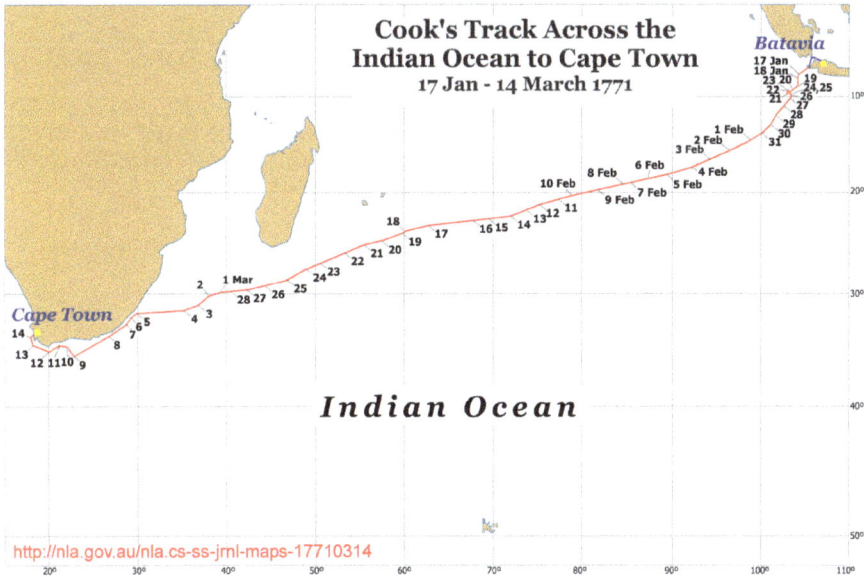

Cook's Track Across the Indian Ocean to Cape Town
17 Jan - 14 March 1771

Batavia

Cape Town

Indian Ocean

A brief landing was made at Prince's Island off the western end of Java on 6 January 1771 where water and wood, as well as supplies of turtles, monkeys, fowls, fish, two deer, vegetables and an assortment of fruit, were available and paid for with Spanish dollars. Illness on board was daily more prevalent but the availability of meat, especially, was treasured because, as Cook explained, it 'was the only salt meat' they had eaten since Savu about four months earlier. Apart from more deaths, which gradually lessened in number, the voyage to Cape Town was uneventful and the *Endeavour* was docked there by 15 March. The Dutch settlement there, as at Batavia, was ruled by a governor and council and was independent of Batavia. Cook duly waited upon the governor who promised to give him all the help 'that the place afforded', which, in Cook's estimate, was firstly lodgings for the sick, but Cook had to find them. He had already given thought to the cause of dysentery and, after eliminating Prince's Island, hesitantly decided that the water taken aboard at Batavia had to bear the blame. He also engaged in, for him, a strange disquisition on the likelihood that the dangers to which the ship and its crew had been subjected would be both exaggerated and enlarged upon 'with many additional hardships we never experienced' by men who tend towards extreme flights of fancy, with the result that 'posterity are taught to look upon these voyages as hazardous to the highest degree'. Surely it must have crossed his mind that the dangers to which both his men and his ship had been exposed on the voyage were of sufficient gravity as to be termed perilous.[1]

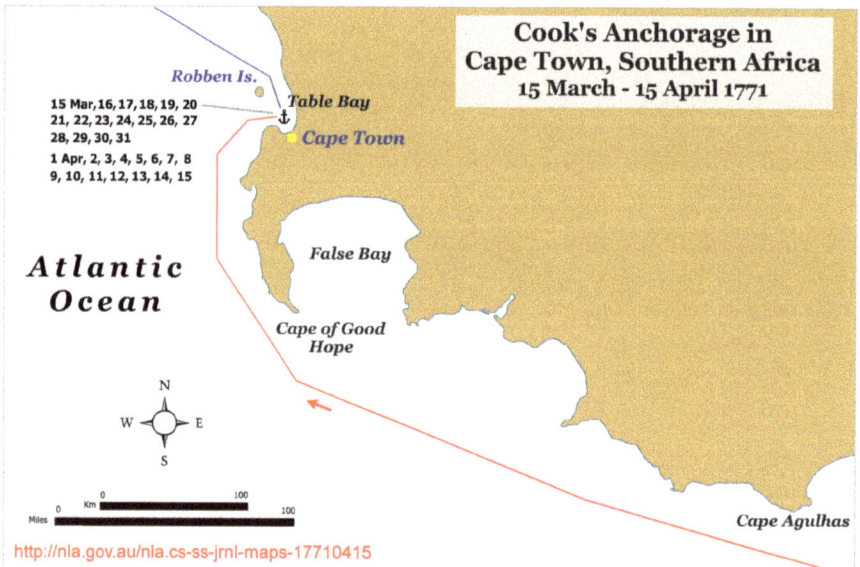

Cook's Anchorage in Cape Town, Southern Africa 15 March - 15 April 1771

Robben Is.

15 Mar, 16, 17, 18, 19, 20
21, 22, 23, 24, 25, 26, 27
28, 29, 30, 31
1 Apr, 2, 3, 4, 5, 6, 7, 8
9, 10, 11, 12, 13, 14, 15

Table Bay

Cape Town

Atlantic Ocean

False Bay

Cape of Good Hope

N
W E
S

0   Km   100
0
Miles   100

Cape Agulhas

http://nla.gov.au/nla.cs-ss-jrnl-maps-17710415

After three more deaths at the cape, the *Endeavour* set out on the home run on 15 April 1771, with a full complement of crew that had been brought up to normal levels by local recruits. On the following day, Robert Molyneux, the master of the ship, died. To Cook he was 'a young man of good parts but had unfortunately given himself up to extravagancy and intemperance'. On 26 May, the last to die was the young officer who had been the first to sight the coast of New Holland, Lieutenant Zachary Hicks. He died from

---

[1] *Cook*, 6, 7, 31 January; 15, 20 March 1771, pp. 445, 446, 448, 457, 458, 459, 460, 461; *Banks*, pp. 233-41, 243.

consumption, an ailment that had afflicted him for some years 'so that it may be said that he has been dying ever since'. Despite these vicissitudes and the great difficulty of manning his ship, Cook found time to write a description of Cape Town and its inhabitants, though not as fully as Banks did. He judged the cape itself harshly and, oddly, given what he knew of New Holland. He said 'no country we have seen this voyage affords so barren a prospect', which was especially so in respect of agriculture given that the soil was sandy and unproductive while the hills were completely barren of trees, which meant that timber had to brought from Batavia. Nonetheless the Dutch used 'every inch of ground that will bear cultivation' to plant vineyards, orchids and kitchen gardens that produced a wide variety of food. Cook was particularly struck by the fact that the Dutch were also insistent that 'they never disturb the original natives but always leave them in peaceable possession of whatever lands they may have approbated for their own use'. This meant that the new settlers rarely found themselves in conflict with the local population, who frequently became servants, 'mix among them and are useful members to society'. Moreover the townspeople were 'extremely civil and polite', which was appropriate given that the 'whole town may be considered as one great inn fitted up for the reception of all comers and goers'. Provisions were taken aboard costing £921 0s 4p and included 4,500 kilograms of bread while 60 pairs of trousers for £10 5s were a separate item.[2]

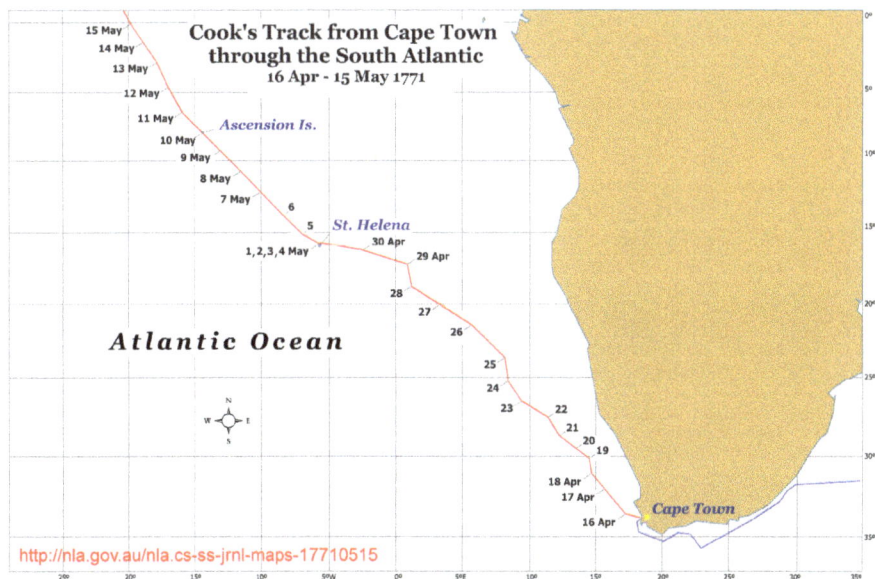

Cook's Track from Cape Town
through the South Atlantic
16 Apr - 15 May 1771

http://nla.gov.au/nla.cs-ss-jrnl-maps-17710515

---

2   *Cook*, 15, 16 April; 26 May 1771, pp. 463-66, 471.

The last port of call was at St Helena, where they met a small English convoy led by HMS *Portland* together with HMS *Swallow* and a dozen vessels of the East India Company. Cook decided to accompany them for the remainder of the voyage and he prudently refrained from commenting on St Helena, which was controlled by the East India Company and was therefore in English hands. Banks could well have been still suffering from the aftermath of his illness because his 4,000-word treatise on St Helena bordered on vilification of his own countrymen. Despite the generally favourable soil and climate of the small island, to the shame of the English inhabitants, its pastures and gardens were 'almost totally neglected' and what was grown fell into the hands of the 'greater people' and the East India Company's captains. This prompted Banks to assert that were 'the Cape now in the hands of the English it would be a desert, as St Helena in the hands of the Dutch would as infallibly become a paradise'. He was as much appalled at the presence of 'very numerous' slaves drawn from 'most parts of the world' as he was at the 'wanton cruelty … exercised by my countrymen over these unfortunate people than even their neighbours the Dutch, famed for inhumanity, are guilty of'. His final comment was, 'One rule however they strictly observe which is never to punish when ships are there'. Given his loyalty to the Empire and its citizens, Beaglehole passed over the matter with 'Banks as usual explored, botanised and conversed', while avoiding any comment on the terminology in which Banks had conversed.[3]

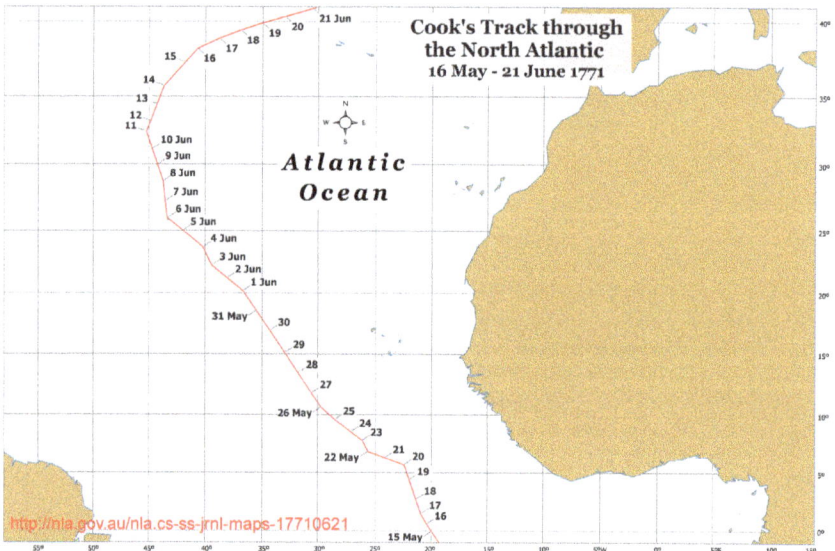

---

[3]   *Cook*, 1-4 May 1771; *Banks*, pp. 263-70.

After Cook's departure in 1772 on his second voyage he was unfortunate in that John Hawkesworth's account of his first voyage had begun its course of wide circulation. Hawkesworth used not only Cook, but extracts from Banks, and other explorers of the period including John Byron and Samuel Wallis of the *Dolphin* and Philip Carteret of the *Swallow*, in writing his book. He also adopted the first-person form so that much of the book seemed to be Cook's own work. The final production was an extraordinary mismatch of the authentic texts combined with frequently absurd flourishes by Hawkesworth, but it had wide popular acclaim. Cook was unaware of this fiasco until he read Hawkesworth while he was at the Cape on the last section of his voyage home in 1775 and found it 'mortifying'. He said that 'I never had the perusal of the Manuscript nor did I ever hear the whole of it read in the mode it was written, notwithstanding what Dr Hawkesworth has said to the Contrary in the Introduction', which seems to indicate that, in the estimation of the Admiralty, Cook was a minor player on their imperial stage. But the book had already circulated among the English at St Helena who, understandably, took Banks's accusations as being made by Cook and they were quick to make their disapproval known. They avoided any refutation of their laziness and neglect of the land, but they took care to set aright their cruelty to slaves, whom they treated with kindness while Cook was among them and he remarked generously on that fact. Nonetheless they were determined to prove that he was mistaken when he, or strictly speaking Banks, had accused them of lacking wheeled vehicles. They parked their carriages 'outside his lodgings day by day to make their point'.[4]

Near Ascension Island, Cook decided that the *Portland* would be likely to arrive home earlier than the *Endeavour*. Thus he made contact and, for delivery to the Admiralty, he gave to its captain 'the Officers' Journals and Charts as I think will give most insight into the voyage, having not a copy of my own ready'. In the event the *Portland* only made home three days earlier than the *Endeavour*. On 19 June a whaling vessel was sighted which proved to be from Rhode Island. Its captain gave the welcome news that peace was restored in Europe and that the disputes with America 'were made up', which he proved by saying that even the 'coat on his back had been made in Old England', thereby making it plain that the American ban on British imports had been lifted. Banks put a light touch on the matter asserting that

---

[4] John Hawkesworth, *An Account of the Voyages Undertaken by the Order of His Present Majesty for Making Discoveries in the Southern Hemisphere: And Successively Performed by Commodore Byron, Captain Wallis, Captain Carteret, and Captain Cook, in the Dolphin, the Swallow and the Endeavour* (1773); Beaglehole, *The Life of Captain James Cook* (1974, p. 268); Nicholas Thomas, *Cook: The Extraordinary Voyages of Captain James Cook* (2003, p. 256).

the Americans said 'King George … had behaved very ill for some time but they had brought him to terms at last'.[5]

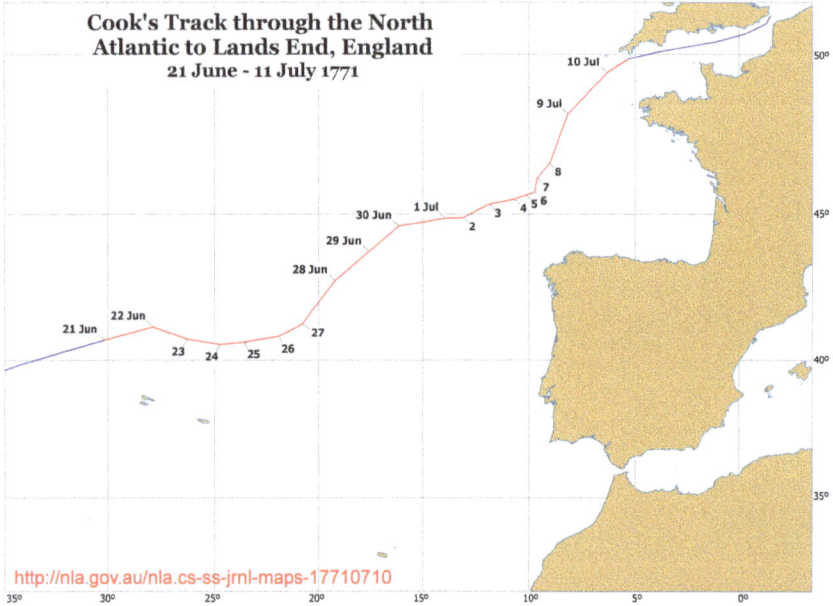

Cook's Track through the North Atlantic to Lands End, England
21 June - 11 July 1771

http://nla.gov.au/nla.cs-ss-jrnl-maps-17710710

In late June the weather turned bad with foul winds, rain and squalls that split sails while the main topmast was 'sprung in the cap'. Cook lamented that 'our rigging and sails are now so bad that something or other is giving way every day'. On 7 July they met a vessel from London and were informed that 'no accounts had been received in England from us and that wagers were held that we were lost', which indicated to Cook that the letters he had sent to the Admiralty from Batavia with the Dutch vessels eight months previously had not been delivered. In the meantime Banks was mourning the loss of his 'Bitch Lady' that, although there was no discernible cause, he found dead in his cabin. On the other hand, the imperturbable and veteran ocean-going goat survived the voyage and was put out into retirement; Dr Johnson was moved to write an amiable, if absurdly grandiose, epigram in Latin in her honour.[6]

Writing on 10 July 1771, Banks said, 'This morning the land was discovered by Nick, the same boy who first saw New Zealand: it proved to be the Lizard'. On the next day Cook recorded that a fresh gale had sprung

5   *Cook*, 10 May, 19 June 1771, pp. 469, 474; *Banks*, p. 274.
6   *Cook*, 22 June, 7 July 1771, pp. 474-75, 476; *Banks*, p. 274. For the epigram, see Johnson in Alan Villiers, *Captain Cook, The Seaman's Seaman: A Study of the Great Discoverer* (1967, p. 188).

up so that they were able to 'run briskly up the Channel … and at noon we were abreast of Dover'. Two days later Cook stood fast by his nautical date, which gave him 13 July, when for Banks it was but 12 July. With his reputation vastly enhanced as a man of the sea beyond compare, James Cook simply declared, 'At three o'clock in the PM anchored in the Downs, and soon after I landed in order to repair to London'.[7]

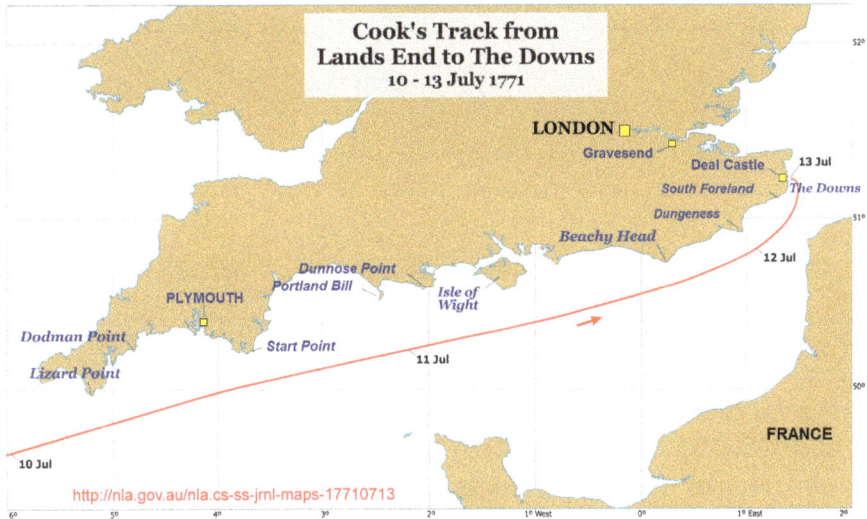

Nevertheless, true to the tradition of the Royal Navy, Cook had to report on the human complement aboard the *Endeavour* who were numbered 88 and of whom 19 were sick. He was not called upon to record that, of the 94 aboard on 26 August 1768 when she sailed from Plymouth, only 54 survived the voyage, which had lasted a few weeks less than three years. He summed up the condition of his vessel as 'foul', which meant little more than that it needed another careening. The remaining provisions were meagre, and flour, suet, oil, vinegar and beer had all run out. In making this report and being already in port he reverted to civil time and dated the day of his arrival as 12 July. Among the various 'curiosities' he had collected he numbered a 'bundle of New Holland fish gigs' that, together with other unremarkable objects from the Society Islands and New Zealand, he passed into the care of Secretary Stephen 'to dispose of as you think proper'.[8]

In that manner, Cook's relationship with the valiant *Endeavour* ceased

---

[7] *Banks*, p. 275; *Cook*, 11, 12, 13 July, p. 477.

[8] Cook's report, 12 July 1711, pp. 478-79; Cook to Stephens from his home at Mile End, London, 13 August 1771 in *Historical Records of New South Wales*, vol. 1, pt 1 (1893, pp. 342-43).

and it is not recorded whether he felt any regret at its passing. Unsung and forgotten the vessel rapidly passed into oblivion, although she was cleansed and refitted immediately to carry stores for the next three years to the Falkland Islands. Renamed the *Lord Sandwich*, she came into private hands but was used as a troop transport in the American War of Independence. Regarded in 1788 as having no further practical use, at Newport, Rhode Island, she was scuttled with other similar vessels to serve as a blockade of the bay. She was called back into history when, in 1989, the space shuttle *Endeavour* was named in her honour. A worthy replica, based mainly in Sydney Harbour, still sails the high seas under her name.

Banks and, to a lesser degree, Solander, were hailed as the heroes of the voyage far and wide, but especially in the press in which one newspaper helped coalesce public opinion by referring briefly to 'Lieutenant Cook of the Royal Navy, who sailed around the Globe with Messrs Solander, Banks etc'. The voyage itself was generally recounted by all the press as if Cook had been a kind of supernumerary attending to the practical arrangements of transporting the heroes from one victory to the next. They were lauded as the discoverers of about 40 islands and, more worthily and truthfully, as the gatherers of more than a 1,000 species of unknown plants and 17,000 others that had never been seen in Britain. One paper only, the London *Evening Post* of 29 August 1771, mentioned New Holland in printing an anonymous letter from 'a gentleman on board the *Endeavour*'. In part the letter is ridiculous remarking that. 'Upon this barbarous shore' the 'savages … are a warlike, stout people, ever jealous of our encroachments; nor would they suffer us to land without various attacks'. Perhaps the most pertinent remark, however, which must have dampened the enthusiasm of financial interests in London, the heartland of mercantile capital, was in the *Public Advertiser* of 2 August 1771: 'It is observable, that in all the Ports and Islands … in the South Seas, there was not the least appearance of gold or silver ores to be discovered.' Nevertheless Banks was presented to George III and the 'Farmer King', aged only 33 and who owned thousands of farms, immediately warmed to him, then 28 whose farms ran to only 200. In this amiably bucolic atmosphere they were able to engage in a later conference at which Banks and Solander explained their botanical deeds to His Majesty and met him subsequently several times to show him specimens and explain their nature. Oxford University duly gave them honorary doctorates of civil law, and the great master of botany, Carl Linnaeus, rejoiced at it all from Uppsala. He thought that a statue greater than the pyramids should be raised in honour of the 'immortal Banks' or, failing that, at least he should be remembered by changing the name of New South Wales to Banksia. Banks's betrothed, Miss Harriet Blosset, was unlikely to have been impressed by these extravagances, nor perhaps even by the £5,000 he offered in exchange for their broken engagement after they had met on his return and he had told her that 'he was of too volatile a temper to marry'. Throughout his life Sir Joseph Banks maintained a benevolent and watchful interest over New South Wales. He was elected president of the Royal Society in 1788 and held that high office until his death. In 1789 he married Dorothea Hugessen, a wealthy heiress. He made an indelible mark on the world of botany while helping to maintain good relations with the scientific world in France, even in times of conflict. He died, childless, in 1820. Harriet was not left to grieve her love and, in 1775, she married a clergyman and member of the Royal Society, Henry de Salis. A branch of the same family later settled at

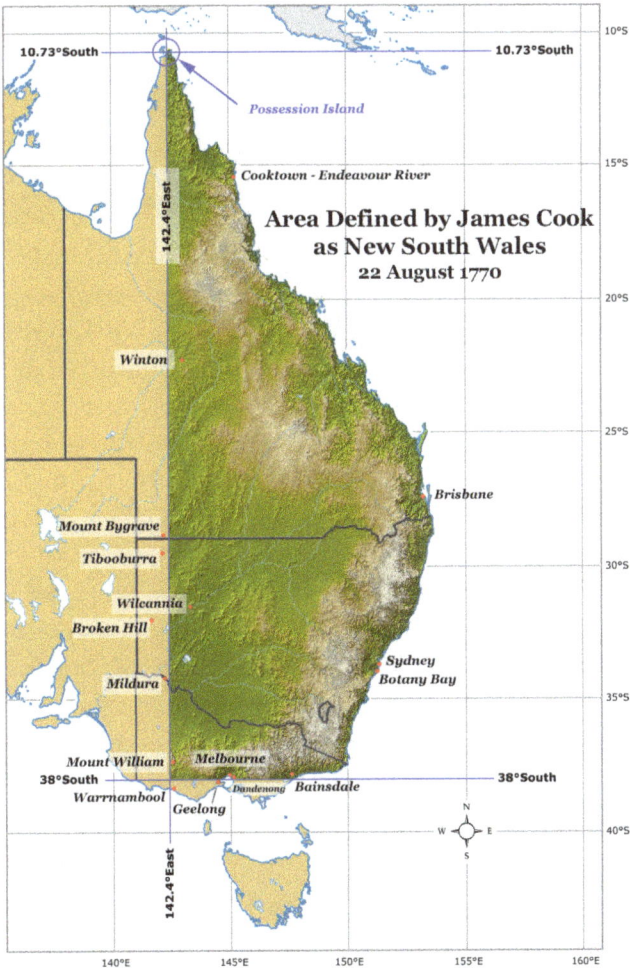

Michelago in New South Wales.[9]

Alexander Dalrymple, who had been granted some measure of access to Cook's journal, lost no time insisting unwearyingly, indeed almost obsessively, that much more needed to be done to find the dreamt of continent in the south, which he had tentatively indicated on a chart drawn by him and marked with 'Signs of Continent' near the Society Islands. This information probably came to him from reports of the Quiros voyage, but mere sightings of floating wood, birds and, much less, cloud formations would never have led Quiros to make any absurd conclusions. Dalrymple, however, eagerly consumed all this fanciful speculation and he was outraged that Cook had been consistently lax in his pursuit of said continent. Indeed he remained unimpressed by all Cook had done. This meant that Dalrymple cursorily dismissed the genuine search for the mythical land undertaken by Cook on his voyage from the Society Islands to New Zealand in which he went down below 40° south into territory in which Dalrymple thought the southernmost point of the new land might be situated.[10]

Cook, finding nothing at that southern location, had given up the chase as futile and headed north to pick up the land discovered by Tasman in 1642. Nonetheless, in circumnavigating and charting New Zealand, Cook had been careful to establish that it had no connection with any land to its south. On one point, however, it was possible to question Cook's judgement, but not his integrity. Dalrymple had come across some knowledge in old Spanish documents of Torres's voyage and he now pointed out that Cook had at his side on the *Endeavour* a copy of his own work, *An Account Of the Discoveries Made in the South Pacifick Ocean, Previous to 1764* in which there is a strait north of Cape York and south of New Guinea that Dalrymple clearly marked as Torres's Track 1606. With reason, because so little was known about the matter, Cook was entitled to be cautious about Dalrymple's claim of the existence of the strait and he remained deeply anxious, given its grave importance to him as a quicker route to Batavia. He also had some justice on his side given the secrecy that veiled earlier exploratory voyages, although the strait was set down on many of the old maps even though 'the kings of Portugal forbad, upon pain of death, the exportation of any marine

[9]   See J.C. Beaglehole, *The Life of Captain James Cook* (1974, pp. 273-74); Patrick O'Brian, *Joseph Banks: A Life* (1997, pp. 148-49); and Nicholas Thomas, *Cook: The Extraordinary Voyages of Captain James Cook* (2003, pp. 141-42). For clippings from the London *Evening Post*, 15 July, 23 July 1771; *Public Advertiser*, 16, 19, 22, 27 July 1771 and other papers, see Beaglehole in *Cook*, pp. 642-55.

[10]   See Dalrymple's chart in *Cook*, Figure 18, opposite p. clxii.

charts which showed the way to Calicut' and the new world in general. In the end Cook merely claimed that he had cleared up a doubtful point as to the strait's existence and that it was safe to take passage through it. That it could become a valuable and time-saving passage from the west into the Pacific and vice versa was self-evident.[11]

The chart of New Holland seen by Cook in the Vaugondy work was a mere conjectural line drawn down from Cape York to Van Diemen's Land. It runs far out to the east of the actual coast and joins Quiros's Australia del Espiritu Santo. Thus the Vaugondy chart did little more than depict a presumed east coast of New Holland, which anyone in their right senses already knew was there. Otherwise the continent would have no terminal given that almost all of its remainder was already charted. Therefore, as a chart, the Vaugondy bore little relevance to the true chart done by Cook, who was nowise dependent on it. Dalrymple further asserted that the name Botany Bay was merely the English version of the French name on the Rotz Dieppe chart, Coste des Herbiages, and he erroneously claimed that Cook must have been aware of this when naming Botany Bay.[12]

This is unfair to Cook because there is no possibility in 1770 that he knew that the Rotz existed, which also was true for Dalrymple. Frederick Watson, appointed editor of the *Historical Records of Australia* in 1922, later published a book on Cook's first voyage that Beaglehole, with some acerbity, labelled as 'a rather silly, though fortunately, small book'. Watson claimed that Cook's journal was officially added to and changed in London, especially in naming both Botany Bay and New South Wales. Yet, if the name Botany Bay, which never appeared in any of the original accounts of either Cook or his officers, was a rendering of the French, it of necessity indicates that the changing of the name took place in the Admiralty in 1771, where the Rotz chart by then was assuredly known. Also it could well be the fact that the reception given in London to the remarkable discoveries of new plants by Banks and Solander prompted the authorities to rid Cook's journal of the pedestrian 'Sting Ray' and turn it into a more acceptable tribute to the science of botany and especially to the two men who so greatly enhanced knowledge of it. It is surely not too much a stretch of the imagination to suggest that Banks

---

[11] See Alan Villiers, *Captain Cook, The Seaman's Seaman: A Study of the Great Discoverer* (1967, pp. 189-90), and Dalrymple's chart in *Cook*, Figure 18, opposite p. clxii.

[12] This matter is discussed at some length in F.M. Bladen's introduction and notes to the *Historical Records of New South Wales: Cook 1762–1780*, vol. 1, pt 1 (1893, pp. xxv–xxvi). Bladen states without equivocation in respect of the naming of Botany Bay that it 'appears beyond any reasonable question, either Captain Cook did not, or, if he did, it was an afterthought'.

himself, who never used Botany Bay or Stingray Bay while there might have had a hand in the change.[13]

Cook promptly attended to his duties on the day after landing by reporting to the secretary of the Admiralty, Stephens, who warmly, but briefly, received him while he passed over his journal and all other records of the voyage. The lord commissioners of the Admiralty met on 1 August and Stephen wrote to tell Cook that he had set before them the journals and letters Cook gave him. Stephen reported that 'their Lordships extremely well approve of the whole of your proceedings'. The fortitude and courage, as well as the unswerving loyalty and devotion the crew gave to their captain was summed up by the lords in their own restrained manner. They expressed their 'great satisfaction in the account you have given them of the good behaviour of your Officers and Men and of the cheerfulness and alertness with which they went through the fatigues of their late voyage'.[14]

It is reasonable to surmise that Cook would hastily have made his way to his home to Mile End Road, where Elizabeth and his family awaited him, although it can only be supposed whether they even knew of his safe arrival. From that home not a word had passed to the father for three years and no word of his had reached them. Probably because he was hesitant to burst in upon them unannounced he sent a message to Elizabeth that he was safe home and would be with her on the following day, Monday 14 July 1771. Of what transpired on that day little is known. A baby boy, Joseph, had scarcely survived Cook's departure, dying just days after his father had bade farewell to him as he did to his other sons Nathaniel (8) and James (6), and daughter Elizabeth (1) when he set forth to join the *Endeavour* in May 1768. By 1771 the two boys were in healthy good spirits, but his darling daughter, Elizabeth, whom he had only known and rejoiced in for a year before his departure, had died. She did so while he was sailing up from the Cape of Good Hope and thus only a few weeks before his arrival home. As a devoted mother, Elizabeth assuredly grieved deeply the loss of their two children. Cook, to whom they were shadows whose faces he could scarcely envisage, grieved also but in the manner of a man to whom, especially since Batavia, death had become a part of life.

During the intervening year between Cook's arrival and his departure on his second voyage, daily life followed a routine broken by the tragedy

---

[13] See *Historical Records of New South Wales: Cook 1762–1780*, vol. 1, pt 1 (1893, p. 161).
[14] Stephens to Cook, 2 August 1771, in J.C, Beaglehole, *The Life of Captain James Cook* (1974, p. 275).

of memory. Cook and Elizabeth were not given to ostentation and forms of entertainment in their home, the warmth of which was unlikely to have been shared beyond their closely knit family and intimate friends. One thing, however, had been achieved in that Cook had begun to enjoy a measure of moderate economic stability together with the respect shown to those judged to have enriched the nation and its people.[15]

Lord Sandwich presented Lieutenant Cook to the king on 14 August, an honour indeed for an officer of that rank who, though a decade older than George III had never stood before such an august personage. Their meeting lasted an hour during which Cook explained his charts and George approved of his contribution to the successful outcome of the voyage. This encounter Cook found 'extremely pleasing'. As a grateful leader of his men, Cook made several suggestions for the promotion of some members of his crew, all of which were accepted including those that the death of others had forced him to promote while still at sea. His own promotion from lieutenant was less clear and not as forthcoming. The next rank was that of commander, which lay below that of post-captain. The difference between the two ranks was in name only in that a commander was paid the same as a post-captain and had the same authority when in service. Lord Sandwich had again become the First Lord of the Admiralty, this for the third time, despite his naming in the House of Commons as 'the most profligate sad dog in the kingdom'. Justice however demands that, in his biography of Cook, the much respected and scholarly parson, Andrew Kippis, said that Sandwich was 'the great patron of our navigator, and the principal mover in his undertakings'. Curiously the origin of the name sandwich, often assigned to him because he was well known to request that meat between pieces of bread be brought to him so as to not interrupt his gambling on a hand of cards, is as difficult to unravel as is that of the naming of Botany Bay.[16]

In any event, after the visit to the king, Sandwich had told his close friend, Banks, of Cook's forthcoming promotion to commander. Cook wrote to Banks thanking him for 'the very great assistance I received therein from you' and declaring that he had never expected to be raised to a rank of such honour, 'unsolicited to a man of my station in life'. He thereby made it plain that he bowed to the social system prevailing in English society, which generally debarred a man of Cook's humble origins from receiving such a distinction, despite the greatness of the service he had given to his country.

---

[15] The multitude of books on Cook all refer to his homecoming with varied details of the family with which this account generally concurs.

[16] Andrew Kippis, *The Life and Voyages of Captain James Cook* (1840, p. xii).

His commission as commander of the *Resolution*, the vessel he captained on his second voyage, was only made formal on 27 November 1771. Whether he was paid a commander's salary from August is uncertain, although it is clear that he was not on active service apart from the ongoing responsibilities he had to wind up affairs at the Admiralty and prepare for his second voyage. It is not unreasonable to suppose, however, that Cook, having being reared in frugality, had arrived home with a modest sum saved on the voyage. He had received £105 as an honorarium for his contribution to observing the Transit of Venus and £120 a year for victualing Charles Green and himself and he might have been able to save something in other quarters so that buying the accoutrements demanded by his rank, perhaps even a new sword, demanded no great sacrifice. Above all, middling comfort at Mile End Road was now ensured. The consequence of a new pregnancy, were such to ensue, would help in some measure at least to fill the missing places at the family table and bring joy to Elizabeth despite her certain knowledge that James would only briefly sit at its head.[17]

In respect of some of those who had lived and laboured at his side for three years, Cook bore the painful burden of writing letters of consolation to their parents and loved ones. George Monkhouse's two sons, William the ship's surgeon, and Jonathon, a midshipman, had died on the voyage and that letter in particular was difficult for Cook to write. He received a letter from his old mentor John Walker of Whitby, which probably contained an invitation to visit him at home. Cook replied graciously saying that were he able to come to the north he would certainly accept the warm gesture. The letter made it plain that Cook was in some measure at odds with the Admiralty as to the degree to which he was permitted 'to make my voyage public'. He indicated that otherwise he would have written sooner to Walker and in some detail but even now, 17 August 1771, he had not received permission to do so and thus he 'lay under some restraint'. He 'ventured', however, to inform Walker that 'the voyage has fully answered the expectations of my superiors' and, although he had 'made no very great discoveries yet I have explored more of the Great South Sea than all that have gone before me so much that little remains now to be done to have a thorough knowledge of that part of the Globe'.[18]

In London, Cook visited the Royal Society and the Admiralty regularly

---

[17] See J.C. Beaglehole, *The Life of Captain James Cook* (1974, pp. 274-75); Nicholas Thomas, *Cook: The Extraordinary Voyages of Captain James Cook* (2003, pp. 178-80); *Historical Records of New South Wales: Cook 1762–1780*, vol. 1, pt 1 (1893, p. 345, fn. 1; p. 346, fn. 4).

[18] J.C. Beaglehole, *The Life of Captain James Cook* (1974, p. 276).

while working on his journal and charts to bring them up to the measure demanded by his own rigorous standards and the requirements of the Admiralty. In the wake of Matra's account of the voyage of the *Endeavour*, which came out in late September 1771, the Admiralty could not postpone the matter of publication of the voyage further. Hawkesworth was given the task and there is no indication as to whether Cook was happy or not about the decision, but he was in no position to oppose it. The more important matter was that a second voyage led by Cook had been decided on in which he would be joined by Banks. Happy that the expedition so carefully pleaded by him to investigate further and finally settle the question of the Great South Land had been officially approved, Cook proceeded to select the ships, assemble a crew and generally prepare for the voyage. Banks, for personal reasons interwoven with petulance connected to the fact that he was not to be the commander, finally refused to be involved. Preparation for departure was so protracted that it did not take place until 13 July 1772.[19]

During the intervening, hectic months, Cook managed in December 1771 to make a visit to his aged father, James, for which he had been obliged to seek Sandwich's permission to 'grant me leave for three weeks'. What kind of a man was he who, in his mid-40s, went to visit his father in 1771? Neither of them were complex men. They were plain, direct, purposeful and honest. The son had gone out to the world and mixed with other men who understood him exactly as he presented himself to them. They could entrust him with their lives and he reciprocated their trust. But that is the Cook of the journals, which say so little of the inner man. What then did his great biographer, J.C. Beaglehole, think of him? He was 'good looking in a plain sort of way', spoke with a 'provincial accent' and had an array of high qualities remarked on by his contemporaries. Thus he was 'Cool, courageous, firm, vigilant, active, resolved, humane, patient', but Beaglehole prefers to insist on his 'stubbornness' to which he devotes over half his paper. Beaglehole also observes that Cook was never seen to be drunk and that he refrained from passionate relations with the women of the islands. He rarely swore and he refused to eat bananas.[20]

James, a widower since the death of his wife Grace in 1765, lived with his daughter, Cook's sister Margaret Fleck, in a small fishing village in north

---

[19] For Cook during this period see Chapter 12 of J.C. Beaglehole, *The Life of Captain James Cook* (1974); *Historical Records of New South Wales: Cook 1762-1780*, vol. 1, pt 1 (1893, pp. 338-67); Richard Hough, *Captain James Cook* (1994, pp. 177-96).

[20] J.C. Beaglehole, 'Cook the Man', in G.M. Badger (ed.), *Captain Cook: Navigator and Scientist* (1970, pp. 11-29).

Yorkshire. Despite Elizabeth's latest pregnancy, Cook took her with him on a difficult three-day coach journey in mid-winter while the boys remained at Mile End Road. Nothing is known of what was surely a happy occasion, but there is an account of the elder James who was visited four years later by a small party that included Banks. James's looks were venerable and 'his deportment was above that usually found among the lowly inhabitants of a hamlet'. It seems that since his son's visit in 1771 the old man had learnt to read 'so that he might gratify a parent's love and pride by perusing his son's first voyage round the world'. At the time of the visit James was 76. He outlived his son, dying aged 84 in 1779.[21]

After a few days in the family circle, Cook rode over to Whitby to visit John Walker. He was warmly welcomed and even vivaciously so by the elderly housekeeper, Mary Prowd, who had fond memories of Cook as a young apprentice, which overcame any inhibitions she felt when greeting the now famous commander. Stretching out her arms to embrace him she said, 'Oh honey James, how glad I's to see thee' and then took delight in hearing of his adventures. While with the Walker household Cook took pains to visit the Whitby shipyards of John Fishburn who had designed and built the *Endeavour*. Cook was warm in his congratulations to Fishburn and assuredly gave him much pleasure by telling him that the two ships he had personally chosen for his forthcoming voyage were also from his shipyard. Returning to his father, only a few days remained before it was time to set out to London where the family arrived in the second week of January 1772.[22]

An account of the further two voyages of James Cook forms no part of this narrative. It is sufficient to say that to journey with him was its own high adventure for those who were with him on the *Endeavour*. At one remove, it becomes the same high adventure for those who are privileged to accompany him almost 250 years later. To the valiant mariner on his return safely to home, the pursuit of the mythical Great South Land meant little because Cook had already charted the east coast of a great southern continent that others later called Australia. His purpose never encompassed dreams. His reality was that of the vast oceans and especially of the portent mystery and

21 Cook to Stephens, 14 December 1771, *Historical Records of New South Wales: Cook 1762-1780*, vol. 1, pt 1 (1893, p. 345) and account of meeting with Cook's father, pp. 345-56. See also Richard Hough, *Captain James Cook* (1994, pp. 180-81) on the visit to Cook's father and Hawkesworth, *An Account of the Voyages Undertaken by the Order of his Present Majesty for Making Discoveries in the Southern Hemisphere: And Successively Performed by Commodore Byron, Captain Wallis, Captain Carteret, and Captain Cook, in the Dolphin, the Swallow and the Endeavour* (1773, pp. 289-91).

22 Richard Hough, *Captain James Cook* (1994, pp. 181-82).

promise of the mighty Pacific. Yet for the rest of his short life James Cook was driven by a higher impulse — a sublime impulse because it knew no bounds. He wanted to sail in waters where no man had ever ventured before him. He did so. His earthly remains rest in those same waters. He lives on among the countless millions who have ranked him as one of the greatest mariners of the ages.

Appendix

The books and charts that travelled on the *Endeavour*, and which had not originally been acquired by Cook, would have been part of the extensive holdings that Banks took aboard. Graeme Powell, former Keeper of Manuscripts at the National Library of Australia and an esteemed scholar of Cook, his life and achievements, compiled a list of 'maps, which depict part of the coasts of Australia', most, if not all, of which were aboard 'HMS Endeavour in 1768–71'. He put the maps in order of publication from 1570 until 1676, and therefore included maps that were available prior to Cook's departure in 1768. They were all small, ranging from the Dampier 15 x 27 cm to the Coronelli, 60 x 45 cm.

Ortelius, Abraham, *Indiae Orientalis*, 1570.

Ortelius, Abraham, *Maris Pacifici*, 1589.

Blaeu, Willem, *India quae orientalis dicitur et insulae adiacentes*, 1635.

Visscher, Nicolaes, *Orbis terrarum nova*, 1658.

Thevenot, Melchisedech, *Hollandia Nova*, 1663.

Duval, Pierre, *Carte des Indes Orientales, incl. Nouvelle Hollande*, 1677.

Coronelli, Vincenzo, *Asia et parte del Mare Pacifico*, 1696.

Dampier, William, *Captain Dampier's new voyage to New Holland*, 1699.

Bowen, Emmanuel, *A complete map of the Southern Continent*, 1774.

Bellin, Jacques, *Carte réduit des Terres Australes*, 1753.

de Vaugondy, Robert, *Carte réduit de l'Australasie*, 1756.

Dalrymple, Alexander, *Chart of the South Pacifick Ocean*, 1767.

None of the above maps pertain to the charts and atlases that were drawn at Dieppe from 1540 to 1584 by cartographers of the famous French school, which depict a large landmass lying below New Guinea. Named Java la Grande, it was taken by some scholars to be the Australian continent. There is no evidence that Cook had access to any of the Dieppe maps on his first voyage from 1768-71.

Powell also compiled a list of books that were certainly, or likely, to have been on the *Endeavour* and held by Cook or by Banks who had 60 to 70 titles in his own library, which made up over 100 volumes on board. It is also probable that the Admiralty sent to the *Endeavour* copies of *The English Pilot*, the third edition, which was published in London frequently in the eighteenth century, in which Cook concluded that 'everything seems to be very accurately delineated' as well as *The Nautical Almanac and Astronomical Ephemeris* (1767) about which he said that 'without it the calculations (of longitude) are laborious and discouraging to beginners'.[1]

Powell first lists the published works that Cook and Banks referred to in their respective journals:

de Brosses, Charles, *Histoire des navigations aux terres australes*, 2 vols, Paris, 1756.

A collection of voyages undertaken by the Dutch East India Company, for the improvement of trade and navigation, London, 1703.

Commissioners of Longitude, *The Nautical Almanac*, edited by Nevil Maskelyne, London, 1767.

Dalrymple, Alexander, An account of the discoveries made in the South Pacific Ocean previous to 1764, London, 1767.

———, *A collection of voyages*, 3 vols, London 1729.

———, *A new voyage round the world*, London, 1697.

———, *A voyage to New Holland*, London, 1703.

Frèzier, Amèdèè François, *Relation du voyage de la mer du sud aux côtes du Chili et du Pérou, fait pendant les années 1712, 1713, et 1714*, Paris, 1716.

Hacke, William, *A collection of original voyages*, London, 1699.

Maskelyne, Neville, *The British Mariner's Guide*, London, 1763.

Narborough, John, *An account of several late voyages and discoveries*, 2 vols, London, 1694.

Osbeck, Pehr, *Dagbok öfwer en ostindisk Resa åren 1750, 1751, 1752*, Stockholm, 1757.

Pingrè, Alexandre, *Mèmoire sur la choix et l'état des lieux et où le passage du Vénus de 3 Juin 1769, pourra tre observé avec le plus d'advantage*, Paris, 1767.

---

[1]   *Cook*, 26 December, 23 August 1770, pp. 443, 392.

Shelvocke, George, *A voyage round the world, by the way of the Great South Sea, performed in the years 1719, 20, 2, 22*, London, 1726.

Thorton, John, *The English Pilot, the third book describing the sea-routes, capes, headlands, straits … and ports in the Oriental navigation*, London, 1761.

Valentijn, François, *Oudt en Nieuw Oost-Indien*, 5 vols., Dortrecht. 1724–26.

A voyage round the world in His Majesty's Ship the Dolphin, commanded by the Honourable Commodore Bryon, London, 1767.

Walter, Richard, *A voyage round the world in the years MDCCXL, I, II. III, IV by George Anson, Esq.*, London, 1748.

Denis John Carr thoroughly researched the evidence regarding the books aboard the *Endeavour* and concluded that the Admiralty gave Cook a transcript of Samuel Wallis's journal written on the *Dolphin* during his voyage to the Pacific, principally to Tahiti, in the years 1766–68. Powell found 'no reason to doubt his statement', although Wallis's journal was not published until 1773. He drew up a further list of books belonging to Banks, which were possibly on the *Endeavour*.[2]

Après de Mannevillette, Jean Baptiste, *Le Neptune Oriental, ou routier général des côtes des Indes Orientales del la Chine*, Paris, 1745.

Biron, Claude, *Curiositez de la nature et de l'art, aportées dans deux voyages, l'un aux Indes d'Occident en 1698 & 1699, & d'autre aux Indes d'Orient en 1701 & 1702*, Paris, 1703.

Cooke, Edward, *A voyage to the South Sea, and round the world, performed in the years 1708, 1709, 1710 and 1711*, 2 vols, London, 1712.

Dampier, William, *A continuation of a voyage to New Holland in the year 1699*, London, 1709.

Harris, John, *Navigantium atque Itinerantium Bibliotheca, or a compleat collection of voyages and travels*, revised by J. Campbell, 2 vols, London, 1744–48.

Herbert, William, *A new directory for the East Indies*, London, 1767.

Osbeck, Pehr, *Reise nach Ostindien und China*, Rostock, 1765.

Rogers, Woodes, *A cruising voyage round the world, first to the South Seas, thence to the East Indies, and homeward by the Cape of Good Hope, begun in 1708 and finished in 1711*, London, 1718.

---

[2]   See D.J. Carr, 'The Books that Sailed with the *Endeavour*', in *Endeavour* (Oxford), vol. 7, no. 4, 1983, pp. 194-201.

Thèvenot, Melchisdech, *Relation des divers voyages curieux*, 2 vols, Paris, 1663–64.

It is unlikely that Cook was able to read works in any language other than English, but he was more than capable of understanding and mastering any of the charts contained in them. Between Banks and Solander the works in Latin, French, German, Dutch and Swedish could be read and relevant passages translated to Cook's advantage. The charts and the narratives and observations by the authors on their voyages would have been of considerable value to Cook and his officers. Together, this collection illustrates in a decisive manner that, although much of the knowledge gained by firsthand experience remained imperfect, the first steps had been taken towards an understanding of hitherto unknown parts of the world.

Bibliography

Primary sources

An Historical Account of the Circumnavigation of the Globe: And of the Progress of the Discovery in the Pacific Ocean, From the Voyage of Magellan to the Death of Cook, Oliver & Boyd, London; Simpkin, Marshall & Co., Edinburgh, 1836.

Beaglehole, J.C. (ed.), *The Endeavour Journal of Joseph Banks, 1768–1771*, 2 vols, Public Library of NSW, Sydney, 1962.

——, *The Journals of Captain James Cook on his Voyage of Discovery*, vol. 1, *The Voyage of the Endeavour 1768–1771*, Cambridge University Press, London, 1955.

Cook, James, *Journal of the HMS Endeavour, 1768–1771*, National Library of Australia, Manuscripts Collection, MS 1.

Currey, John (ed.), *The Endeavour Journal of Zachary Hicks Lieutenant 13 April 1770–22 August 1770*, with notes by F.M. Bladen, Banks Society, Malvern, Vic., 2006.

Dampier, William, *A Voyage to New Holland &c. in the Year 1699*, James Knapton, London, 1703.

——, *A New Voyage Round the World*, London, 1697.

David, Andrew, Rüdiger Joppien & Bernard Smith (eds), *The Charts and Coastal Views of Captain Cook's Voyages*, vol. 1, *The Voyage of the Endeavour, 1768–1771*, Hakluyt Society in association with the Australian Academy of the Humanities, London, 1988.

de Brosses, Charles, *Histoire des navigations aux terres Australes*, 3 vols, Durand, Paris, 1756.

de Vaugondy, Robert, *Carte Générale qui représente Les Mers des Indes, Pacifique, et Atlantique et principalement le Monde Austral divisé en Australasie, Polynésie et Magellanie. Pour servir à L'Histoire des Terres Australes*, Chez Durand, Paris, 1756.

Flannery, Tim (ed.), *Terra Australis: Matthew Flinders' Great Adventures in the Circumnavigation of Australia*, Text, Melbourne, 2000.

Flinders, Matthew, *A Voyage to Terra Australis*, 2 vols, G.& W. Nicol, London, 1814.

Hawkesworth, J., *An Account of the Voyages Undertaken by the Order of his Present Majesty for Making Discoveries in the Southern Hemisphere: And Successively Performed by Commodore Byron, Captain Wallis, Captain Carteret, and Captain Cook, in the Dolphin, the Swallow and the Endeavour*, 3 vols, W. Strahan & T. Cadell, London, 1773.

Heeres, J.E. (ed.), *Abel Janzoor Tasman's Journal*, Gutenberg Australia, eBook no 0600571, April 2006, produced by Colin Choat & Bob Forsyth. Tasman's journal runs to 59 pages and is followed by J.E. Herres, *Abel Janszoon Tasman: His Life and Labours*, http://gutenberg.net.au/ebooks06/0600571h.html.

Historical Records of New South Wales: Cook 1762–1780, vol. 1, pt 1, with a preface by Alexander Britton and an introduction by F.M. Bladen, C. Potter, Government Printer, Sydney, 1893, reprint 1978.

Historical Records of New South Wales: Phillip 1783–1792, vol. 1, pt 2, C. Potter, Government Printer, Sydney, 1893, reprint 1978.

Matra, James, *The Anonymous Journal (A Journal of a Voyage Round the World in his Majesty's Ship Endeavour)*, attributed to James Mario Matra (New York 1748?–Tangier 1806), foreword by Prof. G.M. Badger and introduction and biography of the reputed author by A. Giordano. From the original first edition copy in the Mitchell Library, Sydney. Antonio Giordano Adelaide, 1975 (1771).

Parkinson, Sydney, *Journal of a Voyage to South Seas*, London, 1773, facsimile edition, http://southseas.nla.gov.au/journals/parkinson/contents.html.

Selected sources

Badger, G.M. (ed.), *Captain Cook: Navigator and Scientist*, ANU Press, Canberra, 1970.

Beaglehole, J.C., *The Life of Captain James Cook*, Stanford University Press, London, 1974.

——, *The Exploration of the Pacific*, 3rd edition, Stanford University Press, London, 1966.

——, 'Some Problems of Editing Cook's Journal', *Historical Studies Australia and New Zealand*, vol. 8, no. 29, Nov. 1957, pp. 20–31.

Carr, D.J., 'The Books that Sailed with the *Endeavour*', *Endeavour* (Oxford), vol. 7, no. 4, 1983, pp. 194–201.

Carter, Harold, *Sir Joseph Banks (1743–1820): A Guide to Biographical and Bibliographical Sources*, British Museum, London, 1987.

Carter, Paul, *The Road to Botany Bay: An Essay in Spatial History*, Faber and Faber, London, 1987.

Cook's Endeavour Journal: The Inside Story, National Library of Australia, Canberra, 2008.

Collingridge, George, *The Discovery of Australia*, facsimile edition, Golden Press, Sydney, 1987 (1895).

Dalrymple, Alexander, *Historical Collection of the Several Voyages and Discoveries in the South Pacific Ocean*, 2 vols, London, 1770–71.

——, *An Account of the Discoveries Made in The South Pacifick Ocean, Previous to 1764*, London, 1767.

Fernández-Armesto, Felipe, *1492: The Year our World Began*, Bloomsbury, London, 2011.

Fisher, Robin & Hugh Johnson (eds), *Captain James Cook and His Times*, ANU Press, Canberra, 1979.

Fox, James J., *Out of the Ashes: Destruction and Reconstruction of East Timor*, 2nd edition, ANU Press, Canberra, 2003.

——, *Harvest of the Palm: Ecological Change in Eastern Indonesia*, Harvard University Press, Cambridge, Mass., 1977.

Frost, Alan, *The Precarious Life of James Mario Matra: Voyager with Cook, American Loyalist, Servant of Empire*, Miegunyah Press, Melbourne, 1995.

——, 'Towards Australia: The Coming of the Europeans 1400–1788', in D.J. Mulvaney & J. Peter White (eds), *Australians to 1788*, Fairfax Simon Weldon, Sydney 1987, pp. 368–412.

——, 'New South Wales as *Terra Nullius*: The British Denial of Aboriginal Land Rights', *Historical Studies*, vol. 19, no. 77, 1981, pp. 513–23.

Gammage, Bill, *The Biggest Estate on Earth: How Aborigines Made Australia*, Sydney, Allen & Unwin, 2011.

——, 'Early Boundaries of New South Wales', *Historical Studies Australia and New Zealand*, vol. 19, no. 77, pp. 524–31, Melbourne, 1981.

Gascoigne, John, *Captain Cook: Voyager Between Worlds*, Hambledon Continuum, London, 2007.

Greenlee, William Brooks (trans.), *The Voyages of Pedro Alvares Cabral to Brazil and India*, Hakluyt Society, London, 1937.

Hiatt, Alfred, *Terra Incognita: Mapping the Antipodes Before 1600*, The British Library, London, 2008.

Hough, Richard, *Captain James Cook*, Hodder and Stoughton, London, 1994.

Joppien, Rüdiger & Bernard Smith, *The Art of Captain Cook's Voyages*, vol. 1, *The Voyage of the Endeavour, 1768–1771*, Oxford University Press in association with the Australian Academy of the Humanities, 1985–87.

Kippis, Andrew, *The Life and Voyages of Captain James Cook*, Thomas Nelson, Edinburgh, 1840 (1788).

Maclean, Alistair, *Captain Cook*, Collins, London, 1972.

McCalman, Iain, *The Reef: A Passionate History*, Viking, Melbourne, 2013.

Mapping our World: Terra Incognita to Australia, National Library of Australia, 2013.

Mulvaney, D.J., *Encounters in Place: Outsiders and Aboriginal Australians, 1606–1985*, University of Queensland Press, St. Lucia, 1989.

——, 'The Australian Aborigines 1606–1929: Opinion and Fieldwork', *Historical Studies Australia and New Zealand*, vol. 8, no. 30, Nov. 1958, pp.131–51; vol. 9, no. 31, pp. 297–314.

Mundle, Robert, *Cook*, HarperCollins, Sydney, 2013.

Nugent, Maria, *Captain Cook was Here,* Cambridge University Press, Port Melbourne, 2009.

O'Brian, Patrick, *Joseph Banks: A Life*, The Harvill Press, London, 1997.

O'Sullivan, Dan, *In Search of Captain Cook: Exploring the Man through His Own Words*, I.B. Tauris, London, 2008.

Parkin, Ray, *H.M. Bark Endeavour: Her Place in Australian History*, Miegunyah Press, Melbourne, 2006.

Pike, Douglas (ed.), *Australian Dictionary of Biography*, vol. 1, 1788–1850, Melbourne University Press, Carlton, 1966.

Ramson, W.S. (ed.), *The Australian National Dictionary*, Oxford University Press, Melbourne, 1988.

Richardson, Matthew, *The West and the Map of the World: A Reappraisal of the Past*, The Miegunyah Press, Melbourne, 2010.

Robertson, Jillian, *The Captain Cook Myth*, Angus & Robertson, London, 1981.

Robson, John, *Captain Cook's War and Peace: The Royal Navy Years, 1755–1768*, University of New South Wales Press, Sydney, 2009.

Smith, Bernard, *European Vision and the South Pacific, 1768–1850: A Study in the History of Art and Ideas*, Clarendon Press, Oxford, 1985.

Spate, Oscar, 'Terra Australis – Cognita?' *Historical Studies Australia and New Zealand*, vol. 8, November 1957, no. 29, pp. 1–19.

Thomas, Nicholas, *Cook: The Extraordinary Voyages of Captain James Cook*, Walker & Company, New York, 2003.

Villiers, Alan, *Captain Cook, The Seaman's Seaman: A Study of the Great Discoverer*, Penguin, Ringwood, 1967.

Virga, Vincent, *Cartographia: Mapping Civilizations*, Little, Brown & Co., New York, 2007.

White, John, *The Ancient History of the Maori: His Mythology and Traditions*, vol. 5, Wellington, 1888.

Williams, Glynder, '"Far more happier than we Europeans": Reactions to the Australian Aborigines on Cook's Voyage', *Historical Studies Australia and New Zealand*, vol. 19, no. 77, pp. 499–512.

Index